Author Biography

Mr. C.I.D Clark (JP) was born on 24 September 1946 at Kiagbodo town in Burutu Local Govt Council Area of Delta State, Nigeria. He attended Govt College, Ughelli, Delta State from 1960 to 1966 where he studied for his Ordinary and Advanced level certificates. He earned his WASC in 1964 and H.S.C.(A.L.) in 1966. Mr. Clark attended the university of Ibadan where he undertook his undergraduate studies in sociology from 1967 to 1970 and obtained a 2nd class Honours Upper division B.Sc. Degree in sociology. As a result of his impressive degree result, the authorities of the University of Ibadan sponsored Mr. Clark with a Rockefeller Foundation of New York scholarship to study a Masters in Sociology at Indiana University, Bloomington Indiana, USA; he graduated with an M.A. Degree in Sociology in 1974.

Mr. Clark is happily married to Dr. Mrs. Anthonia O. Clark, who is Head of the Department of the Vocational and Technical Education Faculty of Education, University of Benin, Benin City, Nigeria, and they have six children and seven grand-children. Mr. Clark has been a lecturer and researcher at the University of Benin since January, 1976. Mr. Clark has also served in Government as an Honourable Commissioner for Education, and later for Health, in Delta State from February 1994 to November 1997.

HANDBOOK OF PSYCHOLOGY CONCEPTS

Second edition

Compiled and Edited by
CYRIL I.D. CLARK
University of Benin, Benin City, Nigeria.

Published 2011 by Abramis academic publishing

www.abramis.co.uk

ISBN 978 1 84549 497 1

Printed and bound in the United Kingdom

Abramis is an imprint of arima publishing.

arima publishing
ASK House, Northgate Avenue
Bury St Edmunds, Suffolk IP32 6BB
t: (+44) 01284 700321

www.arimapublishing.com

First published by Omega Publishers Limited,
No. 5, Benin Technical College Road,
P.O. Box 351, Benin City, in 1985

PREFACE

This handbook provides *brief and standard definitions and short notes* on many of the *concepts* that are frequently used in modern psychology and other behavioural sciences, namely, sociology and anthropology.

Many people helped me in many different ways in the production of this handbook. I am very grateful to all of them. But my greatest gratitude goes to Dr. Marida Hollos, who was Williams Fulbright Visiting Associate Professor, Department of Sociology and Anthropology, University of Benin in 1985 when I produced the first edition of this book. She read and vetted the whole manuscript for that publication. She did all of that very expertly and expeditiously. I'm extremely grateful to Dr. Hollos.

However, in the final analysis, I must say that both the initial conception and final shape of this book are entirely my own hand work. Consequently, I accept full responsibility for whatever merits and/or demerits that are in it.

C.I.D. Clark
University of Benin
Benin City, Nigeria
2010

AN OVERVIEW OF MODERN PSYCHOLOGY AND THE RELEVANCE OF CONCEPTS IN MODERN PSYCHOLOGY

Introduction

This essay provides a general introduction to this handbook. It attempts to accomplish two major inter-related objectives, as follows:

> 1. To provide a brief overview of the distinctive nature, objectives, and scope of modern psychology; and

> 2. To show the nature, scope, and relevance of the various technical concepts that are frequently used in modern psychology.

WHAT IS PSYCHOLOGY?

There are many different plausible definitions of psychology in the literature of modern psychology. For example, American psychologists Robert M Liebert and John M. Neale define "psychology" in their textbook titled *Psychology* (New York: John Wiley Sons, Inc., 1977, page 10), as follows:

> *Contemporary psychology is best defined as the scientific study of behaviour and related mental and physical processes.*

While British psychologist Abraham Sperling defines "psychology" in his textbook titled *Psychology Made Simple* (London: Heinemann, 1982, page 269), as follows:

> (Psychology is) *the science of individual behaviour and experience.*

Taking these definitions of psychology as our major points of departure in this essay, I would like to proceed therefore and say that psychology thus defined is an academic discipline. It specializes in studying and providing relatively standard, accurate, and reliable bodies of scientific information about the nature, scope, causes, patterns, courses, objectives, purposes, opportunities and problems or obstacles, and consequences (both positive and negative) of the behaviours, experiences, and mental and physical processes of different individual human beings, such as infants, children, adults, men, women, leaders, followers, rich and poor people, law-abiding individuals as well as deviants, delinquents, criminals, and psychotics, etc., in their different physical, social, and cultural environments, such as in poor, developing black Africa; or, in old, tired, rejuvenating Caucasian Europe; or in industrious, affluent, confident, multiracial Northern America; or else where throughout the whole world.

The range of the variety of the substantive subject matters, that ie, the different aspects of the behaviours, experiences, and mental and physical processes of individual human beings that trained psychologists study and write about is very wide indeed. These include psycho-physical sensations, stimuli, responses, perceptions, learning, cognition or knowledge, aggression, punishments, sufferings, motivation, achievement, happiness or enjoyment or pleasure, consciousness, unconsciousness, dreams, mental and physical disorders, fantasies, madness, etc

Types of Scientific Research Methods that are used in Modern Psychology

In the course of looking for and gathering information and data together, to use for analyzing the different aspects of the behaviours, experiences, and mental and physical processes of individuals, psychologists use different standard scientific research methods. There are *eight* major scientific research methods (among others) that are thus used in modern psychology, as follows:

1. Archival research method.
2. Survey research, method;
3. The Field study method.
4. The Natural experiment.
5. Quasi-experimental research method.
6. The Field experiment.
7. Simulation research method.
8. The Laboratory experiment.

Table 1: Psychology as a Professional Occupation

Occupational Environment	Occupational Title	Responsibilities
Schools, Colleges, Universities	Counselling Psychologist Clinical Psychologist School Psychologist	Administer and interpret intelligence tests, aptitude tests, achievement tests for student placement and guidance. Educational guidance. Career planning. Group, individual therapy.
	Instructor, Professor	Teach courses on psychological topics at colleges and universities.
	Experimental Psychologist	Plan, carry out, interpret, and report on surveys, observations, case studies, and experimental studies of behaviour and experience.

Industry, Business, Government, Military Service	Industrial Psychologist	Develop and administer on-the-job training programs. Study and modify work environment to reduce fatigue, tension, and accidents and increase productivity. Develop programs to foster employee morale.
	Personnel Psychologist	Administer and interpret job aptitude and skills tests. Personnel selection and placement. Counselling guidance.
	Consumer Research	Conduct surveys, interviews, experiments to determine product acceptance and consumer needs.
	Survey Researcher	Design and administer public opinion polls and interviews.
Schools, Hospitals, Private Practice	Clinical Psychologist	Diagnose and treat non-physical-based behavioural and emotional disorders. Give and interpret psychological tests.
Community Action, Nonprofit Organization	Many jobs in social clinical, industrial, and academic settings	Carry out many functions to help communities in areas of ecology, mental health, crisis clinics, halfway houses, drug rehabilitation centers, child guidance centers, etc.

Source: Mednick *et al* (1975), page 23.

Types of Scientific Theories that are used in Modern Psychology

Psychologists, as scientists, do not write about the various subject-matters of the discipline in any how manner. But rather they use certain standard scientific theoretical perspectives that are available in the discipline. There are *eight* major scientific theoretical perspectives (among others) that are thus used in modern psychology, as follows:

1. Structuralist theory.

2. Functionalist theory.

3. Psychoanalytic theory.

4. Behaviourist theories.

5. Gestalt theory.

6. Role theory.

7. Exchange theory.

8. Symbolic Interaction theory.

The Major Fields of Specialization in Modern Psychology

The foregoing analysis shows (among other things) that modern psychology is very wide, complex and technical. It is subdivided into different semi-autonomous fields of specialization, as follows:

1. Psychobiology or physiological psychology.
2. Clinical Psychology.
3. Experimental Psychology.
4. Educational Psychology.
5. Developmental Psychology.
6. Social Psychology.
7. Personality or Individual Psychology.
8. Applied Psychology.
9. Quantitative or Research Psychology.
10. Analytical or Theoretical Psychology.

Most practicing psychologists receive their professional training in different combinations of these fields of specialization in modern-psychology.

Most practicing modern psychologists are experts in either one, two, or some of these fields of specialisation in modern psychology.

WHAT ARE CONCEPTS?

Definition of "Concept"

A "concept" is a unit of meaning, a symbol which supplies a label for a particular segment, or aspect, of reality. For example, *iroko* is *the name* of a tree. It is, therefore, a concept, because it is a symbol that supplies a specific label to represent or to tell us about the distinctive nature of a particular segment of reality. *Every relatively unitary term or symbol is a concept, because it is a "name" or a "label", which represents of stands for a particular aspect of reality.*

Major Characteristics of Concepts

There are *two* major characteristics, or properties, of concepts, as follows:

> (a) *Unitariness:* By this is meant that it is mostly one single term or word which properly makes up any one particular concept. In fact, most concepts are one word, e.g., "role", "status", "motivation", "perception". However, two or more words which are used "conjointly" or in a "collective" sense can also represent a concept e.g. "impression management", "Social Psychology", "Democratic Leadership", "Convergent interests", etc. The most important thing to bear in mind is that in order for either the "one word" or the "collection of words" to qualify to be regarded as a concept or they must actually specifically be a "name" which designate(s) something which has a clear-cut or distinctive identity of its own.

(b) *Clarity and Objectivity:* By this characteristic is meant that in order for any one single word, or set of words or symbols, to qualify to be regarded as a concept, it must be *defined* and *used* in a clear and *unambiguous* way and manner. It should mean the same thing to most of the people who come across it. For example, the word "role" is a concept, because it has a "general" or "uniform" meaning for all the psychologists and other interested intellectuals who use it in their respective analyses or discussions.

The Functions or Uses of Concepts

There are several different functions or uses of concepts, but there are *two* major ones, as follows:

(a)   Concepts are *names* or *labels*, which are used *to designate* or *to identify*, and, therefore, to *distinguish* one thing from all other things. By so doing, we are in a better position to easily "recognize" or "pinpoint" the specific identity of the particular phenomenon that has been thus designated. For example, the concept and definition of "conscience" definitely help one to identify and distinguish the particular psychological phenomenon that is so called in the midst of all the other psychological phenomena. As a result, one can no longer have any difficulty in identifying the psychological phenomenon called "conscience" in the midst" of different psychological phenomena.

(b)   Concepts also serve as the *building-blocks* which all academicians use *for constructing* their various statements, propositions/ hypotheses, theories, and models/ perspectives/paradigms, by means of which they attempt to describe, explain, predict, or generally to give any account of the various subject-matters which they are interested in writing about from time to time. For example, the concepts of "Id", "Ego", and "Superego", represent some of the relevant conceptual "blocks" which Sigmund Freud first of all "molded", and which he used for constructing his own particular brand of the scientific theory which shows the nature of the basic "personality structure" of each individual human being.

In sum, the most important point to note here is that concepts, like cement-blocks, are relatively "unitary" phenomena, which are usually used for building more "complex" phenomena. Cement-blocks are used for building the various houses in which we live, hold lectures, or work; while concepts are used for constructing hypotheses, models, and theories, which describe/explain/ predict any of the various aspects of the world, such as motivation and human behaviour. In fact, without concepts, there can be no statements, hypotheses, models, theories, or communication as a whole. Concepts are the "nitty-gritty" materials which psychologists use for propounding all the theories in psychology.

"General" Versus "Technical" Concepts

All concepts can be classified into *two* broad categories, namely, "general" and "specific" or "technical" types of concepts. General concepts are the words which the generality of human beings use for communicating amongst themselves in their everyday lives – for example, words like "society", "community", "role", "sex", "social group", "government", "the state", "individual", human beings", tribe", etc. One big problem with general concepts is that they do not usually have any one specific, precise, or objective meaning. But rather, they are frequently used by different people to convey different meanings to different people. For example, the term "status", as a general concept, is frequently used to convey several widely divergent types of meanings.

On the other hand, however, "general concepts" can be borrowed by academicians to use in their various disciplines. When they do so, they usually "adapt" them, that is, they carefully "re-define" such general concepts to convey more precise meaning in the light of the context(s) in which they are being applied in that discipline. In fact, it is important for the students who are studying psychology and all other social science courses to note carefully that these disciplines study human behaviours which virtually *every human being* claims to know at least something about, and which they actually discuss everyday. A majority of the concepts which all the practitioners of the social and human behavioural disciplines use for writing their "technical" or "scholarly" analyses or theories about human behaviours are adapted from our *general language – for* example, concepts like "society", "production", "distribution", "goods", and "services", etc. But the most important point to note in this regard is that when "general concepts" are properly adapted for use in any academic discipline, they assume a new dimension, and they become called "technical" concepts.

"Technical" concepts are the relatively precise, specific, and specialized concepts which exist in each academic discipline (e.g.. Chemistry, Physics, Biology, Economics, Psychology, etc.), which the practitioners of each academic discipline have borrowed or carefully and painstakingly *evolved* by themselves over several years to use foe, referring to the various empirical phenomena, that is, the various substantive subject matters, that they specialize in studying in that academic discipline, from time to time. Since each academic discipline has its own relatively distinctive set of substantive subject matters which its practitioners specialize in studying, each academic discipline also, therefore, has its own relatively distinctive corresponding set of "technical" concepts. For example, psychology, medicine, nursing and midwifery, political science, sociology, accounting, law, engineering, etc., have their own relatively distinctive sets of "technical" concepts, The various *key or core set of technical* concepts of each academic discipline constitutes each discipline's *set of "technical" or "specialized" vocabulary.*

As a result, one of the first and foremost important steps which *all* new or beginning students must take in their attempts to study a new academic discipline, such as psychology, business administration, etc; (no matter for how short or long the period of the study), is for such students to make all of the necessary efforts to learn and acquire that academic discipline's set of key or core "technical" concepts, or vocabulary.

The specific nature of the key or core Technical Concepts of Psychology

As indicated earlier above, psychology, like every other relatively distinctive and autonomous academic discipline, has its own relatively distinctive set of "technical" or "specialized" concepts. The discipline's practitioners have been very carefully and painstakingly *evolving* most of these technical concepts over the past several years, to name, refer to, designate, or represent the various specific sets of substantive subject-matters which psychologists specialize in studying. Therefore, we cannot over-emphasize the importance of the fact that all the different categories of students who are either studying psychology as a major subject, or all those who are studying psychology – related–courses in other departments or faculties – such as.

Social Psychology, Educational Psychology, Industrial Psychology, Management Psychology, Clinical Psychology, etc. – must make it a point of duty to very carefully study and master as many of the "technical" concepts that are used in modern psychology as they can possibly do.

Two Major types of Technical Concepts in Psychology

All the different types of technical concepts that are used in modern psychology may be classified into *two* major categories, as follows:

(a)   Psychological concepts, and

(b)   Non-psychological concepts.

Psychological Concepts

Psychological concepts are the various technical concepts which authorities in psychology have actually considered as appropriate to use for designating the various psychological phenomena that they study and write about. For example, the terms "organism", "individual", "emotion", "perception", "cognition", "role", "behaviour", etc., are strictly psychological concepts, because they are mainly used to refer to, or to represent, strictly psychological phenomena, that is, individual behaviours, experiences, mental and physical processes. Consequently, all the psychological concepts in this dictionary are the concepts that strictly refer to psychological phenomena.

Non-Psychological Concepts that are used in Psychology

All the technical concepts that are used in psychology are not necessarily psychological concepts. In addition to the psychological concepts, there are also many non-psychological concepts that are frequently used in contemporary psychology. Examples of non-psychological concepts that are commonly used in psychology include "measurement scale", "variable", "experiment", "neurosis", "collective behaviour", "social norm", etc. All of these and other non-psychological concepts that are commonly used in psychology are called "non-psychological concepts" because they designate, or refer to, non-psychological phenomena. Many non-psychological concepts are frequently used in psychology because they refer to non-psychological phenomena that are inextricably intertwined with psychological phenomena. Psychologists cannot give adequate accounts of the various psychological phenomena that they are primarily and directly concerned with, without their referring to many of the different non-psychological phenomena that are related to or connected with individuals' behaviours and experiences, such as the "environment" or "society" in which the individual organisms that psychologists study directly, live in, and interact with.

In using most of the non-psychological concepts that psychologists use, psychologists usually borrow them from their different parent disciplines. Furthermore, psychologists usually use the borrowed non-psychological terms as they were originally defined and developed in their different parent disciplines. See Table 2 for examples of the various academic disciplines from which psychologists have borrowed most of the non-psychological concepts that abound in modern psychology, and examples of some non-psychological concepts that psychologists have actually borrowed from them,

It is worthwhile to note that generally all academic disciplines always borrow concepts, ideas, techniques, etc., from one another. Just as psychology has borrowed all of its non-psychological concepts from other disciplines, that is also how many academic disciplines have likewise borrowed and used many psychological concepts.

In conclusion, it is important to emphasize that both the purely "psychological concepts" and the "non-psychological concepts" that are frequently used in psychology are integral or bona fide component parts of the total vocabulary of psychology.

Similarly, this dictionary principally comprises both the purely "psychological concepts" as well as the various "non-psychological concepts" that are widely used in the different fields of specialization in modem psychology.

Table 2: Examples of other academic disciplines that are closely related to psychology, and the concepts that have been borrowed from them and used in modern psychology.

	Examples of academic disciplines that are closely related to psychology	Relevant subject-matters that are shared between these academic disciplines and psychology	Examples of relevant concepts that were developed by these academic disciplines and borrowed for use in modern psychology
1	**Biological Sciences** – e.g. zoology, microbiology, genetics, anatomy, physiology, biochemistry, etc.	The biological features of organisms.	Brain, gland, hormone, cell, gene, phenotype, eye, ear.
2	**Health-care Sciences** – e.g. medicine, psychiatry, pharmacy, nursing, etc.	The illnesses of organisms and their managements by health-care experts.	Psychopathology, anxiety, neurosis, psychosis, schizophrenia, ablation, acupuncture, *anorexia nervosa*, etc.

3	**Social or Behavioural Sciences** – e.g. sociology anthropology, economics, political science etc.	Inter-personal and social behaviours.	Society, community, social group, organization, interaction, status, role, exchange, power, cost, beliefs, knowledge, symbols, deviant behaviour, norm, attitude.
4	**Epistemological Sciences** – e.g. philosophy, methodology, statistics, logic, etc.	The elements and principles of scientific analysis, research methods, technique, statistics, computer simulation, etc.	Concepts, hypothesis, theory, data, research, experiment, measurement scale, sample correlation, variable, validity, reliability.

The Relevance of the various Technical Concepts that are used in Modern Psychology

It is necessary and important for all the different categories of professional psychologists and the students who are studying either pure psychology or psychology – related courses, and all other people who are interested in knowing at least something about psychology, to always endeavour to carefully study and master as many of the various technical concepts that are used in modern psychology as possible, because of the following *two major reasons* (among many other plausible reasons):

1. Virtually all the important ideas, latest discoveries, information, analytical and methodological principles and procedures of modern psychology are embodied in the discipline's various technical concepts.

   Therefore, the professional psychologists, psychology students and other people who make some extra efforts to carefully study and master many of the technical psychological and non-psychological concepts that are used in modern psychology would actually be thereupon studying and mastering much of the relevant substantive subject-matters, discoveries, ideas, information, and the analytical and methodological principles and procedures of modern psychology.

2. Concepts or words have their own relatively independent potentialities, dynamics, and relevance in the development of human intellect and communication. In fact, it is generally accepted throughout the whole world that the greater the quantity and variety of "words" or "vocabulary" that academicians, students, and other people have studied and mastered and know how to use effectively, the cleverer or more intelligent, competent, and successful such academicians, students, and other people are in their various fields of study and endeavour.

That is largely because words or concepts are among the major tools or means of human communication and understanding. Psychological words or concepts are especially important for all human beings because they refer to the various psychological behaviours, experiences, mental and physical processes of all human beings.

Consequently, all the different categories of professional psychologists and students of psychology, and all other people who are interested in psychology, would actually be increasing and improving upon their psychological vocabulary, and their knowledge and ability to understand better and communicate more effectively about the behaviours, experiences, mental and physical processes of human beings, if they make some extra efforts to carefully study and master most of the technical psychological and non-psychological concepts that abound in modem psychology.

On the whole, therefore, it is the cardinal responsibility of all professional psychologists and students of psychology, as well as other people who are interested in psychology, to always endeavour to carefully study, master, and know how to effectively use both the purely psychological and the no n-psychological concepts that are available in modern psychology.

The Problem of Lack of Reference Books on the Technical Concepts that are used in Modern Psychology in Nigeria and Africa

It is probably ironical that despite the great importance of technical concepts in modern psychology, it is very difficult to find a good variety of books that adequately provide for them in Nigeria and other African countries,

By contrast to the situation in Nigeria and Africa, in the United States of America in particular, and in the other Western countries in general, there abound numerous and varied assortments of standard reference books, such as encyclopaedias, dictionaries, and handbooks, as well as introductory textbooks, specialized research books, and academic journals, in the whole fields of psychology. Many American and European professional psychologists, psychology students, and other people, can easily buy these books from their numerous bookstores, or borrow them from their numerous libraries, in order for them to study and master many of the technical concepts that are used in modern psychology.

In Nigeria and other African countries, most of the available technical concepts that are relevant to psychology exist in a very piecemeal and fragmentary manner in extremely few and poorly circulated introductory textbooks in psychology and allied disciplines. Worse still, a majority of these few psychology books that are available in Nigeria and Africa were mainly imported from the United States of America, Britain, and other Western countries. There are many cogent reasons why the various psychology books that -are imported from America and Western Europe are not suitable for teaching and learning psychology in Nigeria and other African countries. However, the most relevant reason that I should like to mention at least in this present context is that the imported Western psychology books were written by Western psychologists. Most of the subject – matters, ideological and analytical points of views, and the examples and illustrations in such books are mainly derived from American and/or European societies. Most Nigerian and other African students cannot easily visualize and properly understand the predominantly American and/or European *contexts* and *contents* of those imported Western psychology books, because they are not familiar with them.

Thus, it is quite obvious that the situation of the lack of adequate and sufficient psychological books in Nigeria and other African countries poses a great deal of problem to most professional psychologists, psychology students, and other people in the country and continent, who wish, or need, to get adequate and relevant reference books that contain both purely psychological and non-psychological concepts that are used in modern psychology, for them to study or use for whatever other purposes.

The situation of the acute scarcity of books on psychological concepts in Nigeria and Africa is especially unfortunate because from the past two decades to date interests in academic psychology have been increasing rapidly in the country and continent. Proofs of this observation are as follows:

Firstly, in Nigeria in particular, and in other African countries in general, the various academic areas in which psychology is taught and learnt have expanded a great deal. For instance, psychology courses are presently taught and learnt in the Departments of Psychology, Sociology, Business Administration, Public Administration, Educational Psychology, Mental Health (or Psychiatry), Social or Community Health, and in some other Departments and Institutes in the various Universities, Colleges of Education, Polytechnics, and in some other allied educational institutions in the country and continent.

Secondly, students' enrolments in both purely psychology courses and psychology – related courses in all the above – mentioned departments and educational institutions are also always increasing.

Thirdly, nowadays; more of trained and qualified psychologists are now found in lectureship and research jobs in all these educational institutions. In addition, many trained and qualified psychologists can also be found nowadays in many different administrative and professional jobs in Government ministries and parastatals; in management and professional jobs in private companies, e.g., in advertising, marketing, personnel management, public relations, guidance and counselling, and other suitable jobs; and also in private consultancy jobs.

And, fourthly, psychological concepts and ideas are also frequently acquired and freely used in an *ad hoc* manner by different categories of analysts, interpreters, and commentators, on current and public affairs, in the various modern media of mass communication – such as, in the newspapers, magazines, radios, and televisions.

The Main Objectives of this Handbook

Largely because of the increasing interests in and demand for standard textbooks and reference or supplementary reading materials for the teaching and learning of psychology in Nigeria and other African countries, and the acute shortage of these types of books in the country and continent, I have, therefore, decided to assemble together many of the technical psychological and non-psychological concepts that are commonly used in modern psychology in this compact hand book. It is hoped that it will be easily accessible to most of the people who want, or need, to use it in Nigeria in particular, and elsewhere in general.

Consequently, the major objective of this handbook is to make a large collection and wide range of good, standard, and reliable definitions of most of the technical psychological and non-psychological concepts that are often used in modern psychology, available in this relatively compact and accessible handbook for professional psychologists, psychology students, and other people, to study or use for whatever other purposes, in Nigeria, and elsewhere in Africa, and beyond.

The Distinctive Nature of this Handbook

This Handbook is mainly a supplementary reference book of concepts in the field of academic psychology. Most books that serve as reference sources for specialized academic concepts and subjects are of *three major types;*

1. Encyclopaedias,
2. Handbooks, and
3. Dictionaries.

Each of these three types of books has its own relatively distinctive nature and characteristics, as well as strengths and weaknesses. As the title of this present book succinctly shows, it is exclusively a handbook of concepts that are used in modern psychology. However, in order for me to properly clarify the distinctive nature of this handbook I shall briefly compare and contrast the major characteristics of encyclopaedias, dictionaries, and handbooks that primarily serve as reference books, as follows:

An encyclopaedia is usually a comprehensive, multivolume, reference book. It provides relatively detailed and informative articles on the various concepts and topics that it covers, arranged in an alphabetical order. There are two main types of encyclopaedias: (a) specialized, and (b) general encyclopaedias. A specialized encyclopaedia focuses specifically upon one particular field of study. Examples of specialized encyclopaedias include *The International Encyclopaedia of the Social Sciences*, edited by David L. Sills.

In contrast, a general encyclopaedia covers a very wide range of subjects. Examples of general encyclopaedias include the famous *Encyclopaedia Britannica*.

A *dictionary* is a relatively comprehensive reference book that contains concise definitions of important words of a language, such as English, or of a field of study, such as psychology. It identifies the phonetic, grammatical, and semantic value of each word, often with etymology, citations, and usage guidance and other information. Like in an encyclopaedia, the words in a dictionary are also arranged alphabetically. Furthermore, there are likewise two major types of dictionaries: (a) specialized, and (b) general dictionaries. Specialized dictionaries provide definitions of and/or short notes on the various technical concepts in any particular field of study, such as psychology, medicine, education, social science, etc. Examples of specialized dictionaries include *A New Dictionary of Sociology.* Edited by G. Duncan Mitchell.

In contrast, general dictionaries provide definitions of important words in a whole language. Examples of general dictionaries include *The American Heritage Dictionary of the English Language,* edited by Williams Morris; and *The World Book Dictionary* (in two volumes), edited by Clarence L Barnhart and Robert K. Barnhart.

A *handbook* is a sort of concise, self-contained study book, hi any specific field of study, such as psychology, physics, medicine, or engineering, A handbook attempts to provide the essence of the subject-matter of the area of study that it focuses upon, and also the essence of success in that area of study. It supplies detailed but precise set of information in the particular subject area, without unnecessary padding and superfluous semantic embellishments. A handbook supplements leading textbooks and voluminous reference books, such as encyclopaedias and dictionaries, by providing only the most relevant digest of the subject-matter in a brief note-form. It provides its readers with ready-made short-notes that save scarce and valuable time that would have been otherwise spent in cumbersome private note taking.

There are several different types of handbooks. However, the most notable ones are as follows:

1. *Textbook handbooks:* these are like regular introductory textbooks in a field of study, However, they are generally more concise than most standard introductory textbooks. Examples include the Macdonald and Evans Limited Handbook series, that are published at Estover, Plymouth PL6 7PZ, Great Britain. Some of their products include *Labour*

Law, by M. Wright; and *Basic Sociology,* by F. J. Wright and F. Randall.

2. *Conceptual handbooks:* These are like dictionaries and encyclopaedias. However, conceptual handbooks are generally more concise than dictionaries and encyclopaedias. In contrast to a dictionary, a conceptual handbook would concentrate in providing a sufficiently explicatory definition of a concept, but it would tend to dispense with identifying the phonetic, grammatical, and semantic details of the concept, While in contrast with an encyclopaedia, a conceptual handbook would aim at providing very precise and basic definitions of a concept or subject, rather than detailed and expository descriptions of the concept.

From the foregoing comparisons and contrasts between encyclopaedias, handbooks, and dictionaries, I can now validly or convincingly say that this present book, psychology handbook   is neither an encyclopaedia nor a dictionary, but rather it is a specialized handbook As a result, it mainly attempts to provide the reader with the most basic, standard, and reliable 'definition' and "meaning" of each of the various concepts that are in the book. Consequently, this handbook does not, like a general dictionary, provide such additional details as the phonetic, grammatical, semantic, etymological, and usage guidance aspects of each of the various concepts that are in this book. Similarly, this handbook does not also, like an encyclopaedia, provide detailed, expository, descriptive notes on each of the various concepts that are in this book. Largely for the purpose of emphasis, I'll like to reiterate what I had just said above, that is, that this book is a specialized handbook of psychology that provides the reader with the most basic, standard, and reliable definition and meaning of each of the concepts that are in it. It is a supplementary reference book.

Therefore, I strongly advise that the reader who wishes to get the best value from his or her reading of this handbook should always endeavour to check for both corroborative as well as fuller details and usage of each of the concepts in this dictionary in some standard introductory textbooks, specialized research books, encyclopaedias, and/or dictionaries in the different fields of psychology, and, also in other allied academic disciplines.

The Scope of this Handbook

This psychology handbook is relatively general and comprehensive, rather than being overly specialized and narrow. By this I mean that this present handbook contains numerous carefully selected definitions of the various current and important technical psychological and non-psychological concepts that are presently frequently used in all the major different branches and fields of specialization in modern academic psychology such as, as follows:

(a) *The major types of technical concepts that are used in the different types of scientific research methods that are used in modern psychology, e.g., the various relevant concepts that are used in archival, survey, field, natural experiment, quasi-experiment, field-experiment, laboratory-experiment, and simulation research methods.*

(b) *The major types of technical concepts that are used in the different types of scientific theories that are used in modern psychology, e.g., the various relevant concepts that are used in structuralist, functionalist, psychoanalytic, behaviourist, gestalt, role, exchange and symbolic interaction theories.*

(c) *The major types of technical concepts that are used in the different fields of specialization in modern psychology. e.g., the various relevant technical concepts that are used in*

(i)   Psychobiology or Physiological Psychology,

(ii)   Clinical Psychology;

(iii)   Experimental Psychology;

(iv)   Educational Psychology;

(v)   Developmental Psychology;

(vi)   Social Psychology;

(vii)   Personality or Individual Psychology;

(viii) Applied Psychology (including Industrial Psychology, Guidance and Counselling Psychology, etc);

(ix)   Quantitative or Research Psychology; and

(x)   Analytical or Theoretical Psychology.

However, the various technical concepts that are mainly used end easily identified with each of the above-mentioned major branches and fields specialization in modem psychology are not arranged in separate sections that reflect each of the above-mentioned major branches and fields of specialization in modem psychology. The main reason why I did not arrange the various technical concepts that presently make up this handbook under different specialized technical sections in the book is that many of the concepts are used across the different branches and fields of specialization in modem psychology. Arranging the concepts under the different branches and fields of specialization of psychology in which they are supposedly mostly used and identified with would have created two formidable problems as follows:

1. Such an arrangement would have created the problem of double-counting many technical concepts. That is, if they must be listed under each of the different possible specialized sections in which they are found to be relevant; and

2. Such an arrangement would have created the erroneous impression that the various technical concepts that might be classified under each specialized branch or field of

specialization in psychology are actually used or are relevant to only each of such specialized branches or fields of specialization in psychology.

Therefore, largely in order to avoid these and other similarly serious problems, I found out that it was more appropriate and convenient for me to simply arrange all the different types of concepts that presently make up this Psychology Handbook in an alphabetical order. In this way the reader is inadvertently saddled with the not too small a responsibility of carefully studying and finding out for himself or herself the various major technical concepts in this handbook that are relevant to whichever particular branch or field of specialization of psychology that he or she might be interested in studying at any particular point in time. Nevertheless, I hope that the fact that I have arranged all the concepts that are in this handbook in an alphabetical order would greatly expedite the reader's task of locating any of the particular concepts that he or she would want or need to look for and study or use for whatever purpose.

The main sources of the concepts and definitions

I compiled most of the concepts and definitions which make up this handbook over the past thirty four years (1976 through 2010), from several different sources, including textbooks, dictionaries, encyclopaedias, and journals. However, the most dependable sources from which I obtained most of the concepts and definitions that make up this book are as follows:-

1. Back, Kurt W. et al, *Social Psychology* (New York: John Wiley and Sons, Inc. 1977).

2. Dushkin, David A. (President and Publisher), *Readings in Social Psychology Today* (Delmar, California: CRM Books, 1970).

3. Hilgard, Ernest R.; Atkinson, Rita L., and Atkinson, Richard C.; *Introduction to Psychology* (New York: Harcourt Brace Javanovich, Inc., 1979).

4. Hollander, Edwin P., *Principles and Methods of Social Psychology, Third Edition* (New York: Oxford University Press, 1976).

5. Krech, David; Crutchfield, R.S.; and Ballachey, F.L.; *Individual in Society: A Textbook of Social Psychology*, (New York: McGraw-Hill Book Company, Inc., 1962).

6. Kuppuswamy, B., *Elements of Social Psychology* (New Delhi: Vikas Publishing House PVT Ltd., 1973).

7. Liebert, Robert M.; and Neale, John M., *Psychology* (New York: John Willey and Sons, Inc., 1977).

8. Mednick, Sarnoff A.; Higgins, Jerry; and Kirschenbaum, Jack; *Psychology: Explorations in Behaviour and Experience* (New York: John Wiley and Sons, Inc., 1975).

9. O'Connel, Peter J. (Editor), *Encyclopaedia of Sociology* (Guildford, Connecticut: The Dushkin Publishing Group Inc., 1974).

10. Price, Richard H., *Abnormal Behaviour: Perspectives in Conflict, Second Edition* (New York: Holt, Rinehart and Winston, 1978).

11. Raven, Bertram H. and Rubin J. Z., *Social Psychology: People in Groups* (New York: John Wiley and Sons, Inc., 1976).

12. Schwartz, Marvin, *Physiological Psychology, Second Edition* (Englewood Cliffs, N.J.: Prentice-Hall, Inc., 1978).

13. Secord, Paul F.; Backman, Carl W.; and Slavitt, David R., *Understanding Social Life: An Introduction to Social Psychology* (New York: McGraw-Hill Book Company, 1976).

14. Severy, Lawrence J.; Brigham, John C.; and Schlenker, Barry R., *A Contemporary Introduction to Social Psychology* (New York: McGraw-Hill Book Company, 1976).

15. Sperling, Abraham, *Psychology Made Simple* (London: Heinemann, 1982).

16. Stones, E. *An Introduction to Educational Psychology* (Ibadan: Spectrum Book Limited, 1979).

17. Wrightsman, Lawrence S., *Social Psychology*, Second Edition (Monterey, California: Brooks/Cole Publishing Company, 1977).

In this book, all the various concepts that I obtained from their different sources are mixed together and re-arranged in an alphabetical order. I have extensively re-defined and/or edited most of the definitions of the concepts that I borrowed from these different sources. I have also drawn several concrete and relevant examples and illustrations from the Nigerian society and elsewhere to help to clarify end substantiate the meaning of many of the concepts in this handbook.

The main objective that guided my definition, editing, and illustration of most of the concepts that are in this book was that I wished to make the definitions of the various concepts to be readily intelligible and relevant to the majority of the book's anticipated Nigerian and other African readers.

However, I have also retained some of the original definitions of some of the concepts that I borrowed from their various sources. The two major reasons for this action are:

1. Some of such concepts are the products of highly specialized researches, and as a result their meanings are precise, fixed and widely accepted by most authorities in their respective fields of specialization.

2. I was not able to provide better alternative definitions to some of the other ones of such concepts as at the time in which this book was ready to go to the press.

I wish to hereby formally express my profound grateful *acknowledgement* to all the various authors, editors, and publishers of all the above-mentioned books (and others that I could not remember to mention in this handbook) for all the many concepts and/or definitions of concepts that I borrowed from their different books and used in this Psychology Handbook.

The Relevance of This Handbook

From all of the foregoing analyses and explanations, it could be said that this book is relevant, useful, or important, in several ways, including the following ones:-

1. This handbook provides a relatively comprehensive assortment of standard, up to date, and reliable definitions of most of the technical psychological and non-psychological concepts that are often used in the whole of modern psychology, throughout the world, in one compact and easily accessible book, for most professional psychologists, psychology students, and other interested people, to study, or use for whatever other purposes, in Nigeria and elsewhere. Thus, this book should help to reduce the problem of the acute shortage of psychology books in Nigeria and Africa.

2. This handbook is relatively comprehensive, rather than being overly specialized or narrow. It includes definitions of technical concepts drawn from all the major branches and fields of specialization in modem psychology. Therefore, this dictionary has attempted to cater adequately for most of the conceptual interests and needs of most of the different

categories of people who may wish to study and know the major technical concepts that are relevant to any of the major branches or fields of specialization in modern psychology.

3. Many of the definitions and examples or illustrations of most of the concepts in this handbook have *indigenous Nigerian and African contexts and contents.* As a result, many of such materials are particularly relevant to enable Nigerians and other Africans to easily visualize and understand the various behaviours, experiences, mental and physical processes of different individual human beings in their different Nigerian and other African social, cultural, economic, political and physical environments.

4. As a supplementary reference source book of key concepts of psychology, the careful study or use of this handbook will assist the reader in studying and understanding other intro-ductory or specialized psychology books and journals much more easily and rewardingly.

Benin City, Nigeria
2010

Ability: Demonstrable knowledge or skill. Ability includes aptitude and concrete achievement. *See also achievement and aptitude.*

Ablation: A method of studying brain functions consisting of removing or cutting tissue and observing its effects on the individual's behaviour.

Abnormal behaviour: *See mental retardation, psychopathology.*

Abortion: The forcible termination of pregnancy in a female organism, most typically in a human organism, before the foetus is capable of survival as an individual. There are many different methods of procuring an abortion, ranging from very crude and dangerous ones to very sophisticated and effective ones. The sophistication and effectiveness of abortion techniques depend largely upon available knowledge, technology, and the legal status of abortion itself in any society. Modern antiseptic methods of abortion minimize the risk of infection when done under medical supervision. Complications and fatalities are minimized when abortion is done during the early periods of pregnancy (one to twelve weeks), but they are very likely to occur during the later periods of pregnancy (more than four months).

Abreaction: In psychoanalysis, this is the process of reducing emotional tension by reliving (in speech or action or both) the experience that caused the tension.

Absolute threshold (1) The smallest amount of physical stimulus energy that is required to produce a sensation. (2) The intensity or frequency at which a stimulus becomes effective or ceases to become effective, as measured under experimental conditions.

Abstraction: A Characteristic that is not necessarily found in any particular individual, but rather it is held in common by several individuals, from whom it is usually abstracted for practical or analytical use.

Acceptance: In cognitive psychology, this term refers to the third and last step of observational learning; the observer uses acquired modeling Cues as a guide for his or her own behaviour, which is either imitative or counter-imitative.

Accommodation: In Piaget's theory of cognitive development, this concept refers to the mental process that produces adjustment and change in response to new information.

Acculturation: This concept refers to both the *process* and *result* of contact between two or more different cultures (such as between Western and traditional African cultures). The quantities and qualities of the substantive elements of culture that pass from one culture to another depend largely upon the method by which the transmission of the culture is effected, the relative powers of the carriers of the different cultures, and the purpose of the transmission of any element of one culture to another culture. If the purpose of a powerful culture in having contact with a weaker culture is to dominate the latter, then the powerful culture (e.g. powerful Western European and American capitalists and imperialists) will likely use force or coercion and blackmail to impose selected inferior aspects of their dominant culture upon the weaker African culture. For example, the powerful imperialist European powers used force to impose upon their colonial African subjects new ways of how they (Africans) should consume and enjoy Western made consumer commodities, such as exotic foods, alcohol, tobaccos, drugs, dresses, jewellery, cosmetics, and perverted sex; how to accept and worship only their deities and heroes; how to consume their outdated and meaningless works of art, music, drama, literature, and the like. As a result of these inferior foreign cultural impositions, Africans now find it difficult to improve upon their own indigenous cultures. Worse still, Americans and Europeans look down upon the Africans who display these sub-standard Western cultures.

Achievement: [1] Any acquired positive ability, e.g., school attainment of ability to correctly spell words, solve problems in mathematics, chemistry, statistics, psychology, etc. [2] Any good thing which any individual gets or obtains through making his or her own positive mental and/or physical effort, e.g. when any individual student actually studies his or her books properly and passes an examination well, without any dubious extraneous influences, such as the student's previous knowledge of the examination's question paper, or an unbecoming act of favouritism that .is practised by the examiner(s) towards the student. Achievement is often contrasted with *ascription. See also ascription.*

Achievement Motivation: The degree to which an individual sets high standards, strives to achieve them, and responds with appropriate feelings to failures or successes in such efforts.

Achievement motive: The social motive to accomplish something of value or importance, to meet standards of excellence in whatever one does. For example, a person's *determination* to do his/her very best and accomplish the best result at home, school, place of work, in games and sports, in entertainment, etc.

Achromatic colours: These consist of black, white and gray colours. *See also chromatic colours.*

ACTH: (Adrenocorticotropic hormone): This term refers to the pituitary hormone which prepares an individual to respond to stress.

Action instructions: Information given to the recipient of a fear-arousing communication about ways of coping with the danger.

Action potential: This concept is synonymous with the concept of *nerve impulse.* Both concepts refer to the wave of electrical activity that is transmitted down the axon of the neuron when the cell membrane becomes depolarized.

Action research: Research whose goal is the understanding or solution of some concrete or practical problems.

Acquiescent response set: A tendency to agree with an attitude statement regardless of the nature of its content.

Acquisition: The stage during which a new response is learned and gradually strengthened. It is the second stage of observational learning, characterized by the observer's ability to recall or re-produce the modeled behaviours to which he has been exposed.

Acrophobia: An abnormally intense fear of being in high places, such as very high buildings (e.g. skyscrapers), air-borne aero-planes, etc.

acupuncture

some facial   some body
puncture points   puncture points

Acupuncture: This is a traditional Chinese method of relieving pain in particular, and curing certain other illnesses in general. The method may involve a variety of procedures, and techniques, but all center around the insertion and manipulation of needles in certain supposedly critical points and parts of the patient's body. The result is said to be elimination or reduction of pain, in some instances to the extent of not requiring pharmacological anaesthetics in order to perform an otherwise painful surgery. The various responses which a patient makes to an acupunctural treatment's various painful stimuli are influenced or mediated by a variety of psychological factors, which include hypnosis, placebos, cultural training, and anxiety.

Adaptation: This concept was derived from the Latin word *adaptare*, which means "to fit". It is now technically taken to refer generally to the process by which animal or human species interact with and become fitted to their environments in order to obtain food, shelter, and protection from predation and, also ultimately, to ensure the biological survival of the species. The peculiarity of the physical characteristics and social behaviours of each species aids in fitting the species to its particular environment. On the individual level, an individual's learning greatly helps to increase the possibilities for his effective adaptation to his environment.

Adaptation-level theory: A theory of content effects, which suggests that the individual's background acts to set standard against which events or objects are perceived.

Addict: Any person who habitually uses drugs, especially morphine, heroin, etc, to the extent that cessation causes severe psychological or physical trauma or both.

Addiction: A physiological dependence upon a drug that is produced by continued use, especially of drugs like morphine, heroin, etc.

Additive mixture: The mixture of coloured lights; two spotlights of different colours focussed on the same spot yield an additive colour mixture. *See also subtractive mixture.*

ADH: *See antidiuretic hormone.*

Adipocytes: Special fat cells in the body. Obese individuals have many more of them and thus, perhaps, a higher body fat base line.

Adjustive behaviour: Behaviour by which an individual attempts to deal with stress and meet his needs; efforts to maintain harmonious relationships with the environment.

Adoption: Accepting another's child as one's own. Legally, the adoptive parents assume the same rights, duties, and responsibilities for the adoptive child that they hold for their natural children.

Single people are allowed to adopt children, as are parents who already have children. There is also a greater concern for the rights of the child as opposed to the rights of his natural parents, who may have neglected the child.

Adoption may be either unofficial or legal. Unofficial adoption is the custom of taking in the children of relatives or friends. Legal adoption procedures officially authorise control of a child by the adoptive parents. The adoptive parents must get formal consent from the natural parents, if possible, and they must give the court evidence that they can care for the child according to the adoption laws of the state.

Adrenal gland: One of a pair of endocrine glands located above the kidneys. The medulla of the gland secretes the hormones epinephrine and norepinephrine. The cortex of the gland secretes a number of hormones, collectively called the adrenocortical hormones, which include cortisone. *See also endocrine gland.*

Adrenalin: A hormone, secreted by the pith of each adrenal gland, that prepares an individual to handle stress. *See also epinephrine.*

American Psychologist Gordon Allport

Adultery: The voluntary sexual intercourse between a married person and a partner other than his or her spouse. Most societies have customs or laws for controlling adultery. Some have treated it as a private wrong to be handled by the families concerned, but others have made adultery a crime subject to severe penalties. Adultery is a crime in Nigeria, but the offended persons, such as cheated husbands, wives, or families, rarely take adulterers to courts. However, adultery is one of the commonest grounds (others include barrenness in women, cruelty of men, and poverty of a couple) for instituting and getting civil divorce in both the Customary and High Courts in the country. There are many types of adultery, such as: (1) a casual "fling"; (2) a preparation for another marriage; (3) an entertainment for both spouses (e.g., in "swingers' parties"); (4) as a way of making money; and (5) as a revenge against the other spouse's infidelity.

Adventurous deviant act: An act violating social norms, which is performed because of a challenge, mild threat, excitement, or pleasant tearfulness.

Advocating a contrary position: A way of changing attitudes, in which individuals are induced to advocate a position that is contrary to those in which they-believe, which often leads them to move towards the new position advocated.

Adjustment: The way in which a person becomes efficiently related to his environment.

Adolescence: In human beings, this is the period of transition from childhood to adulthood. It is the period from puberty to maturity. It roughly includes the early teens to the early twenties.

Affect: A general term that refers to feeling, mood, temperament, emotion. It is a synonym for *emotion*.

Affect display: A category of movement in which feelings or emotions are conveyed by facial expressions.

Affect, flat: A lack of any observable emotional responsiveness to one's surroundings.

Affect, inappropriate: Inappropriate emotional responses to situations, such as crying over a joke or laughing uproariously over a tragedy.

Affectional drive: The point of view that the drive for affection is inborn.

Affectional system: A set of patterned behaviours that displays liking between two individuals.

Affective congruency: A state of consistency among actors' feelings about elements of their self-concept, their related behaviour; and the feelings towards these systems components held by other persons.

Affective disorder: A psychosis that is characterized by disturbances of mood, or affect.

Affective experience: Any emotional experiences, whether pleasant or unpleasant, mild or intense. See *also emotion.*

Affectivity: The dimension of feeling whose two poles are pleasantness and unpleasantness. Sometimes called the P-U scale from the initials of those two words.

Affect structure: The pattern of attraction and repulsion that is displayed by the members of any group towards one another. See *also sociometry.*

Afferent neuron: A neuron, or nerve cell, that conveys messages to the brain or spinal cord from the sense receptors informing the individual about events in the environment or within the body. This concept is usually synonymous with the concept of *sensory neuron. See also afferent neuron, receptor.*

Affiliation: Being attached to other persons. Early helplessness of the infant and child makes affiliation necessary. It is continued even when one is grown up.

Afterimage: The sensory experience that remains when a stimulus is withdrawn. Usually refers to visual experience e.g., the negative afterimage of a picture, or the train of coloured images that results after staring at the sun.

Age regression: In hypnosis, this concept refers to the reliving through fantasy of experiences that are based on early memories or that are appropriate to a younger age. *See also hypnosis.*

Aggression: A type of behaviour in which the goal is to harm or injure another person physically or mentally, or both.

Aggressive Identification: Identification with and taking on the attributes of an aggressive or punitive person.

Aggressiveness: Behaviour that reflects impulsiveness, activity without thought, and forcefulness.

Agoraphobia: Fear of open places. *See* also *phobia.*

Alcohol: A sedative-hypnotic drug that is widely used in most countries that can cause addiction. See *also Alcoholism: Drug Abuse; and Addiction.*

Alcoholism: Compulsive consumption of alcohol as a result of an addiction to it, which itself results from an excessive use of alcohol.

Alienation: A psychological condition in which individuals feel unable to influence or predict future outcomes, have doubts concerning the effectiveness of socially approved means to goal achievement, of the validity of widely held values, and experience a lack of intrinsic satisfaction in daily activities.

All-channel communication network: A decentralized communication network in which each member of a group may communicate with other members.

Allergen: A substance that produces a rash or body reaction when introduced to the skin or blood stream.

All-or-none law of neural transmission: States that a neuron either fires at its fixed intensity or it does not fire at all.

All-or-none principle: The rule that the nerve impulse in a single neuron is-independent of the strength of stimulation, the neuron either responds completely (fires its action potential) or not at all.

Alpha rhythm: A slow, even EEG brain-wave (about 8-13; cycles per second), that is generally associated with a state of relaxed, alert awareness, especially in adults. *See also Electron encephalograph.*

Alpha waves: *See electroencephalogram.*

Altercasting: The process by which another person (an alter) is placed in an identity or a role that requires him or her to behave in a manner advantageous to the manipulator.

Altruism: A special form of helping behaviour that is voluntary, costly, and motivated by something other than the anticipation of reward.

Altruistic suicide: According to French sociologist Emile Durkheim, this is the kind of suicide which an individual— who is tightly bound to a highly integrated group with a strong sense of solidarity – commits to sacrifice his/her life for the group's objectives, goals, ideals, or welfare. In highly integrated societies where there is a strong sense of social solidarity; self-destruction may be looked upon as self-affirmation and self-fulfillment; both life and death are believed to have equal or the same meaning and value. *See also anomic, egoistic, and fatalistic suicides.*

Ambiguous situation: A situation which is not clearly structured; so it produces a sense of frustration.

Ambivalence: Simultaneous liking and disliking of an object or person; the conflict caused by an incentive that is at once positive and negative. *See also conflict.*

Ambivert: A person whose personality is a balanced mixture of extravert and introvert traits.

Amentia: The condition of subnormal mental development.

Amnesia: The partial or total loss of memory of past experiences, especially through shock, psychological disturbance, brain injury or illness. The memories lost in amnesia have not been completely destroyed, for the forgotten events may again be remembered when the person recovers from the amnesia. Thus, amnesia is mostly associated with hysteria and illness. *See also Repression; Hysteria.*

Amphetamines: A group of stimulating drugs that produce heightened levels of energy and in large doses, nervousness, sleeplessness, and paranoid delusions. Dexedrine sulfate ("speed") and methamphetamine ("meth") are two types of amphetamines. *See also depressants, stimulants.*

Ampulla: The enlarged area at the base of each semicircular canal that contains the receptors for the perception of body rotation.

Amytal: This is a trade name for amobarbital, a sedative and hypnotic that acts as a depressant on the central nervous system.

Anaclytic Identification: Identification arising out of the loss, or threatened withdrawal, of a loved object. Closely related to developmental identification.

Anal retentive character: According to psychoanalytic theory, this is a person who tends to hoard material and personal assets and to be stingy towards others because withholding his or her bowel movements during the anal stage of development led to the control of others.

Anal stage: (1) In psychoanalytic theory, this is the second stage of psychosexual development. It is believed that during this stage the child focuses on the pleasures and tensions that are associated with the anal region and comes into conflict with his parents because of their desire to toilet-train him.

(2) The second stage according to the psychoanalytic theory of psychosexual development, following the oral stage. The sources, of gratification and conflict have to do with the expulsion and retention of faeces. *See also psychosexual development.*

Analysis-by-synthesis: A theory of perception assuming that the perceiver analyses a stimulus into features and then uses the features to synthesize, or construct, a percept that best fits all of the information.

Anatomy: The science of the structure of animals and plants, such as the human body.

Androgens: The collective name for male sex hormones, of which testosterone, secreted by the testes, is best known. See *also gonads.*

Androgyny: The state of possessing both masculine and feminine traits; it generally refers to *psychological* rather than *physical* characteristics.

Anorexia nervosa: This is a Latin word which means "nervous noneating".

Animism: The tendency, that is especially but not exclusively characteristic of pre-school children, to attribute qualities such as motives and feelings to inanimate objects.

Annal aggressive character: According to psychoanalytic theory, this is the character of an adult who, when provoked, exhibits hostile or other inappropriate emotional outbursts because a similar tactic (inappropriate elimination) worked when he or she was at the anal stage of development.

Anomie: Without a feeling of belonging. Feeling that the values and norms of a group or society from which one has drawn a sense of security have fallen apart and are no longer reliable.

Antagonism: The opposite effect, upon a given organ of the body, of impulses sent along the sympathetic nerves, to the effect of impulses sent along the parasympathetic nerves.

Anterograde amnesia: The inability to learn, or retain, new information; presumably because new information is not encoded into long-term memory. *See also dualmemory theory, encoding, long-term memory, retrograde amnesia.*

Anticonformity: Any behaviour that is directly antithetical to any group's normative expectations.

Antidepressant: Drug that is used to elevate the mood of depressed individuals: Examples include – imipramine (Tofranil), isocar-boxazid (Marplan), and tranylcpromine (Parnate).

Antidiuretic hormone (ADH): Hormone secreted by the pituitary gland that signals the kidney to reabsorb water into the blood stream instead of excreting it as urine.

Anti-intraception: Opposition-to the subjective, the imaginative, and the tender-minded. A characteristic of the authoritarian personality syndrome.

Antisocial personality: *See psychopathic personality.*

Anthropology: The "science that studies chiefly proliferate ("primitive") societies. Its main divisions are archaeology (the study of the physical monuments and remains from earlier civilizations), physical anthropology (concerned with the anatomical differences among men and their evolutionary origins), linguistic anthropology and social anthropology (concerned with social institutions and behaviour). *See also behavioural sciences.*

Anthropomorphism: The attribution of human motivation, characteristics, or behaviour to inanimate objects, animals, or natural

Annulment: Court declaration that a marriage has never legally existed. There are many grounds for annulment. Some of the commonest grounds for annulment include the fact that one or both parties was under the legal age for marriage, bigamy, and fraudulent intent – for example, refusal to have children after agreeing before the marriage.

Anxiety: (1) A state of apprehension or uneasiness, that is related to fear. The object of anxiety (e.g., a vague danger or foreboding) is ordinarily less specific than the object of real fear (e.g., a vicious animal), (2): Neurotic fear of anticipated trouble, called 'worry' when mild but continuous, and 'panic' when occasional but intense.

Anxiety hierarchy: A list or situations or stimuli to which a person responds with anxiety ranked in order from the least anxiety-producing to the most fearful. Used by behaviour therapists in systematically desensitizing patients to feared stimuli by associating deep relaxation with the situations rather than anxiety. *See also behaviour therapy, systematic desensitization.*

Anxiety neurosis: A disorder in which anxiety is felt in so many situations that it appears to have no specific cause; in addition to diffuse anxiety, the patient may suffer acute attacks. It is often referred to as free-floating anxiety.

Anxiety reaction: A form of neurosis that is characterized by a diffuse dread, often accompanied by tenseness, palpitation, sweating, or nausea. *See also neurosis.*

Apathy: Listlessness, indifference; one of the consequences of frustration. See *also frustration.*

Aphagia: Inability to eat. See also *hyperphagia.*

Aphasia: Impairment or loss of ability to articulate words *of* comprehend speech.

Apnea: A sleep disturbance that is characterized by inhibited breathing during sleep.

Apparent motion: *See autokinetic effect, phil phenomenon, stroboscopic motion.*

Appetitive behaviour: Seeking behaviour. See *also aversive behaviour.*

Approach-approach conflict: A situation in which there are two stimuli that are both attractive and incompatible.

Approach-avoidance conflict: A situation in which the stimulus to approach and the stimulus to avoid are simultaneous. It is tantamount to an ambivalent situation.

A priori: That which is presupposed, self-evident, or taken for granted; that which is a necessary given before knowing.

Aptitude: The capacity to learn; e.g., typing aptitude prior to practice on a typewriter. Aptitude tests are designed to predict the outcome of training, hence to predict future ability on the basis of present ability. *See also achievement*

Aqueous humour: The liquid that fills the space in the eye between the cornea and the lens.

Archetype: In the psychology of Carl Jung, this refers to any basic idea, such as "God" or "mother", which is said to characterize a universal unconscious.

Archival research: Analysis of existing documents or records, especially those consulted in public archives.

Area sampling: A form of probability sampling in which a geographic area serves as a basis of selection of a stratified random sample. For instance, a few districts, and within each district a few precincts, and within each precinct a few dwellings, may be randomly chosen for a sample.

Arousal: A state of heightened emotion.

Artifact: (1) Any man-made object, e.g. a motor car, a book, a statue, etc. (2) Any device that is constructed to simulate any desired form of behaviour from any organism. (3) Any research finding that does not reflect the true state of affairs in an area of population, but instead reflects the results of an arbitrary methodological approach.

Artificial intelligence: The performance by a computer of tasks that have hitherto required the application of human intelligence.

Ascendent (also-Ascendant): Tending to take the lead or to dominate the behaviour of another person or group.

Asch situation: An experimental situation in which a subject is led to believe that his or her perception is different from that of jail the other subjects. Used to test the extent of conformity to group opinion.

Figure 1: Typical comparison lines used in Asch's study of group effects on judgments

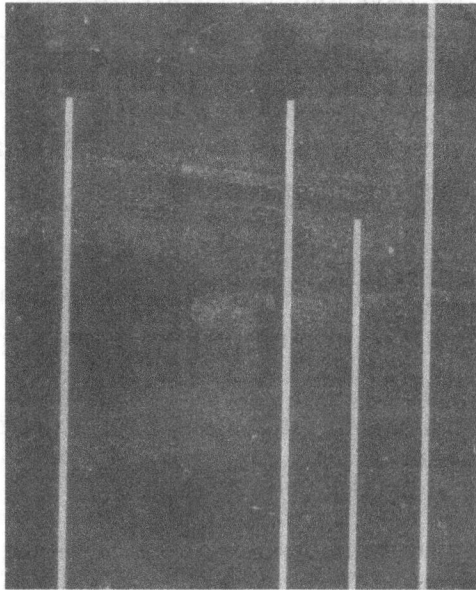

Source: Raven and Rubin (1976), page 316.

Source: Raven and Rubin (1976), page 317

Ascriptive Status: The social position which an individual occupies within a stratification system that is attributed to the characteristics over which he or she has no control, such as tribe, race, sex, age, or circumstances of birth. The individual can hardly change his or her ascriptive status. For example, most people remain forever in the tribe, race, or sex into which they are born until the end of their lives.

Asnomia: Complete absence of the sense of smelt in an individual.

Assertive training: A form of counter-conditioning in which assertive or approach responses are reinforced in an attempt to extinguish passivity or anxiety in certain situations. *See also behaviour therapy, counter-conditioning.*

Assimilation: In Piaget's theory of cognitive development, this refers to the individual's incorporation of new information into his or her over-all cognitive structure.

Association areas: Areas of the cerebral cortex that are not directly concerned with sensory or motor processes; they integrate inputs from various sensory channels and presumably function in learning, memory, and thinking.

Associative learning: Learning that certain contingencies (or relations) exist between events; learning that one event is associated with another.

Associative Organization: The extent to which materials to be remembered are associatively related *(for example, table-chair)*.

Assumed similarity: Correspondence between one's judgments or ratings of another person and one's own characteristics. A response set in person-perception tasks. Sometimes called *projection*, because it represents an attribution of one's characteristics to another person.

Assumption about human nature: Belief that people in general possess certain common characteristics.

Asymptote: The stable level to which a variable tends over the course of time; e.g., in learning, the final response strength after an extended period of acquisition.

Ataraxics: The so-called tranquillizing drugs. From a Greek word meaning calmness.

Attachment: The tendency that is especially but not exclusively characteristic of the young individual to seek closeness to particular individuals and to feel more secure in their presence.

Attention: The focusing of perception leading to heightened awareness of a limited range of stimuli.

Attitude: A relatively enduring disposition towards any characteristic of a person, place, or thing that is largely based upon one's beliefs and emotional feedings.

Attraction: A characteristic attributed to a person or group; such that a person tends to approach and interact with other persons or groups.

Attribution; The process by which we attempt to explain the behaviour of other people. Attribution theory deals with the rules which people use to infer the causes of observed behaviour. See *also dispositional attribution, situational attribution.*

Attribution proems: The process of assigning stable, enduring characteristics or dispositions to another person on the basis of his observed behaviour. By observing an individual's action and its effects – in relation to the situational demands, and our awareness of his knowledge, abilities, and past behaviour – we draw inferences about that person's intentions, and thence about his dispositions or personal characteristics.

Attribution theory: A theory which postulates that we make evaluative attributions concerning the reasons for the behaviour of others, in order to determine whether another person's words or behaviour reflect his true feelings or are elicited by the situation.

Audition: The sense or art of hearing. See *also hearing.*

Auditory canal: The passage that leads from the pinna to the eardrum.

Authoritarian aggression: A tendency to be on the lookout for and to condemn, reject, and punish people who violate conventional values. A characteristic of the authoritarian-personality syndrome.

Authoritarianism: A basic personality style that includes a set of organized beliefs, values, and preferences, including submission to authority, identification with authority, denial of feelings, cynicism, and others.

Authoritarian leadership: (1) A style of leadership that is somewhat similar to *directive leadership* and to *autocratic leadership*. (2) A set of attitudes and characteristics which occur together in prejudiced individuals. The Authoritarian leader determines the task, the members of the group, the way in which the problem has to be tackled, etc.

Authoritarian personality: (1) A personality characterized by a high need for unquestioning obedience and subordination, frequently associated with acceptance of strong leaders, scorn of weakness, nonconformity, and hostility to out-groups. (2) A personality syndrome that disposes a *person* towards a fascist ideology; to be deferent towards superiors but authoritarian towards those considered inferior. Likely to be prejudiced against minority groups and to sea the world as divided into the weak and the strong.

Authoritarian submission: A submissive, uncritical attitude towards the idealized moral authorities of the in-group. A characteristic of the authoritarian-personality syndrome.

Autism: Absorption in fantasy in order to avoid interest in objective reality; a symptom of schizophrenia. *See also schizophrenia.*

Autistic hostility: Hostility between two parties that arises from fears, fantasies, and negative expectations. By means of a mutual process of escalating aggressive acts and restricting friendly communications, the basis for hostility between the two parties becomes real, although it actually originated with the autistic thinking of each side.

Autistic thinking: This concept refers to an individual's wishful thinking in which his/her primary concern is with his/her needs or desires, at the expense of objective reality. It prays a prominent part in fantasy, as well as in day and night dreaming.

Autocratic leadership: The type of leader of a group who makes all of the decisions pertaining to the group's activities on his own; communicates these decisions, plans, and goals piecemeal, without letting the .members have an over-all picture or understanding of the group's ultimate goals; remains aloof from active cooperative participation; and gives praise and criticism arbi-arbitrarily. This type of leader resembles the *authoritarian leader* and uses some of the methods of the *task – centred leader*. Compare with *democratic leadership* and *laissez-faire leadership*.

Autokinetic-effect: (1) The apparent movement of a stationary spot of light when viewed in a totally dark room. (2) A perceptual illusion in which a stationary point of light, as seen by an observer in a dark room, seems to move.

Autokinetic Phenomenon: The observation that a stationary pinpoint of light in an otherwise completely dark room appears to move. This phenomenon was utilized by Sherif to study the development of group norms. During the course of successive judgments, groups of subjects tended to agree about how far "the light had moved-

Automatic: writing: Writing that the writer is unaware of; i.e., he or she does not know what he or she is producing; familiar in hypnosis. *See also hypnosis.*

Autonomic nerves: A division of the nervous system that serves the endocrine glands and the involuntary muscles of the internal organs.

Autonomous. Guided or controlled from within, i.e., self-regulated.

Autonomous man: This is the viewpoint which states that each individual human being has real control over his behaviour and destiny. Man is seen as an active agent with the capacity to voluntary and purposive action.

Autonomous nervous system (ANS): This is the part of the nervous system that innervates the endocrine glands, the heart, the smooth muscles of the stomach, the intestines, and other organs (that are collectively called the *viscera)* into action. It controls the patterns of behaviours that are usually thought to be involuntary, such as salivation, heartbeat and respiration rates, etc. It plays an important rote in influencing emotions, and also in preparing the body to deal effectively, with stress, relaxation, and rest.

Autonomous stage of morality: A later stage of moral development in which rules are seen as modifiable in order to fit the needs of a given situation.

Autonomy: This refers to the individual's capacity for self direction and a sense of inner freedom. This concept lies between the concepts of *rebellion* and *conformity*.

Average: See *measure of central tendency*.

Aversive behaviour: Avoidance behaviour. See *also appetitive behaviour*.

Aversive conditioning: A form of conditioning in which an undesirable response is extinguished through association with punishment; has been used in behaviour therapy to treat alcoholism, smoking, and sexual problems. See *also behaviour therapy, counter- conditioning*.

Avoidance: A behaviour pattern that is designed to keep an individual from making contact with an unpleasant stimulus.

Avoidance – avoidance Conflict: This refers to a somewhat complex conflict situation in which an individual is attempting to simultaneously avoid two negative stimuli. He is thereby in a sort of "double bind" or a "no-win" situation.

Avoidance learning: (1) Learning to avoid unwanted results by producing certain responses before the noxious event occurs. (2) A form of learning that is controlled by the threat of punishment. The learning is motivated by the anxiety raised by the threat and the reduction of anxiety when the punishment is avoided. *See also escape learning.*

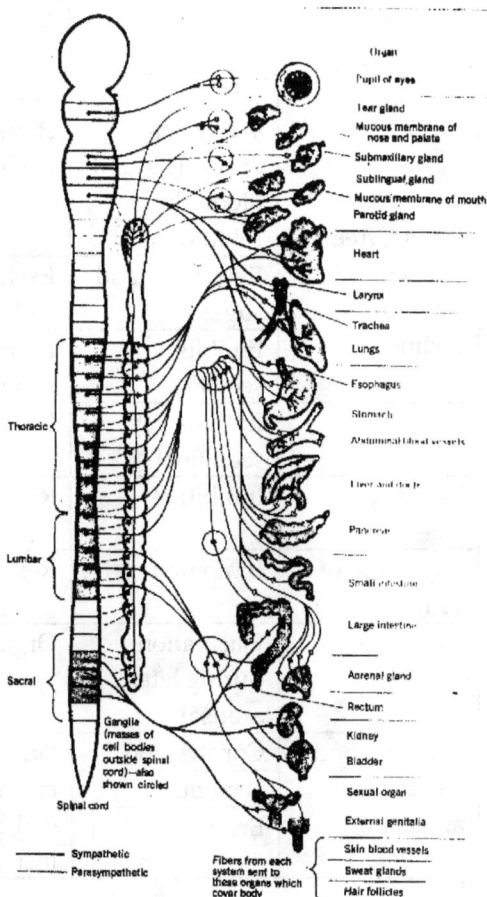

Parasympathetic system		Sympathetic system	
Function	Experience	Function	Experience
Constriction	Diminished light	Dilation	Increased light
Stimulates secretion		Inhibits secretion	Dryness in nasal passage, mouth, and throat
Deceleration, constriction of blood vessel		Acceleration, dilation of blood vessels	Increased blood pressure, heart pounding
	Relaxed throat, lower pitch		Tense throat, higher pitch
Constrict bronchi	Relaxed breathing	Dilate bronchi	Rapid breathing
Stimulates secretions and peristalsis		Inhibits secretions, peristalsis, and blood flow	Butterflies in stomach, heavy, tense feeling, indigestion
Liberates bile	Light, "free", relaxed internal feeling	Inhibition	
		Releases blood sugar	Excited, energetic feeling
Stimulates secretion		Inhibits secretion	Butterflies in stomach, heavy, tense feeling, indigestion
		Inhibits secretion	
Excitation	Expulsion of faces	Inhibition	Retention of faces
Excitation	Expulsion of urine	Inhibition	Retention of urine
Erection during early arousal	Excitation	Ejaculation during later arousal	Orgasm
Dilation	Skin and body feel relaxed and calm	Constriction	Skin feels cold and clammy, hairs and on end, perspiration increases
Inhibition		Secretion	
Relaxation		Erection	

Source: Mednick *et al* (1975), pages 116-7.

B

Background expectations: Those aspects of interactions that are taken for granted by everyone, and are so well accepted that their violation often produces incredulity and bewilderment.

Bad habit: This is a general concept that refers to any behaviour pattern which is irritating to both oneself as well as to other people.

Balance theory: A theory of interpersonal attraction and attitude change which hypothesizes that people will tend to be consistent in their attitudes and beliefs, and that they will experience discomfort or tension if these are inconsistent. Thus there are pressures on an individual to change his beliefs and attitudes to bring them into balance. [Example: If I paint a landscape and my base friend doesn't like it, I will experience tension or discomfort. I may then (1) try to convince her that the painting is truly a work of art, (2) change the painting so that she will like it, (3) deny that it was the "real" me who painted it (perhaps I painted it under pressure), (4) conclude that she isn't really such a good friend after all, (5) decide that she is a wonderful friend in many ways, but that she just doesn't know anything about art, and/or (6) decide that she has a right to her own opinion but that our relationship is based on our common interest in psychology, not an, and thus our differences on this issue are irrelevant).

Barbiturates: A class of synthetic sedative drugs that are addictive; in large doses, they can be lethal because they cause the diaphragm to relax almost completely.

Bargaining: In exchange theory, this is a process in which each of two or more persons attempts to negotiate a definition of the situation and of the resultant relationship that will *maximize* the outcomes for all involved.

Barnum effect: Refers to the readiness of most people to believe general descriptions, as given in astrological characterizations, and to use them personally.

Basal ganglia: Clusters of interconnected nerve cell bodies in the brain that control such important behaviour as the functioning of the heart.

Basal mental age: In individual tests of the Binet type, this term refers to the highest age level at which, and below which, all tests are passed. *See also mental age.*

Base line: A measure of the frequency of behaviour to be modified, taken before any treatment begins.

Base rate: The rate of response in the general population, or frequency of occurrence of an action or attitude in the general population.

Basic Personality: The underlying framework or core of behavioural patterns, attitudinal traits, and cognitive structures which apparently remains relatively stable and permanent during an individual's adult – life, and which manifests itself in a consistent or repetitive manner throughout the wide variety of different social contexts in which an individual finds himself or herself. Although, this basic personality" may not sometimes seem to be as permanent and immutable as is sometimes assumed, a major category of individuals actually do appear to have persistent, pervasive, and integrating behavioural patterns or attitudinal sets that serve to make comprehensible a wide range of seemingly unrelated individual personality traits which are unmanifested in actions and which thus enable some degree of predictability concerning human behaviour. An individual's "basic personality" is probably the result of a combination of biogenetic factors, unique individual socialization experiences, societal and specific group memberships, and certain general cultural orientations.

A Second View: An alternative meaning of the concept of "basic personality" was developed in the writings of American social psychologist Abram Kardiner, who referred to common personality traits possessed by a significant number of individuals who share the same cultural background or experiences. Used in this sense "basic personality" is essentially synonymous with the concepts of "national character," "modal personality," or "social character." *See also Modal personality: Personality structure.*

Basilar membrane: A membrane of the ear within the coils of the cochlea supporting the organ of Corti. Movements of the basilar membrane stimulate the hair cells of the organ of Corti producing the neural effects of auditory stimulation. *See also cochlea, organ of Corti:*

Basket-shaped nerve endings: The receptors for pressure sensations that are located around the base of the hair cells.

Behaviour: This concept refers to any bodily movements and the internal and external responses which each individual makes in any environment. These movements and responses include secreting from glands, talking, walking, writing, fighting, playing, – in short, the whole gamut of the actions which an individual enacts in society. See also *Normal behaviour; Abnormal behaviour.*

Behavioural sciences: The sciences that are concerned in one way or another with the behaviour of humans and lower organisms; especially social anthropology, psychology, and sociology, but including some aspects of biology, economics, political science, history, philosophy, and other fields of study. See *also anthropology, psychology sociology.*

Behaviour genetics: The study of the inheritance of behavioural characteristics.

Behaviourism: A school or system of psychology associated with the name of John B. Watson; it defines psychology as the study of behaviour and limits the data of psychology to observable activities. In its classical form it was more restrictive than the contemporary behavioural viewpoint in psychology.

Behaviourists: A school of psychologists who ignore both conscious and unconscious experiences as being too subjective for scientific study, and concentrates on such patterns of behaviour as conditioned responses. Led by the American psychologist John B. Watson. An influential present-day behaviourist is American psychologist, B. F. Skinner.

Behaviour modification, also called (behaviour therapy): A type of psychotherapy which, in the narrow sense, applies classical or operant conditioning to help resolve a patient's problems; in the broader sense, it is applied experimental psychology.

Behaviour settings: A term used in ecological psychology to refer to every location-activity combination. Thus the term "behaviour settings" refers not only to physical localities (a gymnasium, a street comer, a drugstore) but also to the activities that take place within them.

Behaviour therapy: A method of psychotherapy that is based on the principles of learning theory. It uses such techniques as counter-conditioning, reinforcement, and shaping to modify behaviour (syn. behaviour modification).

Belief: The attribution of a cognition to an object. The statement, "Breast-feeding makes for happier babies" attributes happy babies to the object, breast-feeding. A belief is based more on fact or presumed fact than an attitude, but several beliefs are usually associated with a given attitude.

Belief component: One of the two parts of an attitude, consisting of the content of the attitude, typically expressed in verbal statements.

Belongingness: Identification with a group and the feeling of being accepted by that group.

Benzedrine: This concept refers to amphetamine sulfate, a strong amphetamine known in slang as "bennies". It is medically used to treat certain childhood disorders as well as to control obesity.

Bestiality: The act of human beings having sexual intercourse with animals. Bestiality mainly occurs in rural areas and most frequently although it does not exclusively involve male adolescents and farm or domestic mammals.

Beta rhythm: The low voltage, high frequency [14-25 cycles per second] brain rhythm in an alert adult.

Bias: The emotional or sentimental or ideological preconceptions of individuals or groups, which substantially influence the way they perceive and interpret any subject-matter, and which lead them to reach conclusions that are significantly different from the objective "nature of the subject-matter in question".

Bigotry; The-altitude or behaviour of a person of strong bias or prejudice. The bigot's behaviour is often characterized by stubbornness and emotionality. He or she most commonly displays intolerant feelings and behaviours towards other people who differ with him or her on most matters, such as political, religious, racial, and ethnic matters.

Binet – Simon Scale: This is an intelligence test that was first developed by a French Psychologist (called Binet) and a psychiatrist (called Simon) to assess mental abilities in individuals, in order to know when to provide *special education* facilities for those of them who are found to be mentally retarded persons. It principally comprises a series of verbal and performance items that become increasingly difficult to answer.

Binocular depth cue: Information about depth that requires the use of both eyes (for example, retinal disparity).

Binocular (retinal) disparity: A binocular depth cue that is produced by the disparity between the images reaching each eye.

Binocular disparity: The fact that an object projects slightly different images on the two retinas due to the different positions of the right and left eyes.

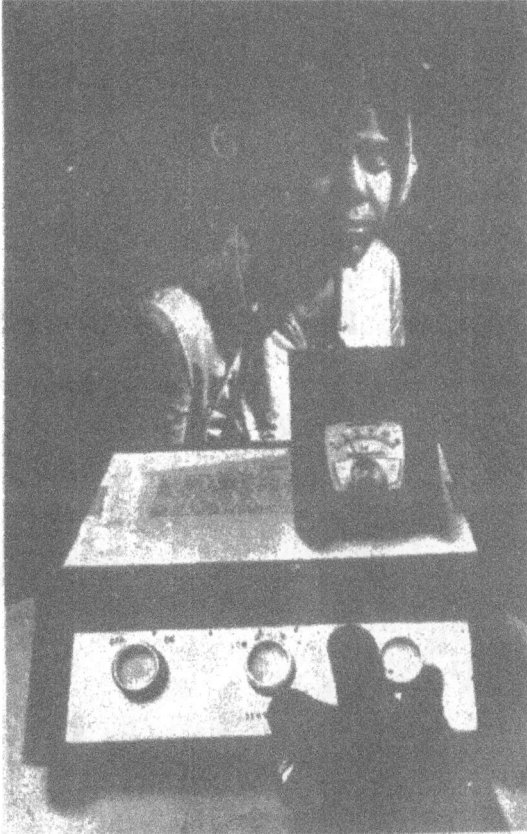

Source: Liebert and Neale (1977), page 35.

Biofeedback: A procedure that permits individuals to monitor their own physiological processes (e.g., heart rate, blood pressure), which they are normally unaware of, and to learn to control them.

Biological determinism: This is the belief which is held by some people that qualities or characteristics that are inherent in an organism cause his or her behaviour.

Biological drive: This term refers to a set of characteristics that are inherent in organisms, that impel them to engage in the types of behaviours that would preserve them and their species. Biological drive is frequently correlated with such specific physiological states as hunger, thirst, and body temperature. Examples of biological drives include the drives for food, water, air, sex, and, avoidance of pain.

Biological feedback control: This consists in providing an individual with information about a bodily response (such as heart-rate, skin temperature, blood pressure, etc) by some mechanical or electronic means so that the individual can learn to adjust or change that response.

Biological therapy: Treatment of personality maladjustment or mental illness by drugs, electric shock, or other methods directly affecting bodily processes. See *also psychotherapy.*

Blind Spot: [1] The point at which the optic nerve joins the retina. Since neither rods nor cones are present, this spot is blind to any light.

[2] The area where the optic nerve leaves the eye; it contains no visual receptors.

[3] An insensitive area of the retina where the nerve fibers from the ganglion cells join together to form the optic nerve.

Blood pressure: The pressure of the blood against the walls of the blood vessels. Changes in blood pressure following stimulation serve as one indicator of emotion.

Body Language: This concept is synonymous with the concept of *nonverbal communication.* The most typical and obvious forms of body language are gestures. Other important forms of body language include the way individuals walk, the positions in which they choose to sit and stand in any occasion, and their facial expressions.

Body Types: The various categories or classes into which some scholars classify different forms of human beings' bodily shapes, looks, and other characteristics. For example, American William Sheldon's classification comprises three major categories, each of which he also related to a characteristic temperament. The *endomorph* is flabby and easy-going; the skinny *ectomorph* is inclined to be introspective; and the *mesomorph* is restless and tends to translate impulse into action.

Boomerang effect: A social influence situation in which persons who have received a communication that was designed to change their attitude or behaviour in a certain direction actually change their attitude or behaviour in the opposite direction. A boomerang effect is particularly likely to occur when the positive influence of the message is overbalanced by the even greater negative influence of the agent himself, e.g. suspicion or dislike for the communicator.

Brain stem: The structures lying near the core of the brain; essentially all of the brain with the exception of the cerebrum and the cerebellum and their dependent parts.

Brainstorming: A process in which group members are encouraged to list all the ideas which come to mind, even the most ridiculous, and to avoid evaluating their quality.

Brainwashing: An intensive attitude-change programme notably utilized by any country fighting a war, to try to change the political views of their prisoners of war. This method utilizes isolation and physical strain, as well as political indoctrination, arousal of guilt, peer pressures, and the foot-in-the-door technique. *See also coercive persuasion.*

Branching programme: A teaching programme often implemented by a computer in which the students' path through the instructional materials varies as a function of their performance. Students may move rapidly through the material if their responses are generally correct or go off to remedial loops if they encounter difficulties. *See also CAL, linear programme.*

Brightness: The dimension of colour that describes its nearness in brilliance to white (as contrasted with black). A bright colour reflects more light than a dark one. See *also hue, saturation.*

Brightness constancy: The tendency to see a familiar object as of the same brightness, regardless of light and shadow that change its stimulus properties. *See also colour constancy, object constancy.*

British Ability Scales: A comparatively recent measure of intelligence which can be used with children up to the age of seventeen years.

Broca's area: A portion of the left cerebral hemisphere that is said to control motor speech.

Bystander apathy: This means any situation in which bystanders (the various people who are around in any place) are reluctant to give help to other persons who are in need. There are several different reasons why bystanders display such apathetic or indifferent behaviour. However some of the commonest reasons include diffusion of responsibility, perceived loss of control, fear of personal injuries and reprisals, etc. The extent to which bystanders would get themselves involved in any problematic situation also depends on a variety of reasons which include the following: people who are perceived as sick, well-dressed, socially well-placed, and females are more likely to make bystanders to help them whenever they are in need, than other types of people, such as drunkards, poor or wretched – looking people, or mates. Thus, for example, females are more likely than males to get lifts or rides in cars that are being driven by male owners or male drivers.

Bystander effect: The finding that a person is less likely to provide help when in the presence of other witnesses than when alone.

Bystander intervention phenomenon: The observation that a person will be less likely to offer assistance to someone in need of help when there are other people present.

CAL: A common abbreviation for computer-assisted learning: i.e. instruction carried out under computer control. *See also branching programme, linear programme.*

Canalization: This concept was first professionally, that is, technically, used by the American psychologist Gardner Murphy to refer to his account of the relationship between human drives and goal attainments. According to Murphy, canalization is the process in which individuals engage in certain appropriate types of behaviours or lines of actions that enable them to achieve their desired goals or objectives and thereby reduce their drives. For example, if a person is hungry (a drive), and he/she finds and eats enough food, and he/she is satisfied (goal attainment), then that person's hunger has been canalized, at least as at that particular point in time.

Cannabis: The source of marijuana and hashish is the Indian hemp plant that is technically called in botany as *Cannabis sativa,* a herbaceous annual growing wild in many parts of the world, including Nigeria. Marijuana and hashish can have sedative, euphoriant, or hallucinogenic effects.

Cannibalism: This means the eating of human flesh by some human beings. It is not a universal practice. There are no available reliable scientific evidence to show the exact origin of this practice, and the various parts of the world in which it actually occurs. However, the various available bits and pieces of evidence show that the various societies in which cannibalism is practised, differ widely in their choice of whom they eat (relatives or enemies), the parts of the body that they eat, how they prepare the food, and the reasons or purposes for their eating the flesh of their fellow human beings.

Cannon-Bard theory: A classical theory of emotion proposed by Cannon and Bard. The theory states that an emotion-producing stimulus activates the cortex and bodily responses at the same time; bodily changes and the experience of emotion occur simultaneously. *See also cognitive-physiological theory, James-Lange theory.*

Cardinal dispositions: In Allport's trait theory, these are an individual's most pervasive traits; they tend to dominate his or her personality completely.

Career: The sequence of movements which persons normally make from one position to another as in an occupation or any other way of life. For example, training to become and working as a professional psychologist, an engineer, a medical doctor, etc.

Career contingencies: Those factors on which sequential movement from one position to another depend.

Case history: A biography obtained for scientific purposes; the material is sometimes supplied by interview, sometimes collected over the years. *See also longitudinal study.*

Case study: In Psychology, this is a research procedure by which current, historical, and biographical information is collected for a single individual.

Castration; Surgical removal of the gonads; in the male, removal of the testes; in the female, removal of the ovaries.

Castration anxiety: In psychoanalytic theory, this is the anxiety experienced by a little boy that his penis will be cut off or injured, especially by his angry father who detects that the boy would like to have an incestuous relationship with his mother.

Castration Complex: Supposed fear on the part of boys that they will be (and on the part of girls that they already have been) deprived of their external male genitals, as a punishment for incestuous desires.

Cat: An identity which recognizes some elements in the dominant culture, such as being affluent and living in style, especially in more deviant or extreme forms, but which involves achieving this without working. Instead, the cat lives by his wits outside the law. Central here is a life-style which emphasizes the "kicks" the cat gets from his exploits.

Catatonia: [1] The maintenance of a fixed posture, sometimes grotesque, for long periods of time, accompanied by muscular rigidity, a trance-like state of consciousness, and waxy flexibility. [2] Hostile form of schizophrenia, characterized either by inhibition of response, or by extreme violence.

Categorical organization: The extent to which materials to be remembered can be grouped together in categories (for example, horse-cow-dog (four-footed animals).

Catharsis: The reduction of frustration-induced tendencies towards aggressive behaviour through the expression of hostility or tension in behaviour, verbal expression or fantasy. The catharsis theory holds that the observation of hostility or aggression in others (such as in a football game or a violent film) may serve to dissipate one's tendencies towards more direct aggression.

Cathartic effect: A supposed reduction in the tendency of a viewer to perform aggressive behaviour, brought about by a vicarious release of aggressions through viewing the aggressive behaviour of other persons in fictional media or other events.

Causal relationship: A relationship in which one event is not only antecedent to, but the cause of, the occurrence of a second event.

Ceiling effect: An artificial limit on the highest possible score, due to some characteristic of the measure.

Central core: The most central and the evolutionally oldest portion of the brain. It includes structures that regulate basic life processes, including most of the brain stem. See *also brain stem, cerebellum, hypothalamus. reticular system.*

Central dispositions: In Allport's trait theory, these are the few really distinctive traits that characterize a person.

Central fissure: A fissure of each cerebral hemisphere that separates the frontal and parietal lobes (syn. fissure of Rolands).

Centrality: A characteristic of a *position* in a group structure (usually a *communication network).* The fewer the number of communication linkages from a given position to all of the other positions, the greater the centrality. Thus, in a five-person *wheel communication network,* the hub position is most central, since its occupant is only four steps removed (one to each of the other four positions) from reaching the occupants of those positions. Less commonly centrality also applies to other structural dimensions, such as *sociometric* and *structure interdependence.*

Centralized communication network: A *communication network* in which one or a few members of a group (the central members) can readily receive communications from all or most of the others (the peripheral members), but in which the peripheral members cannot communicate well among themselves. This is the opposite of a decentralized communication network in which everyone can fairly easily communicate with everyone else. The degree of centralisation in communication affects morale, effectiveness in problem-solving, leadership and other group variables. The following communication networks range in order from highly centralized to highly decentralized: *Wheel, Y, chain, circle,* and *all-channel.*

Central nervous system: In vertebrates, the brain and spinal cord, as distinct from the nerve trunks and their peripheral connections. See *also autonomic nervous system, peripheral nervous system.*

Table 3:- **The central nervous system**

Structure	Function
1.The Brain Cerebrum Corpus Callosum Thalamus Hypothalamus Cerebellum	Sense perception, control of voluntary movements, learning, memory, thinking, consciousness. Connecting left and right cerebral hemispheres. A relay station for impulses to cerebral cortex. Control of or influence on such functions as endocrine balance, temperature regulation, appetite, metabolism, emotions. Coordination of voluntary movements, body balance, muscle tone.
2. The Brain Stem (The upper portion of the spinal cord) Reticular formation Pons Medulla	Activating cerebral cortex; its impulses play an important role in consciousness, awareness, sleep. Connecting the two hemispheres of the cerebellum via 12

	cranial nerves, extending brain control over breathing, swallowing, heart heat, digestion, etc.
3. Spinal Cord	Carrying brain impulses to body and impulses from body to brain, controlling many reflexes.

Mednick, et al (1975), page 68.

Figure 5: The central nervous system

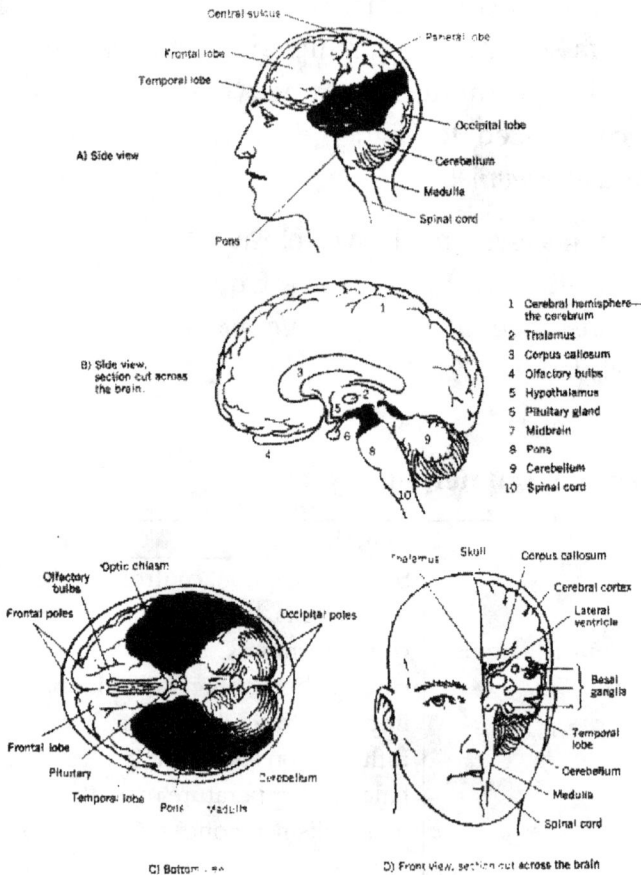

Source: Mednick et al (1975), page 69.

Central trait: A personal characteristic that strongly influences a perceiver's impressions of the person possessing it. Asch showed that the *warm-cold* personality dimension is a good example of a central trait.

Cephalocaudal: The principle that physical growth in the head (or cephalic) region proceeds well ahead of growth in the tail (or caudal) region.

Cerebellum: This is the lobed structure attached to the rear of the brain-stem that is responsible for regulating muscle tone and coordinating intricate body movements, balance, and posture.

Cerebral cortex: The surface layer of the cerebral hemispheres in higher animals, including humans. It is commonly called gray matter because its many cell bodies give it a gray appearance in cross section, in contrast with the myclinated nerve fibers that make up the white matter in the centre. The cerebral cortex is involved with higher mental processes such as speech, learning, problem-solving, perception, and movement.

Cerebral hemispheres: The two large masses of nerve cells and fibres .hat constitute the bulk of the brain in humans and other higher animals. The hemispheres are separated by a deep fissure, but connected by a broad band of fibres, the corpus callosum (syn. cerebrum). *See also cerebral cortex, left hemisphere, right hemisphere, split-brain subject.*

Cerebrotonia: In Sheldon's type theory, this concept refers to temperament (which is associated with the ectomorphic body type) that is characterized by privacy, secretiveness, postural restraint, and social inhibitions.

Cerebrum: The two cerebral hemispheres.

Chain communication network: A *communication network* in which the channels form a chain (A – B – C – D – E).

Figure 6: Chain communication network

Source: Raven and Rubin (1976), page 271.

Charisma: A particular appeal or personal magnetism that is attributed to certain persons.

Charismatic Leader: A leader with extraordinary power of personality so that he is looked upon by other people as a superhuman or divinely conditioned individual.

Chauvinist: One who displays excessive pride and devotion to his or her own group. For example, a male chauvinist is one who believes that men are better than women in nearly all respects.

Childhood: (1) Legally, any person who has not yet reached his eighteenth birthday anniversary. (2) Commonly, any person whose adolescence has not yet begun. (3) In psychology, the period of life between infancy and adolescence.

Choice Dilemma Questionnaire (CDQ): An instrument that is used to study risky shift. A subject is given a series of problems in which he must choose between one alternative that is safe (with little risk of harm or loss) but that only offers the prospect of a small reward, and another alternative that offers great risk as wed as the possibility of a large reward.

Choleric: Irritable. One of Galen's 'four temperaments.'

Chromatic Colours: All colours other than black, white, and grey; e.g., red. yellow, blue. *See also achromatic colours.*

Chromosome: A chromosome is a threadlike particle that exists in pairs in the nucleus of each cell that exists in each individual's body. A chromosome is made of RNA and protein. The chromosomes carry the genes which transmit the basic hereditary .information from parents to their offspring. Each human being has 46 chromosomes, arranged in 23 pairs, one member of each pair derives from the mother, one from the father. *See also gene.*

Chronic personality characteristics: The characteristics of an individual that are relatively enduring. They are present at different times and in different situations.

Chronic suicide: A slow self-murder which an individual inflicts upon himself/herself, when he/she dies as a result of his/her engaging in some unbecoming behaviour, such as alcoholism, drug abuse, reckless sexual indulgence, compulsive eating etc.

Chronological age (CA): Age from birth; calendar age. *See also mental age.*

Chunk: The largest meaningful unit of information that can be stored in short-term memory; short-term memory holds $7 - 2$ chunks. *See also short-term memory.*

Circadian rhythm: A cycle or rhythm that is roughly 24 hours long Sleep-wakefulness, body temperature, and water excretion follow a circadian rhythm, as do a number of other behavioural and physiological variables.

Circle communication network: A *communication network* in which the channels of communication form a circle: A communicates with B, B with C, C with D, D with E, E with A. Thus the, circle is a decentralized communication network.

Figure 7: Circle communication network

Source: Raven and Rubin (1976), page 271.

Circular reaction: A process whereby the emotions of others elicit he same emotions in oneself. This reaction, in turn, serves to intensify the emotions of others.

Clairvoyance: (1) A form of extrasensory perception in which the perceiver is said to identify a stimulus that is influencing neither his nor her own sense organs nor those of another person, (2) The ability to perceive objects or events that cannot be perceived by the conventional senses. See *also extrasensory perception, precognition, psychokinesis. telepathy.*

Classical conditioning: In psychology, this concept refers generally to all *conditioned-response experiments* which conform to Ivan Pavlov's experiment. Their main feature comprises a procedure by which a neutral stimulus (such as a bell) becomes strongly associated with a stimulus which can elicit a response (such as food, which will elicit salivation from an animal). By pairing the two stimuli for a period of time, it is possible to condition the organism so that the originally neutral stimulus (the bell) will elicit the same response as the unconditioned stimulus (the food). (Syn. stimulus substitution). See also *operant conditioning-*

Class interval: In statistics, this concept refers to a small section of a scale according to which scores of a frequency distribution are grouped; e.g., heights grouped into class intervals of a half metre. See also *frequency distribution.*

Claustrophobia: Fear of being in small, closed places, such as rooms, elevators, etc. See *also phobia.*

Client-centred therapy: A method of psychotherapy designed to let clients learn to take responsibility for their own actions and to use their own resourcefulness in solving their problems (syn. nondirective counseling). It is essentially a humanistic-existential insight therapy, developed by Carl Rogers, which emphasizes that the therapist should try to understand the client's subjective experiences in order to help him or her become more aware of the current motivations for his or her behaviour; the goal is to reduce the client's anxieties and to encourage the actualization of potentialities.

Climacteric: This term refers to the so-called change of life. It is called 'menopause' in the female.

Clinical psychologist: A psychologist, usually with a Ph.D. degree, trained in the diagnosis and treatment of emotional or behavioural problems and mental disorders. See *also counseling psychologist, psychiatrist.*

Clique: A subgroup whose members have many mutual choices and few choices of persons outside of the clique. The clique is usually technically identified by means of sociometric measurement See *sociometrv.*

Closed-ended question: Any question that presents two or more response alternatives for the respondent to choose between.

Closure: An organizing tendency to perceive an incomplete pattern as a complete pattern.

Coalition: A subgroup whose members cooperate with one another in order to work towards a common goal and to exert control over others who are not in the coalition and with whom the subgroup is in *competition.*

Coalition formation: The development of an alliance between two members of a three-person group.

Cocaine: A pain-reducing and stimulating drug obtained from coca leaves; it increases one's mental powers, produces euphoria, and heightens one's sexual desire.

Cochlea: The coiled, bony structure in the inner ear that contains the primary receptors for hearing. *See also basilar membrane, organ of Corti.*

Clinical psychological method: A study method in psychology that takes advantage of data that are obtained from counselling and psychotherapy.

Coefficient of correlation: A numerical index used to indicate the degree of correspondence between two sets of paired measurements. The most common kind is the product-moment coefficient designated by r. See *also rank correlation.*

Coercive persuasion: The use by communicators of complete control over respondents, with respect to both communication and sanctions, to bring about desired attitudes or behaviours.

Coercive power: The ability to punish another person. In social psychology, it means the *social power* that derives from the *influencing agent's* ability to punish the person who is being influenced, and where it is clear that the agent will punish that person if he does not comply. Impersonal coercive power utilizes an impersonal commodity such as a poor grade, a spanking, a fine, or an arrest; personal coercive power utilizes disapproval, hate, or rejection as commodities.

Cognition: An individual's thoughts, knowledge, interpretations, understandings, or ideas, and related mental activities concerning the environment and oneself. A cognition is a discrete bit of knowledge, an element of understanding.

Cognitive: Referring to thought or mental, rather than emotional, orientation.

Cognitive complexity: The use of many dimensions of knowledge in interpreting other people's behaviour.

Cognitive consistency: A situation in which a person's cognitions (beliefs, values, attitudes, etc.) tend to be logically and psychologically consistent with one another. When this is not so, he will experience discomfort or strain. The general consistency notion is basic to many models of attitude structure and change. *See also Cognitive dissonance.*

Cognitive consonance: A state of comfort experienced by an individual because he holds two or more cognitions whose implications are consistent with one another. This is the opposite of *cognitive dissonance.* (Example: The cognition that I am living in Kiagbodo town is consistent with the cognition that the weather here is very sunny and pleasant and with the cognition that other parts of Nigeria are facing heavy rainfall and cold weather).

Cognitive controls: The constraints on any person's behaviour that result from his or her acceptance of norms or standards as guides.

Cognitive dissonance: (1) According to American psychologist Leon Festinger, this is the condition in which one has beliefs or knowledge .that disagree with each other or with behavioural tendencies; when such cognitive dissonance arises, the subject is motivated to reduce the dissonance through changes in behaviour or cognition.

(2) An uncomfortable situation in which one's attitudes are inconsistent with one another or with one's behaviour; as a consequence, one is motivated to try to reduce the inconsistency in some way.

(3) An unbalanced arid uncomfortable state in which a person holds two conflicting or mutually exclusive ideas. According to the American psychologist Leon Festinger, the person will relieve the dissonance by changing one of the beliefs to make it consistent with the other or by adding other beliefs which lessen the dissonance.

Cognitive dissonance, theory of: A theory advanced by Leon Festinger stating that, because cognitive dissonance is unpleasant, an individual experiencing it will tend to change his cognitions or behaviours, or that he will add new cognitive elements in order to reduce his dissonance and unpleasant experiences.

Cognitive element: A discrete piece of information, thought, belief, observation, or opinion that *an* individual has about himself or his environment.

Cognitive learning: Learning that involves reorganization of one's perceptions, knowledge, and ideas.

Cognitive map: A hypothetical structure in memory that preserves and organizes information about the various events that occur in a learning situation; a mental picture of the learning situation. *See also schema.*

Cognitive norms: These norms refer to beliefs about objects, issues, etc. For example, traffic rules, rules of a game, rules of marriage, etc.

Cognitive reorganization: A person tends to seek harmonious relations among his cognitions and behaviour. He accepts ideas that are consistent with previous attitudes. Instabilities in the cognitive field produce …………….. These feelings of restlessness persist until there is a reorganization and restructuring of ideas, etc.

Cognitive structure: The organization of any set of relevant per-ceptions, information and interpretations into a meaningful and integrated pattern.

Cognitive restructuring: Restoring a state of congruency by misperceiving how other persons see one, by misinterpreting one's own behaviour, or by restructuring the situation to change the evaluation of the relevant behaviour.

Cognitive-physiological theory: A theory of emotion proposed by Schachter which states that emotion is bodily arousal in interaction with cognitive processes. Emotion is determined by the label a person gives to his or her state of bodily arousal. *See also James-Lange theory, Cannon-Bard theory.*

Cognitive process: The process by which concepts, interpretations and understandings are achieved.

Cognitive processes: The mental processes that occur during perception, learning, and thinking.

Cognitive psychology: A point of view in psychology that stresses the dynamic role of cognitive processes. An emphasis is placed on "knowing" and "perceiving" as contrasted with simple associative learning.

Cohesiveness: The force that acts on the members of a group that keeps them in it. It is a product of (1) the attractiveness of the interaction with group members, (2) the inherent value to the individual of the group activities themselves, (3) the extent to which membership achieves other ends, and (4) the extent to which attractive outcomes are available in alternative relations outside the group.

Collective Behaviour: The activities of a number of persons who are confronted with the same stimulus. It is a general term that refers to the behaviour of a number of individuals who form crowds, audiences, mobs, riots, rebellions, social movements, etc.

Collective unconscious: According to Carl Jung, this concept refers to an unconscious mind that is impersonal and held in common by most human beings.

Colour blindness: The inability of any person to distinguish between chromatic colours. Total colour blindness is rare, but two -colour vision occurs in one out of every fifteen men. See *also dichromatism. monochromatism red-green colour blindness, trichromatism.*

Colour circle: An arrangement of chromatic colours around the circumference of a circle in the order in which they appear in the spectrum, but with addition of non-spectral reds and purples. The colours are so arranged that those opposite each other are complementaries in an additive mixture. *See also colour solid.*

Colour constancy: The tendency to see a familiar object as of the same colour, regardless of changes in illumination on it that alter its stimulus properties. See *also object constancy.*

Colour-mixture primaries: Three hues chosen to produce the total range of hues by their additive mixture. A spectral red, green, and blue are usually selected. See *also psychological primaries.*

Colour solid: A three-dimensional representation of the psychological dimensions of colour, with hue around the circumference, saturation along each radius, and brightness from top to bottom. See *also colour circle.*

Commitment: (1) A personal decision to engage in a line of behaviour. (2) A process in which the actor adheres to normative behaviours because the disruptive consequences of not conforming would interfere with the achievement of socially approved ends or values. (3) In interpersonal attraction, a tacit agreement to give priority to, and maintain an intimate relationship with, a particular individual.

Common fate: A situation in which individuals or groups will win or lose together; it encourages working together and often increases attraction or reduces prejudice.

Common traits: In Allport's trait theory, these are the characteristics that appear frequently enough in a population to permit comparisons among people.

Communication: The process of making common or exchanging ideas, sentiments, beliefs, information, etc. The process of social interaction among human groups is largely a process of communication usually through articulate speech or language.

Communication network: The pattern of communication channels in a group or social organization. Some of the principal communication networks are the *wheel, Y, Chain, circle,* and *all-channel.*

Community Psychiatry: A special field of psychiatry that works to mobilize all the resources of a community to treat mental illness and promote mental health. Specially trained psychiatrists, with clinical psychologists and psychiatric social workers, try to involve all resources of a town in the programme – not just mental hospitals and clinics, but also general hospitals, schools and colleges, courts, welfare agencies, churches, mosques, shrines, labour organizations, and all other interested citizens in general. One aim is to study patterns of mental disorders in the community with a view to planning prevention. Another is to treat as many cases as possible outside in the community rather than inside mental institutions – using clinics and home care, for example.

Community psychology; A therapeutic approach that tries to seek out and prevent potential difficulties rather than wait for troubled individuals to take the initiative. Community psychology tends to be practiced in the person's own environment (e.g. home, school, place of work, neighbourhood, total institution, etc).

Comparison function: A function of reference groups, in which' one individual compares himself with a reference group in order to evaluate his own behaviour and outcomes. See *also Reference groups.*

Comparison level (CL): (1) The net level of benefits (rewards minus costs) that an individual considers appropriate in order for him to join or remain in a group – a standard against which the outcomes in a given group are compared. CL may also be viewed as the neutral point on the individual's subjective scale of "satisfaction – dissatisfaction." If the person's experiences in the group are above the CL, then he is satisfied with the group; however the further his experiences fall below the CL, the greater his dissatisfaction. This term was first technically used by the two American social psychologists John Thibaut and Harold Kelley in their *analyses of interdependence.* (2) In exchange theory, this concept refers to a plane of expectation or expected outcome which is influenced by an individual's past experiences in comparable relationships, judgment of what outcomes other persons similar to oneself are receiving, and perception of outcomes available in alternative relations.

Comparison level for alternatives (CLalt): A standard used by an individual in deciding whether or not to remain in a group; his decision will be based upon the possible benefits that he might receive in various other social relationships (relative to their costs). If his group experiences are below the CLalt, he will be inclined to leave the group; if his experiences are above the CLalt but below the CL, he will be dissatisfied with the group, but he will remain a member. This term was first technically used by the two American social psychologists John Thibaut and Harold Kelley in their analysis of *interdependence.*

Compensation: The adjustment mechanism by which a person obscures the fact of some personal deficiency by concentrating on some other possession.

Compensatory movements: The smooth motion of the eye as the head is turned from side to side to view an object from various angles.

Compensatory reaction: A response that may occur when another person exhibits too much or too little verbal or nonverbal intimacy. It involves an adjustment in one or more signals of immediacy (for example, eye contact, smiling, or proximity). Predicted in a theory by Argyle and Dean (1965).

Competition: (1) A contest in which one individual or group is rewarded at the expense of other individuals or groups. (2) The striving against others for the possession or *use* of limited goods – they may be material objects or matters of social esteem, rank, etc. (3) The behaviour towards one another of two or more persons who have *divergent interests* (negative goals interdependence). Since each person perceives that he can only reach his goal at the expense of the other(s), and vice versa, he will behave in such a way as to enhance only his own progress, and he may even attempt to retard the other(s). *Coordination* is extremely unlikely in situations of pure competition.

Competitive conflict: Conflict between two or more parties (individuals, groups, or larger social entities) arising from *competition*, in which each. party tries to move towards its goals at the expense of the opposing party (parties). As compared with *hostile conflict*, the major focus is on the incompatibility of extrinsic goals. (Example: Two state governments in the federation may struggle over a disputed territory that each believes is rightly its own). Compare *instrumental aggression*.

Competitive motive: A condition that leads an individual to seek personal success and the failure of other participants in a situation.

Competitive reward structure: A reward structure such that not all people striving for a reward can attain it and such that movement towards the goal by one decreases the chances that others will attain it.

Complementary colours: Two colours that in additive mixture yield either a gray or an unsaturated colour of the hue of the stronger component.

Complementarity hypothesis: The hypothesis that two or more persons will tend to be attracted to each other to the extent that their needs and traits complement one another. (Example: A dominant person will be more attracted to a submissive person than to another dominant person). *See also Similarity hypothesis.*

Complementary needs: A state in which each member of a dyad (i.e. a two persons group) has a need which is expressed in behaviour that is rewarding to the other member.

Complex: In Freudian terminology, this concept refers to a system of emotionally charged ideas, existing in the unconscious, which influence thought, perception, and behaviour.

Complex cell: A ceil in the visual cortex that responds to a bar of light or straight edge of a particular orientation located any-where in the visual field by integrating inputs from simple cells. *See also simple cell.*

Compliance: (1) A form of social influence in which an individual conforms outwardly (to obtain a reward or avoid punishment) but does not necessarily believe in the opinions expressed or the behaviour displayed. (2) Overt conformity, the act of openly acceding to another's wishes. Usually contrasted with internalization; one may conform with or without conviction.

Compound schedules. The use of a combination of schedules of partial reinforcement so that a complex sequence of responses may be required in order to obtain rewards.

Compromise process: In forming attractions, this concept refers to a process in which a group moves towards an equilibrium in which each individual's position in the affect structure is the best that he or she can obtain in terms of reward-cost outcomes. The end result is that individuals form relationships with other persons whose worth or desirability matches their own.

Compulsion: A repetitive action that a person feels driven to make and is unable to resist; ritualistic behaviour. See *also obsession, obsessive - compulsive reaction.*

Compulsive personality; A personality syndrome that is characterized by cleanliness, orderliness, and obstinacy. In the extreme behaviour becomes repetitive and ritualistic (syn. anal character).

Concreteness-abstractness: A pervasive quality on which individuals may be characterized. Concrete individuals make extreme distinctions, depend on authority and other extrapersonal sources, and have a low capacity to act "as if." Abstract persons behave in the opposite of these ways.

Concrete operations: This is the third stage in Jean Piaget's theory of cognitive development. During this stage, a child can think about things and their relationships without having actually to reach out and handle the things.

Concrete operations period: The third stage of cognitive development in Piaget's theory, during which children from about 7 to 12 years of age become capable of logical thought and can understand and apply rules such as the conservation of master, but they still cannot grasp truly abstract relationships. *See also conservation.*

Concubinage: Cohabitation without legal marriage. It is a sort of quasi-marital liaison, which men engage in with one or more women, either as their exclusive "marital" way of life, or as a secondary and occasional cohabitational affair, that supplements a legal marriage. Concubinage does not involve strict or rigorous legal ties. A concubine may betaken into a matrimonial residence, or kept outside and maintained separately.

The institution of concubinage exists in all societies. It is practised mostly but not exclusively by middle and upper-class men. In the societies whose marriage laws permit only monogamy, such as the United States, Canada, Western Europe, and South America, concubinage enables their elites to practise covert or disguised polygamy; whereas in the societies whose marriage customs or laws permit polygamy, such as Nigeria, other African countries, and Islamic Arab countries, concubinage serves as a less complicated and inexpensive way by which their elites maximize their propensities to practise overt polygamy.

Concubine: A woman who cohabits with a man without being legally married to him. She may be taken into a matrimonial home in lieu of a legal wife. or in addition to a legal wife or wives; or she may be kept outside and maintained separately. There are usually no strict or rigorous legal ties between a concubine and her man; and as a result, the union between them can be terminated by any one of them without the need for the intervention of other persons, or the observance of legal formalities.

The social status of the concubine varies significantly from society to society, but most commonly she has the right of general maintenance and social respect, her children are legitimate, but she or her children may or may not be allowed to officially bear the father's name.

Conditioned response (CR): In classical conditioning, this concept refers to the learned or acquired response to a conditioned stimulus; i.e., to a stimulus that did not evoke the response originally (such as salivating at the sight of food); in instrumental conditioning, it refers to the response that has been shaped by means of reinforcement. *See also conditioned stimulus, unconditioned response, unconditioned stimulus.*

Conditioned stimulus (CS): In classical conditioning, this concept refers to a stimulus previously neutral that comas to elicit a conditioned response through association with an unconditioned stimulus. See *also conditioned response, unconditioned response, unconditioned stimulus.*

Conditioning: The process of learning by association. There are two general types of conditioning: *classical conditioning* (also known as "Pavlovian conditioning", named after the Russian scientist, Ivan Pavlov, who was the first person to describe the phenomenon at the turn of the century); and *operant conditioning.*

In classical conditioning a stimulus (such as food) that normally evokes a particular response (such as salivation) is repeatedly paired with another stimulus that does not normally evoke the response (for example, a bell). Eventually, the subject will be conditioned to salivate at the sound of the bell.

In operant conditioning the subject engages in various random acts, one of which (such as pressing a lever) is reinforced (by the presentation of, for example, food). Eventually the subject will be conditioned to press the lever.

The school of psychology known as behaviourism, best represented now by the American Psychologist, B. F. Skinner, has elaborated the operant form of conditioning into an encompassing account of human behaviour, which is seen as being largely the product of the conditioning processes.

Confidence Tricks: Persuading a victim to entrust valuables to one as a sign of trust though one is entirely a stranger to the other.

Confidence limits: In statistics, these are the upper and lower limits that are derived from a sample, and used in making inferences about a population; e.g., from the mean of a sample and its standard error one can determine limits that permits a statement that the probability is 95 in 100 that the population mean falls within these limits. *See also statistical inference, statistical significance.*

Conflict: The simultaneous presence of opposing or mutually exclusive impulses, desires, or tendencies. In role expectations, the term conflict means a condition which arises when one expectation requires behaviour of the actor which in some degree is incompatible with the behaviour required by another expectation.

Conflict, interpersonal (or conflict, intergroup, conflict, social): The behaviour towards one another of two or mare parties (individuals, groups, or larger social units) who have negative means interdependence and/or negative goals interdependence. Interpersonal conflict may be subdivided into *competitive conflict* and *hostile conflict;* this subdivision parallels the distinction between *instrumental aggression* and *hostile aggression.*

Conflict, intrapersonal (or decisional conflict): The dilemma faced by an individual who must choose between two or more alternative behaviours that are incompatible with one another. (Examples: An individual may be required to choose between two cars both of which have positive and negative features; a child may have to decide whether to perform a disagreeable chore or be punished). According to Festinger's *cognitive dissonance theory,* after making the decision that resolves such a conflict, the individual will invariably experience some dissonance.

Conformity: In psychology, this term refers to an individual's behaviour and/or attitudes which adhere to the norms and pressures, values, standards, laws, of any human group or the larger society.

Congruency by comparison: A condition that occurs when the behaviour or attributes of O suggest that P possesses a particular self-component.

Congruency by implication: A condition that occurs when perceives that O sees him or her as possessing a particular characteristic corresponding to an aspect of his or her self-concept.

Congruency by validation: A condition that occurs when the behaviour or other characteristics of O allow or call for behaviour on the part of P that confirms a component of P's self.

Conjunctive task: A group task in which success depends upon the performance of the least effective member. (Examples: A team of boat rowers can move only as fast as the slowest member; a task may be accomplished by dividing the work among the members of a group).

Connotative meaning: The suggestive and emotional meanings of a word or symbol, beyond its denotative meaning. Thus naked and nude both refer to an unclothed body (denotative meaning), but they have somewhat different connotations. See *also denotative meaning, semantic differential.*

Conscience: An internal recognition of standards of right and wrong by which each individual judges his or her own conduct. *See also superego.*

Consciousness: Awareness. The totality of experience and mental processes of a person at a given moment.

Consciousness of kind: The awareness on the pan of an individual of important similarities between himself and other persons and the resultant feelings of empathy, identification or belonging. The American Psychologist Franklin Giddings, who coined this term, saw this perception of resemblance as a pleasurable sensation, involving feelings of affection, sympathy, and desire for recognition. When united through consciousness of kind, Giddings claimed, individual minds interact with each other so that they feel the same emotions, arrive at the same conclusions, and often act in concert. Giddings employed the concept as a major explanatory factor in dealing with such basic psycho-social processes as co-operation and competition between various persons, such as husband and wife, relatives, friends co-workers, and the like.

Conscious processes: Events such as perceptions, afterimages, private thoughts, and dreams, of which only the person is aware. They are accessible to others through verbal report or by way of inference from other behaviour (syn. experience, awareness). See *also divided consciousness, focal consciousness, marginal consciousness, nonconscious processes, subconscious processes, unconscious processes.*

Consensual validation: A process by which individuals check their ideas or beliefs against those of other people in order **to** determine their validity.

Conservation: Piaget's term for the ability of a child to recognize that certain properties of objects (e.g., mass, volume, number) **do not change despite** transformations in the appearance of the objects. *See also preoperational stage.*

Consideration: A dimension of leadership; the leader's concern with relationships between himself and other group members in data and the maintenance of group moral and cohesiveness

Construct: A concept, defined in terms of observable events, which is used by a theory to account for regularities or relationships in data.

Constructive memory: Using general knowledge stored in memory to construct and elaborate a more complete and detailed account of some events.

Content analysis: A research technique for the objective, systematic, and quantitative coding of the content of communication. (Examples: Coding newspaper editorials according to their stand on the issue of free education in Nigeria).

Contingencies of reinforcement: In behaviourism, this refers to a relation among the following three elements: (1) the occasion on which a response occurs, (2) the response itself, and (3) the action of the environment on the individual after a response has been made.

Contingency model of leader effectiveness: A theory or leadership proposed by American psychologist Fred E. Fiedler relating the effectiveness of *directive leadership* and *group-centred leadership* to a particular group situation. When the group's activities or membership is either extremely favourable or unfavourable to its leader, the *directive leader* tends to be most effective; on the other hand, when the group's activities or membership is moderately favourable, the *group-centred leader* is most effective.

Control group: A group used for comparison with an experimental group. It undergoes the same experiences as the experimental group except that it is not exposed to the independent variable that is manipulated by the experimenter, and thus constitutes a standard against which the treatment effects can be compared. See *also Dependent variable and independent variable.*

Control processes: Regulatory processes that serve to establish equilibrium or monitor goal-directed activities. *See also homeostasis.*

Controlled experiment: A research method in which the experimenter systematically manipulates certain variables *(independent variables)* while he measures others *{dependent variables)*, thus allowing him to test causal relationships. (Example: to test the hypothesis that congeniality in groups results in greater productivity, the experimenter may create a congenial relationship in some groups by various methods (the independent variable), leave other groups alone, and then measure and compare the resulting levels of productivity (the dependent variable).

Convergence: The motion of the eyes as they adjust to an object moving towards them.

Convergent interests (or common interests; positive interpendence): A relationship in which the movement of one person towards his own goal increases the likelihood that another person or persons will make progress towards their respective goals, and vice versa. Convergent interests may be a function of "positive means interdependence" and/or "positive goals interdependence". Convergent interests usually lead to *cooperation.*

Convergent thinking: In tests of intellect, this concept refers to producing a specified "correct" response in accordance with truth and fact. See *also divergent thinking.*

Conventional level of moral development: The level of moral development, according to American psychologist Lawrence Kohlberg, that is held by most adults. The emphasis is on being "nice" and on conforming to and maintaining the existing Social order.

Conversion reaction: A form of neurotic reaction in which the symptoms are paralysis of the limbs, insensitive areas of the body (anaesthesias), or related-bodily symptoms. The presumption is that anxiety has been "converted" into a tangible symptom, such as deafness or blindness (syn. hysteria). *See also neurosis.*

Co-operation: [1] The behaviour towards one another of two or more persons who have *convergent interests* (positive interdependence). Each perceives that progress towards his own goal will be enhanced by the progress of the other person or persons as well, and each expects reciprocation. In situations of pure cooperation, there is likely to be *coordination.* [2] Social interaction in which persons or groups combine their activities, or work together with mutual aid, in a more or less organized way, for the promotion of common goals.

Co-operative motive: A condition that leads an individual to seek the outcome most beneficial to all participants in a situation.

Co-operative reward structure: A reward structure such that all those who strive must achieve the reward in order for it to be attained by any one participant. Each person's efforts advance the group's chances.

Coping behaviour: Response to a stress-producing situation designed to reduce the stress conditions.

Coping Strategy: A method of direct problem-solving in dealing with personal problems, contrasted with defense mechanisms. See *also defensive strategy.*

Coping with danger: Overcoming a problem—one way of reacting to a fear-arousing communication (e.g., stopping smoking after being warned of the hazard of lung cancer).

Co-ordination: The process by which two or more persons implicitly or explicitly attempt to phase their preferences, intentions, and/or expectations with those of others. Queuing (lining up) or taking turns is a common method of coordination. (Example: Working parents and school-age children must coordinate their use of the one family bathroom in the morning as they will all prepare for a busy weekday.)

Cornea: The clear, tough outer covering of the eye.

Corpus callosum: The large band of nerve fibres that connects the cerebral hemispheres.

Correlation: The degree to which two *variables* are related or vary together. When an increase in one *variable* is related to a corresponding increase in the other (for example, height and weight), the two *variables* are positively correlated. There is a negative correlation between two *variables* when an increase in one is related to a decrease in the other (for example, the amount of money a person withdraws from his savings account and the balance shown in his bankbook). Two *variables* may also be uncorrelated if a variation in one is unrelated to a variation in the other (for example, shoe size and body temperature).

Correlational method: Anon-manipulative, non-experimental method of science; it is used for finding the relationships between or among the naturally occurring characteristics of variables; causality cannot be inferred in studies using this method.

Correlation coefficient: A statistical index (r) that measures the degree of *correlation* between two *variables*. The value of this index is –1.00 if two *variables* are perfectly negatively correlated, 0 if they are uncorrelated, and +1.00 if they are perfectly positively correlated.

Cost: In exchange theory, this concept refers to the undesirable consequences of carrying out an activity or taking an action.

Counselling psychologist: A trained psychologist, usually with a Ph.D or Ed.D. degree, dealing with personal problems not classified as illness, such as academic, social, or vocational problems of students. He or she has skills similar to those of the clinical psychologist, but usually works in a non-medical setting, such as schools, offices, homes, etc. See *also clinical psychologist, psychiatrist.*

Counterconditioning: A type of therapeutic relearning that is achieved by conditioning a new and more adaptive response to a stimulus that had formerly elicited maladaptive behaviour. Counterconditioning can be accomplished by pairing a strong positive stimulus (such as presenting an attractive toy to a child) with a formerly negative stimulus (such as the sight of a feared animal).

Counterformity: The individual who resists group pressure for conformity not only by expressing his independent judgment but also by actively opposing the group; he is negativistic and hostile to the group. *(See Compliance and Conformity).*

Counternorm effect: Those aspects of the influence process which produce resistance to the influence attempt.

Counterphobic behaviour: This term refers to the form of behaviour which occurs when a person is driven to master or conquer some particularly dangerous challenge.

Covert responses: Responses that at not readily observable, like silent speech.

Covert sensitization: A form of aversive therapy in which the patient is asked to imagine those situations and activities that he or she finds attractive (though undesirable) and then is given other descriptions of those activities that elicit unpleasant feelings.

Craze: A deep concern for some new or revived recreational activity. Though temporary the people are highly emotionally involved in the activity. For example, wearing of jeans by both men and women, and perming of hair by women have been popular craves in the 1980s in Nigeria.

Creativity: In psychology, this term refers to a situation in which an individual is able to produce new combinations of some elements from old elements. The combinations either meet specified requirements or are in some way useful. The more mutually distant the elements, the more creative is the resulting combination.

Credibility: The degree to which a communicator is believable. One's credibility is a function of one's personal characteristics, one's position or status, the nature of the communication, the context in which it is delivered, one's relation to the listener, and the listener's characteristics.

Criterion: [1] A set of scores or other records against which the success of a predictive test is verified. [2] A standard selected as the goal to be achieved in a learning task.

Critical period: A stage in development during which the organism is optimally ready to learn certain response patterns. It is closely related to the concept of maturational readiness.

Critical ratio: A mean, mean difference, or coefficient of correlation divided by its standard error. It is used in tests of significance. See *also statistical significance.*

Cross-cultural: Pertaining to a study or method that compares responses of people from different societies to the same stimulus.

Crowd: A temporary aggregation of human beings at a particular spot; the members are aware of a common emotional interest, have their attention concentrated in that direction, are in rapport or consensus and tend to reinforce each other in behaviour. As a result of these processes the ordinary "rational" controls of personality are released or are in abeyance.

A crowd

Crowd contagion: Mass imitation in which feelings and/or behaviour are spread from one person to another in a crowd.

Crowding: A psychological state of stress that sometimes accompanies high population density. (A similar term, *crowded;* refers to situations in which population density is relatively high).

Cue: A stimulus that symbolizes a more complex stimulus.

Cue trait: A quality of a stimulus person which is used as a basis for making further judgments about the person.

Cultural Anthropology: The branch of anthropology that studies the structure and function of human cultures.

Culture: A people's way of life that comprises their system of shared beliefs, values, symbols, artifacts and performance styles that characterize a group, community or society.

Culture free: Free from biases that invalidly deflate the scores of subjects from certain cultures, ethnic groups, or social classes.

Culture-fair test: A type of intelligence test that has been constructed to minimize bias due to the differing experiences of children raised in a rural rather than urban culture or in a lower-class rather than in a middle-class or upper-class culture (syn. culture-free test).

Cumulative curve: A graphic record of the responses emitted during an operant conditioning session. The slope of the cumulative curve indicates the rate of response.

Curiosity drive: The tendency to explore, seek and investigate.

Custom: Any non-legal but institutionalized pattern of conventional social behaviour that is associated with any social group, community, or society. Customs include particular ways of dressing, eating, marrying, receiving visitors, settling disputes, etc., in every community across the whole world. Customs vary from one community to another community. The various customs of any community are manifested in the attitudes, behaviours, and sentiments of the various individual members of that community in most of the places in which they live and engage in various purposeful interactions.

Cutaneous (haptic) senses: These consist of the senses whose reception lie in or near the skin, such as touch, temperature, etc.

Cytological research: A research that focuses on the study of cells.

D

Dark Adaptation: The increased sensitivity to light when the subject has been continuously in the dark or under conditions of reduced illumination. *See also light adaptation.*

Daydreaming: Reverie: free play of thought or imagination. Because of self-reference. It is usually a form of autistic thinking. *See also autistic thinking.*

Death: The cessation of life in humans and other vertebrates.

Death instinct: Sigmund Freud first introduced and developed this concept in his book titled *Beyond the Pleasure Principle* (1920). According to him, the concept refers to the force which underlies aggressive behaviour. According to him, the death instinct, which he also otherwise called *thanatos*, refers to the tendency of organisms to return to an inanimate or inorganic state, that is similar to catabolism, or biological breakdown. Freud contrasted this concept with his concept of *dual life*, or *eros*, which is the force that underlies sexual behaviour, and regarded the death Instinct as the more dominant force in humans and other organisms. Freud conceded that the death instinct is a hypothetical construct that is not directly verifiable. However, he postulated that the concept is indirectly verifiable through its manifestation in certain phenomena, such as in the various acts of human destructiveness and aggression, and also in the peculiar fusions of destructiveness and sexuality in sadism and masochism.

Debt management: In a social sense, this concept refers to the process by which individuals keep their social debts to a minimum. The social debt depends not only on the rewards and costs experienced by both donor and recipient but also on the degree to which the donor's acts are perceived by the recipient as voluntary, intentional, and without ulterior or sinister motives.

Decibel (db): A unit for measuring sound intensity

Deduction: The process of logical reasoning from premises to conclusions. It is used in deriving predictions from a theory.

Defense mechanism: An adjustment made, often unconsciously, either through action or the avoidance of action to keep from recognizing personal qualities or motives that might lower self-esteem or heighten anxiety. Denial and projection are two examples. See *also defensive strategy.*

Defense reaction: A response pattern, or adjustive mechanism, that tends unconsciously to shield a person from some imperfection in his personality or from some threat from reality.

Defensible space: Refers to multiple-family dwellings and describes space with well-defined boundaries and ample opportunities by residents to maintain surveillance over visitors.

Defensive attribution: Placing blame for a serious and frightening accident on the victim, in order to avoid thinking that similar accident might happen to oneself (e.g., a responsible person would not have such an accident).

Defensive deviant act: An act violating social norms which is a response to some physical or psychological threat.

Defensive identity: A conception of self and one's social roles created to withstand living under conditions of constant threat.

Defensive identification: Similar to the concept of identification with the aggressor. The child internalizes attributes of the more powerful persons, partly to reduce his own powerlessness and partly to produce behaviour that will gain him acceptance and protection.

Defensive identification: In psychoanalytic theory, this is the process by which the child resolves the Oedipus or Electra complex by becoming more like the same-sexed parent and thus vicariously possessing the opposite-sexed parent.

Defensive strategy: Behaviour aimed at defending the person against anxiety when faced with a problem rather than dealing directly with the problem. See *also coping strategy.*

Deferred Gratification: The postponement of immediate satisfaction in anticipation of further rewards; e.g. saving money instead of spending it immediately; sending children to school instead of making them work and earn.

Degradation ceremonies: Formal procedures which emphasize and legitimize an individual's deviant status, such as arrest and imprisonment.

Deindividuation [1] The hiding of one's personal identity, as in a crowd; such reduction of a person's identity tends to increase aggressive tendencies.

[2] The loss of a sense of individual identity in a group, which frequently leads a person to act in a less moral manner. [3] Behaviour performed in or with a group in which an individual's identity is overpowered by identification with the group and the sense of individuality is lost.

Deintensification: An attempt to underplay an emotion, as when a fearful person attempts to look less afraid.

De ja vu: This is a French word which means "already seen". In psychology, the word means the illusion on the part of an individual of having already experienced something that he/she is actually experiencing for the first time.

Delayed conditioning: A classical conditioning procedure in which the CS begins several seconds or more before the onset of the US and continues with it until the response occurs. *See also simultaneous conditioning, trace conditioning.*

Delta waves: *See electroencephalogram.*

Delusion: A false belief that is inconsistent with reality and firmly held in spite of evidence to the contrary; it is common in paranoid disorders... *of control:* The belief that one is being manipulated by some external force such as radar, TV, or a creature from outer space ... *of grandeur:* The belief that one is an especially important or powerful person ... *of persecution:* The belief that one is being plotted against or oppressed by others. *See also hallucination, illusion paranoid schizophrenia.*

Demand Characteristics: (1) The perceptual cues, both explicit and implicit, that communicate what behaviour is expected in a situation. (2) The features of an experiment or of an experimenter's behaviour that convey to the participant the desired outcome of the experiment.

Dementia: Mental deterioration, particularly of intellect and memory,

Dementia praecox: A former term for schizophrenia, describing what was believed to be an incurable deterioration of mental functioning that began in adolescence.

Democratic leader: A leader who leaves all policy making to group discussion and group decision and who participates in the group activities.

Democratic leadership: One of the three leadership styles that was studied in the classic experiment by American psychologists Lewin, Lippitt, and White. The democratic leader of a group was instructed to participate with the group in making decisions, to be friendly and supportive, to assist the group in focusing upon and developing longrange goals, and to communicate in a fair, objective manner. These behaviours are also associated with group-centred leadership.

Demographic: Relating to characteristics by which a population can be classified into separate statistical subgroups (for example, age or sex).

Dendrite: The specialized portion of the neuron that (together with the cell body) receives impulses from other neurons. *See also axon, neuron.*

Denial: A defense mechanism by which unacceptable impulses or ideas are not perceived or allowed into full awareness. *See also defense mechanism.*

Denotative meaning: The primary meaning of a symbol, something specific to which the symbol refers or points (e.g., my street address is denotative; whether or not I live in a desirable neighbourhood is a connotative meaning secondary to the address itself). See *also connotative meaning, semantic differential.*

Deoxyribonucleic acid (DNA): Large molecules found in the cell nucleus and primarily responsible for genetic inheritance. These molecules manufacture various forms of RNA, which are thought by some to be the chemical basis of memory. *See also ribonucleic acid.*

Dependency: A condition in which one person relies on another for need satisfaction. Dependence is thus the inverse of power.

Dependant variable [1] A variable or measure whose value depends upon a particular independent variable. In the expression Y=f(X), Y denotes a dependent variable since its value depends upon the value of X. If Y=x², and X=5, then Y =25. In experimentation, a researcher attempts to predict the value of the dependent variable on the basis of his hypothesis about the effect of an *independent variable. See also controlled experiment.* [2] The variable whose measured changes are attributed to (or correspond to) changes in the independent variable. In psychological experiments, the dependent variable is often a response to a measured stimulus. See also *independent variable.*

Depersonalization: The state in which an individual lacks a clear sense of his personal identity, feels estranged from himself, and senses that his behaviour and personality are irrelevant and meaningless to his own needs. This concept is frequently discussed as a concomitant of increased industrialization and urbanization.

Depth perception: The capacity by an individual to ascertain that some phenomena are closer than others; to see things as rounded or protruding, and to be able to look down (white airborne) and feel a sensation of altitude. *See also distance cues.*

Depth psychology: The psychology of unconscious mental processes.

Depolarization: Change in the resting potential of the nerve cell membrane in the direction of the action potential; the inside of the membrane becomes more positive. See also *action potential; resting potential.*

Depressants: Psychoactive drugs that tend to reduce arousal. *See also stimulants, hallucinogens.*

Depression: An emotional disorder characterized by a conviction that one is totally worthless, valueless, and useless. Also common is guilt of overwhelming proportions, the conviction that one has done 'something' forever unpardonable, and that one is inherently evil.

Depressive neurosis: A reaction marked by excessive sadness that originates with a specific environmental event.

Deprivation: State of lack or loss of desired or needed things, e.g. food, security.

Descriptiveness: The degree to which an item in a psychological research project yields information about a person as an individual.

Desertion, also called abandonment: This concept refers to the wilful separation of one spouse from the other without legal cause or intention of returning. In constructive desertion the misconduct of one spouse forces the end of cohabitation. Under ordinance marriage in Nigeria, desertion of one to two years' duration is sufficient ground for a free divorce.

Destructiveness and cynicism: Generalized hostility; vilification of the human, A characteristic of the authoritarian-personality syndrome.

Determinism: The philosophical point of view that all events are caused, including behavioural events.

Developmental Identification: Identification arising out of problem-solving and reinforcement experience of childhood. The attributes of the parent are internalized because these attributes have acquired secondary reinforcing power. *See also Anaclytic Identification.*

Developmental psychologist: A psychologist whose research interest lies in studying the changes that occur as a function of the growth and development of the individual, in particular the relationship between early and later behaviour.

Developmental quotient (DQ). A measure of the rate of mental development in infants.

Development Versus Social Learning: The controversy between two theoretical orientations as to the major processes underlying and accounting for socialization. Perhaps the question most often debated concerns the acquisition of moral values.

Development Position: Jean Piaget, a Swiss psychologist, has suggested that children go through an invariant and irreversible sequence of stages as they develop. Each stage builds on the cognitive skills of the previous one but is qualitatively different from it. Moving from one stage to the next depends to a great extent on the physical and cognitive maturation of the child's environment. Piaget believes that it is virtually impossible to teach the child the skill of the next stage, he must acquire them on his own.

On the other hand, American Psychologist Lawrence Kohlberg has proposed a series of three basic stages for the development of moral values, as follows:

Pre-conventional: The child's Ideas of what is right end wrong are based on the hedonistic principles of obtaining rewards for oneself and avoiding punishment

Conventional Morality: is based on respect for authority and the approval of others.

Post-conventional: Moral ideas are founded on the concept of the "contract" and the individual's principle of conscience. This Kohlberg's sequence of stages has been found in many cultures of the world.

Social-Learning Position: This viewpoint regards the acquisition of moral values and indeed, almost all of socialization, as a learning experience. The child is taught what to believe by the significant person around him, especially his parents. It is, therefore, the environment and not the rate of maturation of the child that is most important. In contrast to the developmental theory the social-learning position argues that a child can easily be taught to believe in ideas that are at a higher stage of moral development than that in which he currently finds himself.

Deviant behaviour: The behaviour which deviates markedly from the average or the norm of a group or a culture.

Deviation IQ: An intelligence quotient (IQ) computed as a standard score with a mean of 100 and a standard deviation of 15 (Wechsler) or 16 (Stanford-Binet), to correspond approximately to traditional intelligence quotient. *See also intelligence quotient.*

Descriptive statistics: Simplifying or summarizing statements about measurements made on a population. Strictly speaking, "descriptive statistics" should apply solely to populations, rather than to samples, but the term is used loosely for summarizing statements abut samples when they are treated as populations. *See also statistical inference.*

Desocialization: The process of removing persons from the role categories which they have previously occupied.

Destitute children: The children who are neglected by the parents and who are found begging in the streets; children who have no home and no means of subsistence.

Difference threshold: The minimum difference between a pair of stimuli that can be perceived under experimental conditions. *See also absolute threshold, just noticeable difference, threshold.*

Difference threshold (just noticeable difference): The smallest difference in physical energy between two stimuli that will enable someone to judge them as different.

Differentiating item: In the description of persons, a word, phrase, or statement about the abilities, interests, or beliefs, of persons.

Diffusion: An emotional state in which the aroused person makes many useless and exaggerated responses, and performs normal acts with excessive violence.

Diffusion of guilt: The reduced feeling of guilt experienced by someone who is part of a group that has been responsible for an undesirable act. He may feel less guilty because he attributes the act to the group as a whole rather than to himself personally. Diffusion of guilt may be responsible for the *bystander intervention phenomenon* and such extreme group behaviour as gang rape, lynching, and atrocities committed by military personnel against helpless civilians.

Diffusion of responsibility: [1] The tendency for persons in a group situation to fail to take action (as in an emergency) because others are present, thus diffusing the responsibility for acting. A major factor in inhibiting bystanders from intervening in emergencies.

[2] A reduced feeling of responsibility experienced by a person who is a member of a group, so that he may feel free to commit an extreme act or do nothing at all since he shares responsibility with the other members of his group. *Deindividuation* may toad to diffusion of responsibility, and diffusion of responsibility may help to produce the *risky shift* and the *bystander intervention phenomenon.*

Digital computer: A computer that performs mathematical and logical operations with information, numerical or otherwise, represented in digital form.

Diglossic society: A society in which two or more languages are used.

Dominance hierarchy: A stable, relatively enduring pattern of *social power* in a group, in which one or more members exert more control than others.

Dipsomania: Compulsive desire for alcoholic beverages.

Direct counterimitation: Avoiding a specific modeled behaviour

Direct imitation: Copying a model exactly.

Directive leadership: A leadership style characterized by the use of four forms of *social influence: reward power, coercive power, power, expert power,* and *legitimate power.* The directive leader is mainly interested in eliciting compliance in order to bring about the changes that he feels are necessary; he tends to make decisions himself and is relatively unconcerned about being accepted by the other members of the group. This style is the opposite of *group-centred leadership.*

Discrimination: [1] In perception, this concept refers to the detection of differences between the stimuli. [2] In conditioning, it refers to the differential response to the positive (reinforced) stimulus and to the negative (non-reinforced) stimulus. *See also generalization.* [3] In social psychology, it refers to the prejudicial treatment, as in racial or ethnic discrimination.

Discriminative stimulus: (1) A stimulus that indicates that there is a potential change in the relationship between responses and consequences. For example, red traffic light indicates to a motor vehicle driver that he can no longer continue driving with impunity–he risks either apprehension by a law-enforcement officer or a collision with another vehicle.) (2) In Skinnerian behaviourism, this concept refers to a stimulus that becomes, an occasion for an operant response; e.g., the knock that leads one to open a door. The stimulus does not elicit the operant response in the same sense that a stimulus elicits respondent behaviour. See *also operant behaviour.*

Disinhibition: A situation in which a person generalizes positively from specific modeled behaviours to a whole class of behaviours.

Disorientation: A state of mental confusion, in which a person is unsure of his location or identity.

Displacement [1] A defence mechanism whereby a motive that may not be directly expressed (e.g., sex, aggression) appears in a more acceptable form. See *also defense mechanism.* [2] The principle of loss of items from short-term memory as too many new items are added. See *also chunk, short-term memory.*

Displaced aggression: The aggression against a person or object other than that which was (or is) the source of a frustration. See also *scapegoat.*

Display rules: Various movements by which an emotion differing from the real feelings of the individual is presented.

There are four kinds: deintensification, over-intensification, masking, and neutralization.

Disposition: The tendency of an individual to behave in a particular way across a wide variety of situations.

Dispositional attribution: Attributing a persons actions to internal dispositions (attitudes, traits, motives), as opposed to situational factors. See *also situational attribution.*

Dispositional item: In the description of persons, this concept refers to any word, phrase, or statement that labels how the person behaves in a broad class of situations.

Dissociate: To separate one image, idea, or function of the personality, from another,

Dissociation: The process whereby some ideas, feelings, or activities lose relationship to other aspects of consciousness and personality and operate automatically or independently.

Dissociative reaction: An alteration in consciousness that manifests itself as amnesia, fugue, multiple personally, and somnambulism.

Dissonance: [1] In music, an inharmonious combination of sounds; contrasted with consonance. [2] In social psychology, Festinger's term for a perceived inconsistency between one's own attitudes and one's behaviour. See *also cognitive dissonance.*

Distal stimulus: A stimulus that actually occurs in the environment.

Distance cues: [1] In vision, the monocilar cues according to which the distance of objects is perceived – such as superposition of objects, perspective, light and shadow, and relative movement –and the binocular cues used in stereoscopic vision. See *also stereoscopic vision.* [2] In addition, the corresponding cues governing perception of distance and direction, such as intensity and time differences of sound reaching the two ears.

Distributive justice: The notion developed by American sociologist and leading contributor to exchange theory George C. Homans, which states that people expect rewards to be proportional to their costs and investments in a social exchange.

Divergence: The outward motion of the eyes as they adjust to an object that is moving away from them.

Divergent interests (or opposed interests; negative inter-dependence): A relationship in which the movement of one person towards his own goal decreases the likelihood that another person or persons will make progress towards their respective goals, and vice versa. Divergent interest may be a function of negative means interdependence and/or negative goals interdependence. Divergent interests often lead to *competition* and *conflict.*

Divergent thinking: In tests of intellect (or creativity), producing one or more "possible" answers rather than a single "correct" one. *See also convergent thinking.*

Divided consciousness: The state of consciousness as in attending to two activities at once. See *also conscious processes.*

Divorce: The legal dissolution of a legally valid marriage. Although virtually alt societies generally try to protect the family, most societies also have some arrangement for divorce. The divorce procedure may be very simple – as in the ancient Middle East or in Athens, where a husband could divorce a wife simply by giving notice that he was doing so. On the other hand, divorce in modern society (especially in affluent America) may be a costly legal process.

Many marriages are broken by means other than divorce, including annulment or separation, for example- but also by desertion and even by suicide and murder.

There is a strong and widespread popular opinion in contemporary Nigeria, that there is a very high rate of divorce in the country, especially in the urban areas, such as Lagos, and the other eighteen state capitals. The factors that are generally mentioned as being responsible include the adverse influences of the so-called "permissive Western culture", industrialization, education, urbanization, and materialism.

But, unfortunately, there are no available reliable studies, that provide adequate empirical data in support of this general impression about the divorce situation in the country.

However, some of the available fragmentary but reliable divorce statistics indicate that about three-fifths of the divorce cases that are heard in both the Customary and High Courts throughout the country actually involve couples who need help and reconciliation rather than outright divorce. Thus many of these courts permit a cooling-off period or a long legal separation before a divorce will be granted, especially when children, are involved.

Dizygotic (DZ) twins: Twins developed from separate eggs. They are no more alike genetically than ordinary brothers and sisters and can be of the same or different sexes (syn. fraternal twins). *See also monozygotic twins.*

Dogmatism: A closed-minded, rigid style combined with beliefs that are authoritarian in content.

Dominance: The higher status position when social rank is organized according to a dominance-submission hierarchy; commonly found in human societies and in certain animal groups.

Dominance hierarchy: In a group, the ranking of the members in terms of influence or power. The most powerful or dominant member is highest in the hierarchy.

Dominant gene: A member of a gene pair, which, if present, determines that the individual will show the trait controlled by the gene, regardless of whether the other member of the pair is the same or different (that is, recessive). See *also recessive gene.*

Dominant response: The most likely response that an individual will give when exposed to a specific stimulus or situation. The dominant response was probably learned earlier in life in similar situations.

Dominant trait: A trait that will be expressed in any individual who has its gene.

Donation: A helping behaviour in which goods or services are provided to a person or organization in need.

Dopamine: A neurotransmitter of the central nervous system that is believed to play a role in schizophrenia. It is synthesized from an amino acid by the action of certain body enzymes and, in turn, is converted into norepinephrine. See *also neurotransmitter, norepinephrine.*

Dopamine hypothesis: The hypothesis that schizophrenia is related to an excess of the neurotransmitter dopamine; either schizophrenics produce too much dopamine, or are deficient in the enzyme that converts dopamine to norepinephrine. See *also dopamine: norepinephrine, schizophrenia.*

Double-barreled item: A questionnaire item that actually asks two different questions at once. Such items should be avoided because they are ambiguous.

Double blind: An experimental design, often used in drug research, in which neither the investigator nor the patients know which subjects are in the treatment and which are in the nontreatment condition until the experiment has been completed.

Double personality: The alternate identity which is suddenly assumed by some victims of amnesia.

Drive: (1) An aroused condition of an organism that is based on deprivation or noxious stimulation, including tissue needs, drug or hormonal conditions, and specified internal or external stimuli, such as in pain. (2) Loosely, any motive. *See also motive, need.*

Drive-reduction theory: The theory that a motivated sequence of behaviour can be best explained as moving from an aversive state of heightened tension (i.e. drive) to a goal state which the drive is reduced. The goal of the sequence, in other words, is drive reduction. See *also drive, incentive theory, motive, need.*

Dropouts: The young people who choose temporarily or permanently to renounce certain dominant values of their society or community or group cultures or sub-cultures, especially the values which strongly endorse or emphasize the need on the part of the individual to acquire proper educational trainings, authentic educational qualifications (i.e., officially recognized certificates, testimonials, licences, etc.), and respectable as well as lucrative jobs in either the public or private sectors of the county's labour market. Almost invariably most dropouts are the individuals who had tried several times to acquire some good educational qualifications and jobs but continued to fail, hence they were compelled by certain very discouraging forces which are beyond their own personal control (e.g., lack of adequate familial emotional support for their failures, lack of adequate financial sponsor-ships, lack of good remedial educational opportunities, etc.) to withdraw either temporarily or permanently from the very gruelling struggle to gain a prestigious and respectable position in the society's social stratification hierarchy.

Many of such "dropouts" may decide to join "underground" deviant/criminal gangs, and thereafter engage in criminal acts, such as armed robbery, smuggling, etc. While many other dropouts may decide to retire temporarily into their "large and multipurpose family compound – homes", wherein they continue to grumble, regret and brood over their past failures, and also day-dream about how they could have become "graduates", "doctors", etc.; and as well as "build new castles in the air", such as their thinking about how they could still become "politicians", "businessmen", etc. Many of the '"wise" dropouts who nurture the ambitions of becoming politicians, professional thugs and the like, might actually get the opportunity to become political thugs, political henchmen, etc. When they serve their political mentors well, and also ingratiate themselves properly with the grass-roots people, through engaging in conspicuous consumption and "spraying money" all around, they themselves may one day contest and win election, and become legislators, who help to make new laws that would subsequently govern how doctors, academicians, engineers, etc. should behave in the society or community.

Drug: (1) Any substance which is used as medicine in the treatment of disease. (2) A narcotic, especially one that is addictive. *See Table 4: Facts about drugs, pages 104 – 105.*

Table 4: Facts about drugs

Usual dose	Duration of effect	Effects sought	Long-term symptoms	Physical dependence potential	Mental dependence potential	Organic damage potential
Varies	4 hrs	Euphoria, prevent withdrawal discomfort	Addiction, constipation, loss of appetite	Yes	Yes	No[1]
15 Milligrams	6 hrs	Euphoria, prevent withdrawal discomfort	Addiction, constipation, loss of appetite	Yes	Yes	No[1]
30 Milligrams	4 hrs	Euphoria, prevent withdrawal discomfort	Addiction, constipation, loss of appetite	Yes	Yes	No
10 Milligrams	4-6 hrs	Prevent withdrawal discomfort	Addiction, constipation, loss of appetite	Yes	Yes	No
Varies	Varied brief periods	Excitation talkativeness	Depression, convulsions	No	Yes	Yes?[2]
1-2 Cigarettes	4 hrs	Relaxation; increased euphoria perceptions, sociability	Usually none	No	Yes?	No
50-100 Milligrams	4 hrs	Anxiety reduction, euphoria	Addiction with severe withdrawal symptoms, possible	Yes	Yes	Yes

---

[1] Persons who inject drugs under nonsterile conditions run a high risk of contracting hepatitis, abscesses, or circulatory disorders.

[2] Question marks indicate conflict of opinion. It should be noted that illicit drugs are frequently adulterated and thus pose unknown hazards to the user.

			convulsion, toxic psychosis.			
2.5-5 Milligrams	4 hrs	Alertness, activeness	Loss of appetite, delusions, hallucinations, toxic psychosis	No?	Yes	Yes?
100-500 Micrograms	10 hrs	Insightful experiences, exhilaration, distortion of senses	May intensify existing psychosis, panic reactions	No	No?	No?
1-3 Milligrams	Less than 1 hr	Insightful experiences, exhilaration distortion of sense	?	No	No?	No?
350 Micrograms	12 hrs	Insightful experiences, exhilaration distortion of sense	?	No	No?	No?
25 Milligrams	6-8 hrs	Insightful experiences, exhilaration distortion of sense	?	No	No?	No?
Varies	1-4 hrs	Sense alteration, anxiety reduction, sociability	Cirrhosis, toxic psychosis, neurologic damage, addiction	Yes	Yes	Yes
Varies	Varies	Calmness, sociability	Emphysema, lung cancer; mouth and throat cancer, cardiovascular damage, loss of appetite	Yes?	Yes	Yes

Source: Liebert and Neale (1977), pages 378-379.

Table 4: Facts about drugs

Name	Slang name	Chemical or trade name	Source	Classifi-cations	Medical use	How taken
Heroin	H. Horse, Junk, Smack, Scag	Diacetyl-morphine	Semi-synthetic (from morphine)	Narcotic	Pain relief	Injected or sniffed
Morphine	White Stuff, M.	Morphine Sulphate	Natural (from opium)	Narcotic	Pain relief	Swallowed or injected
Codeine	Schoolboy	Methyl-morphine	Natural (from opium), semi synthetic (from morphine)	Narcotic	Ease pain and coughing	Swallowed
Methadone	Dolly	Dolophine Amidone	Synthetic	Narcotic	Pain relief	Swallowed or injected
Cocaine	Coke, Snow	Methylester of Benzoyl-ecogonie	Natural (from coca, not cacao)	Stimulant local anesthesia	Local anesthesia	Sniffed, injected or swallowed
Marijuana	Pot, Grass, Hashish, Tea, Gage, Reefers	Tetrahydro-cannabinol (THC)	Natural (from Cannabis sativa)	Relaxant, euphoriant; in high doses, hallucinogen	None in US	Smoked, swallowed, or sniffed
Barbiturates	Barbs, Blue Devils, Candy, Yellow Jackets, Phennies, Peanuts, Blue Heavens	Phenobarbital, Nembutal, Seconal, Amytal	Synthetic	Sedative hypnotic	Sedation, relief of high blood pressure, epilepsy, hyperthy-roidism	Swallowed or injected
Ampheta-mines	Bennies, Dexies, Speed, Wake-Ups, Lid Proppers,	Benzedrine, Dexedrine, Desoxyn, Methampheta-mine, Methedrine	Synthetic	Sympatho-mimetic	Relief of mild depression, control of appetite and	Swallowed or injected

	Hearts, Pep Pills				narcolepsy	
LSD	Acid, Sugar, Big D. Cubes, Trips	D-lysergic acid Diethyl amide	Semi-synthetic (from ergot alkaloids)	Hallucinog en	Experimen tal study of mental function, alcoholism	Swallowe d
DMT	AMT, Business -man's High	Dimethyl-triptamine	Synthetic	Hallucinog en	None	Smoked or injected
Mescaline	Mesc.	3,4,5-Trimethoxy-phemethyl-amine	Natural (from peyote)	Hallucinog en	None	Swallowe d
Psilocybin		3 (2-Dimethyl-amino) ethylindol-4-oldihydroge n phosphate	Natural (from psilocybe)	Hallucinog en	None	Swallowe d
Alcohol	Booze, Juice, etc.	Ethanol Ethyl alcohol	Natural (from grapes, grains, etc, via fermentatio n)	Sedative-hypnotic		Swallowe d
Tobacco		Nicotiana Tabacum	Natural	Stimulant sedative	Sedative, emetic (nicotine)	Smoked, sniffed, chewed.

Source: Liebert and Neale (1977), pages 378-379.

E

Eardrum: The membrane at the inner end of the auditory canal, leading to the middle ear. See also *middle ear*.

Eclectic: Being selective from a variety of theories, methods, schools of thought, etc.

Ecological manipulation: A form of *manipulation* in which one person influences another by altering some aspect of his environment. (Examples: A hostess may be able to discourage some of her guests from smoking by not providing ashtrays; one person can discourage others from crossing a field by erecting a high electrified fence).

Ecological perspective: A viewpoint that encourages social scientists to study the behaviour of an organism in the environment in which it occurs.

Ecological psychology: A viewpoint in social psychology that encourages us to study the behaviour of an organism in the environment in which it occurs.

Ecology: The study of relationships between organism and environment, where both are viewed as part of an ongoing, dynamic system.

Ectomorph: The third of the three types of physique in Sheldon's type theory. It comprises delicacy of skin, fine hair, and ultrasensitive nervous system. *See also endomorph, mesomorph, type theory.*

Figure 8: Structure of the ear and the auditory stimulus

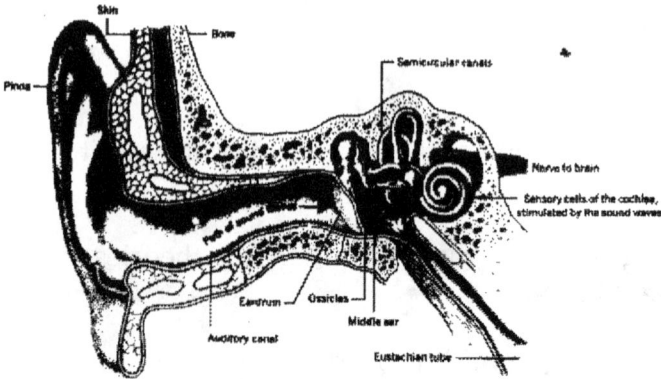

Sound waves enter the external ear (or pinna) and then travel through the auditory canal, a tube approximately 0.7 cm. in diameter and 2.5 cm. long, to the tympanic membrane (or eardrum). They cause this thin piece of tissue to move and press against a series of three small bones called ossicles, which magnify the force of the eardrum's movement; these displacements than reach an opening in the cochlea known as the oval window. The cochlea, a coiled, bony structure, resembles a snail shell. As the oval window moves in and out due to pressure from the ossicles, it presses against fluid in the cochlea, producing disturbances that travel up the cochlea.

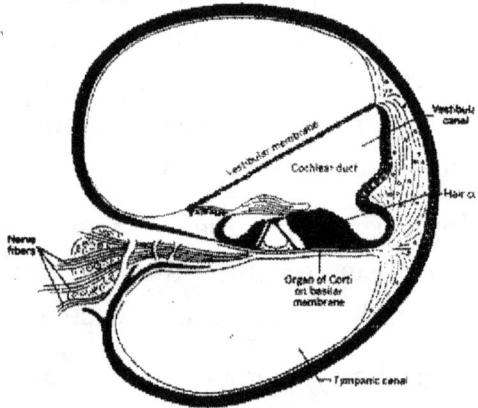

Part of the cochlea. The organ of Corti on the basilar membrane has hair cells that are the actual receptors of auditory stimuli. Movements of the basilar membrane caused by displacements of the liquid in the tympanic canal stimulate these hair cells, thereby producing sensations of sound.

Source: Liebert and Neale (1977), page 73.

Figure 9: The decibel level of familiar sounds

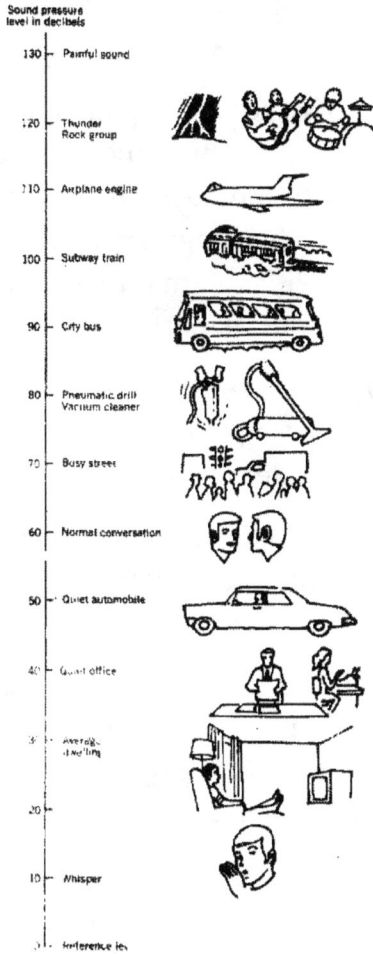

Sound pressure level in decibels

130	Painful sound
120	Thunder / Rock group
110	Airplane engine
100	Subway train
90	City bus
80	Pneumatic drill / Vacuum cleaner
70	Busy street
60	Normal conversation
50	Quiet automobile
40	Quiet office
30	Average dwelling
20	
10	Whisper
0	Reference level

Source: Mednick et al (1975), page 146

Educational psychologist: A psychologist whose research interest lies in the application of psychological principles to the education of children and adults in schools. See also *school psychologist.*

Educationally subnormal: A child whose I.Q. falls within the range of approximately 45-80.

EEG: See *electroencephalograph*

Effect dependences A *form* of dependence on others for the provision of goods protection, etc. See also *Information dependence.*

Effective Group is characterized by an informal, comfortable, relaxed atmosphere, in which there is considerable group discussion in which members listen to each other with respect, and in which disagreements are not suppressed. Such a group provides individual satisfaction and also contributes to efficient task performance.

Effective Leader: One who sees that the members of his group enjoy their membership and also exert themselves to complete the tasks undertaken.

Effector: A bodily organ that is activated by nerves composed of efferent neurons; a muscle or gland. See also *efferent neuron, receptor.*

Efferent neuron: A neuron, or nerve cell that conveys messries from the brain or spinal cord to the effector organs, the muscles, and glands (usually synonymous with motor neuron). *See also afferent neuron, effector.*

Ego: According to Freud, this is that part of the psyche which arbitrates between the demands of the id for gratification and the reality of the external universe; it is the "I" or self, as distinguished from the id and the superego.

Ego-analysis: A variant of traditional psychoanalysis in which greater on people's ability to control themselves and their environments rationally.

Egocentrism: A mechanism by which a person gets attention and obscures inferiority through boastfulness and similar behaviour.

Table 5: Functions of the ego

Ego function	Adequate ego	Inadequate ego
Tolerating frustration	Can substitute another goal for one that is blocked.	Has a temper tantrum
Coping with insecurity, anxiety, and fear	Can develop psychological "defense mechanisms"	Can only flee or attack
Resisting temptation	Can defer gratifications	Seeks immediate gratification
Assessing reality	Adjusts behaviour to particular circumstances and people	Regards authority figures as replicas of parents
Facing guilt	Has guilt feelings and can right a wrong	Has few guilt feelings and tries to evade them.
Establishing inner controls	Can substitute inner control when external supervision is withdrawn	Becomes disorganized when outside controls are removed.
Resisting group intoxication	Is slow to respond to group excitement	Loses control under impact of group excitement
Responding to rules and routines	Interprets rules and routines realistically as necessary to groups	Interprets rules and routines as directed against self.
Dealing with failure, mistakes, and success	Can correct a mistake and is proud of success	Interprets a mistake as worthlessness and success as absolute worth
Maintaining ego integrity	Expresses, but does not lose own values in group activity.	Gives in easily to the authority of the group.

Source: L. Broom and P. Selnick, Sociology: A Test with Adapted Readings. Fifth Edition (New York: Harper and Row, 1973). Page 106.

Ego-defensive function: A reaction to frustration in which an individual deceived himself or herself about his or her real motives and goals to avoid anxiety or loss of self-esteem.

Ego ideal: The person or the self which an individual thinks he or she could and should be.

Eidetic image: A vivid, detailed visual image.

Eidetic imagery: The ability to retain visual images of pictures that are almost photographic in clarity. Such images can be described in far greater detail than would be possible from memory alone. See also *mental imagery.*

Electra complex: According to psychoanalytic theory, a young girl's feeling of attraction towards her father and hence envy of her mother for occupying the place, vis-a-vis her father, that the girl would like to occupy.

Electrodes: Long, thin, insulated wires through which a current can be passed.

Electro encephalograph (EEG): A record that is obtained by attaching electrodes to the scalp (or occasionally to the exposed brain) and amplifying the spontaneous electrical activity of the brain. Familiar aspects of the EEG are alpha waves (8-13 Hz) and delta waves of slower frequency.

Figure 10: Patterns of electrical activity in the brain as recorded by an electroencephalograph

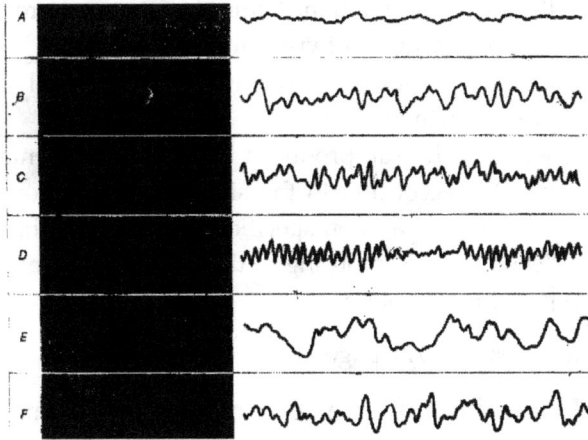

Source: Liebert and Neale (1977), page 35.

Electroshock therapy: (also *Electro-convulsive therapy (ECG):* A form of shock treatment for mental illness in which high voltage current is passed briefly through the head, producing temporary unconsciousness and convulsions, with the intention of alleviating depression or other symptoms. *See also shock therapy.*

Embryo: The fetus during the first 3 months after conception; at this stage, it is highly sensitive to any illness or nutritional deprivation of the mother.

Emergent norm theory: The theory which states that when a number of unrelated people are faced with an ambiguous situation they become a purposeful crowd when they perceive the emergence of a norm to guide their behaviour. For example, when one person throws a stone, or shouts combative slogans, at a policeman.

Emotion: It is a state of feeling, such as anger, fear, love, etc., experienced by individuals for relatively brief period of time, that tends to up set the body's homeostatic baselines.

Table 6: Synopsis of the theories of emotion

James-Lange	Visceral changes produced by an event are noticed, which then lead to emotion. Different emotions are caused by different patterns of visceral activity.
Cannon	Different emotions can arise from identical patterns of visceral activity.
Schecher-Singer	Visceral arousal, produced by an environmental event, is labelled according to the situation the person is in. The arousal is a non-specific mechanism that is then "channelled" according to the person's interpretation into particular emotions.

Source: Liebert and Neale (1977), page 51.

Figure 11: Examples of the brain that influence various emotions and reactions

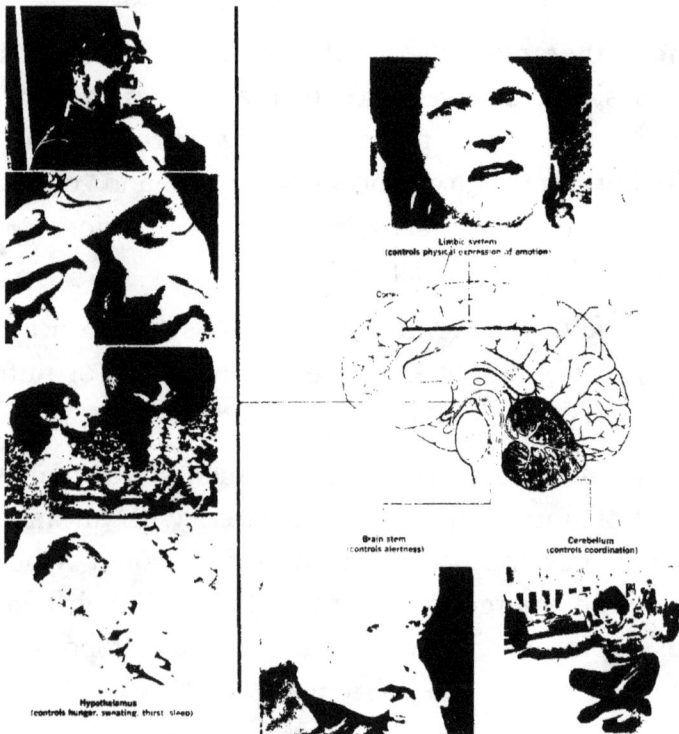

Source: Liebert and Neale (1977), page 33.

Emotional inoculation: A repeated exposure to an anxiety-arousing series of communications which leads to development of resistance to attitude change. *(Same as immunization).*

Empathy: Ability to understand the feelings of another person by putting oneself in his/her position and sharing his/her feelings.

Empirical approach: An active, planned collection of factual information. Contrasted with a rational (or armchair) approach.

Empirical-rational strategy: A strategy of planned change, which holds that publishing the facts that support change is sufficient to initiate that change.

Empiricism: The view that behaviour is learned as a result of concrete. observable experience. *See also nativism.*

Enactive mode: The first mode of mental representation in Bruner's theory; it is nonverbal and based on action.

Encapsulation: An emotional state in which possible alternatives are narrowed down perceptually, and in which the present situation is intensified at the expense of the future.

Encoding: Transforming a sensory input into a form that can be processed by the memory system.

Encounter group: A group whose major purpose is to encourage personal growth and improved sensitivity and communication among its members. The group provides opportunities for intensive interaction, openness, the expression of emotions, and the honest exchange of opinions and feelings. It is essentially the same as a T-group and sensitivity group.

Endocrine gland: The ductless gland, or gland of internal secretion, that discharges its products, hormones, directly into the bloodstream. The hormones secreted by the endocrine glands are important chemical integrators of bodily activity. The endocrine glands are also sometimes referred to as 'ductless' glands, because they do not have any tubes or ducts leading into specific parts of the body, as do such glands as the salivary and tear glands. *See also hormones.*

Table 7: Endocrine glands and their functions

	Endocrine Gland	Hormone	Function and Influence on Behaviour and Experience
1	Pituitary		The master gland: pituitary hormones control the secretion of other glands.
	Anterior Pituitary	Growth Hormone Corticotropin (ACTH)	Growth of skeleton and body Adrenal gland stimulation, influences emotional behaviour.
	Posterior Pituitary	Vasopressin	Blood pressure, water regulation and secretion
2	Thyroid	Thyroxin	Metabolic rate, body weight, level of physical activity, intellectual development, irritability to stimuli.
3	Thymus	Thymus Hormone	Development of body's immunity reactions.
4	Parathyroid	Parathyroid Hormone	Calcium metabolism; maintaining normal reactivity of nervous system
5	Pancreas	Insulin	Sugar metabolism
6	Adrenal		
	Adrenal Cortex	Cortisone	Salt and carbohydrate metabolism; secondary sex characteristics (voice, hair, etc).
	Adrenal Medulla	Noradrenalin (or Norepinephrine) Adrenalin (or	During emotional stress releasing blood sugar, increasing blood pressure, heartbeat, feelings of

		Epinephrine)	tension and anxiety.
7	Gonads (testes, male) (ovaries, female)	Androgen Estrogen Progestin	Primary and secondary sex characteristics are linked to all three hormones. Menstruation, pregnancy, and emotional irritability are linked to estrogen and progestin.

Source: Mednick et al (1975), page 70.

Figure 12: The endocrine glands

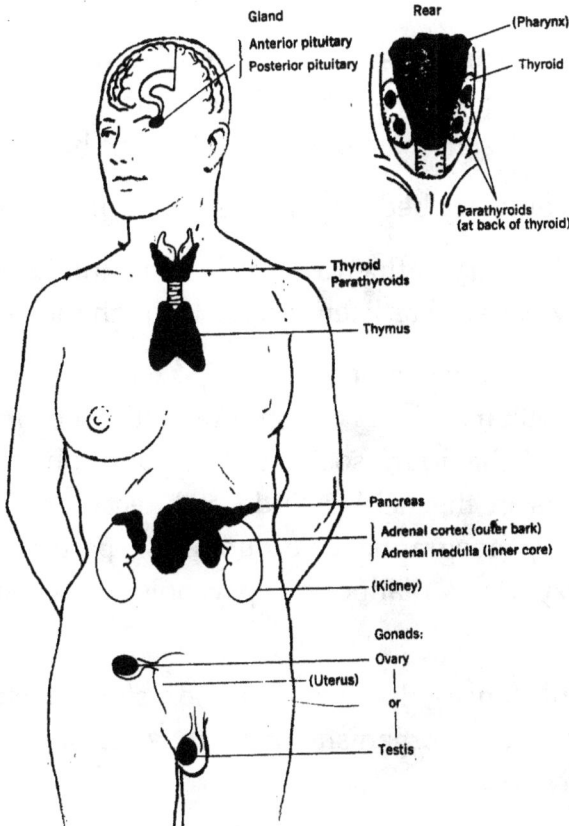

Source: Mednick et al (1975), page 71

Endocrinology: The scientific Study of the hormones secreted by our glands.

Endomorph: The first of three types of physique in Sheldon's type theory. It comprises prominence of intestines and other visceral organs, including a prominent abdomen, as in an obese individual. *See also ectomorph, mesomorph, type theory.*

Endorphins: A newly discovered group of neurotransmitters in the brain that have morphine-like properties and may play important roles in emotion and behaviour and possibly in schizophrenia.

Engineering psychologist: A psychologist who specializes in the relationship between people and machines, seeking, for example, to design machines that minimize human errors.

Enuresis: Involuntary bed-wetting, usually during steep.

Environment: Every influence met by an individual after the hereditary pattern has been receive through the germ plasm.

Environmental psychology: A recently developed, multidisciplinary field concerned with the interplay of individual behaviour, social milieu, and physical setting. Researchers in the field include architects, anthropologists, sociologists, geographers, economists, political scientists, legal experts, planners, psychologists, and other professionals.

Enzymes: Substances that speed up or slow down chemical reactions in an organism: but they remain unchanged themselves.

Epilepsy: A chronic brain disease, with many forms, whose symptoms include convulsions and periods of mental blackouts or unconsciousness.

Epinephrine: One of the hormones secreted by the adrenal medulla that is active in emotional excitement (sny. adrenalin). *See also adrenal gland, norepinephrine.*

Equilibratory senses: The senses that give discrimination of the position of the body in space and of the movement of the body as a whole. *See also kinesthesis, semicircular canals, vestibular sacs.*

Equilibrium, quasi-stationary: An apparently stationary pattern of behaviour that is actually a balance point between two opposing forces. (Example-: A factory worker whose rate of production (number of pieces produced per second) seems to be stable, may actually be responding to pressures to increase his production (such as incentives and personal standards) as well as to equally strong pressures to decrease his production (such as group norms and fatigue).

Equity theory: A minitheory that specifies how people assign rewards to contributions; each person's rewards should be equitable in light of his or her costs.

Table 8: Erikson's eight ages of man

Freud's Stages of Development	Erikson's Stages of Development	Potential Ego Strength
Oral	Basic Trust vs. Mistrust	*Hope*, a belief in the attainability of desires despite one's own conflicting urges and feelings.
Anal	Autonomy vs. Shame and Doubt	*Will*, the courage to employ one's "free choice" despite the danger of the consequent rejection of others.
Phallic	Initiative vs. Guilt	*Purpose*, the courage to

		envision and seek goals despite the frustration of infantile desires.
Latent	Industry vs. Inferiority	*Competence,* the exercise of physical and mental skills in spite of frustration, and difficulties.
Genital (listed below are the genital substages added by Erikson)		
Puberty and Adolescence	Identity vs. Role Diffusion	*Fidelity,* the ability to sustain loyalties despite conflicts.
Young Adulthood	Intimacy vs. Isolation	*Love,* devotion to others in the face of inevitable conflict.
Adulthood	Generativity vs. Stagnation	*Care,* a deep concern for people as they are, regardless of their past action or events beyond their control.
Maturity	Ego Integrity vs. Despair	*Wisdom,* the concern with life despite eventual death.

Source: Mednick et al (1975), page 342.

Erogenous zone: An *area of* the skin or muscous membrane that, when stimulated, produces pleasurable sensations.

Eros: In psychoanalysis, this concept collectively refers to the life instincts.

Escalation of conflict: The increase in conflict between two persons, groups, or any other social units, due to the development of competing goals, threats, and autistic hostility.

Escape learning: A form of learning that is controlled by an actual painful stimulation. Escape from the punishment brings an end to the unpleasant or painful situation and is therefore rewarding. (Note that such a reward is thus technically a negative reinforcer). See *also avoidance learning, negative reinforcer.*

Esprit de corps *(Literally, "spirit of a body (of person)").* The sense of pride in one's group, high cohesiveness, the feeling of common interest and acceptance of group purposes and goals.

Essentializing label: A label which makes a global statement about a person's entire character. To say someone is shy is not to give him an essentializing label; to say someone is a thief is.

Esteem need: According to American psychologist Abraham Maslow, this concept refers to the needs including the desires for attachment, independence, freedom, reputation and prestige.

Estrogen: A female sex hormone that is manufactured and secreted by the ovaries; it is partially responsible for the growth of the female primary and secondary sex characteristics and influences the sex drive. *See also androgens.*

Estrous: The sexually receptive state in female mammals. It is a cyclical state, related to menstruation in the primates and humans (syn. heat). *See also menstruation.*

Ethnomethodology: The investigation of the hidden meanings or the "unwritten social script" used in everyday life. The methodology used by ethnomethodologists, in which unwritten social norms are violated, may be described as a demonstration of the ordinary by use of the absurd.

Ethnocentrism: A rejection of foreigners, aliens, and all out-groups, abetted by a belief that one's own group is best in all respects.

Ethnic group: A group sharing a common culture, customs, and language.

Ethnology: The science of the comparative study of the races of mankind, especially their origin, distribution, and physical differences.

Ethology: The study of the behaviour of animals in their natural settings.

Ethologists: One group of zoologists and naturalists who are particularly interested in the kinds of behaviour that are specific to a species. More of their work has been on insects, birds, and fishes than on mammals to date. *See also imprinting, instinct.*

Etiology: The study of the causes and conditions of a disease or abnormality.

Eugenics: The mating that is deliberately controlled by the application of the laws of heredity in order to breed superior individuals.

Evaluative component: One of the two pans of an attitude, which refers to the positive or negative character of an individual's orientation towards an aspect of his or her world.

Evaluative norms: These are the norms regarding the goodness or desirability of human behaviours, objects, ceremonies, etc., in any human group.

Evaluation apprehension: The concern shown by someone whose performance is being evaluated. This concern may cause the person to perform less well or to act in a way that he believes will be approved by an observer.

Evoked potential: An electrical discharge in some pan of the nervous system that is produced by stimulation elsewhere. The measured potential is commonly based on response averaging by a computer.

Exchange theory: A set of propositions relating interaction of persons to the level *of* satisfying outcomes that they experience, and specifying the consequences of these outcomes for the maintenance or change of the interaction.

Excitatory synapse: A synapse at which the neurotransmitter changes the membrane permeability of the receiving cell in the direction of depolarization. See *also depolarization, inhibitory synapse, synapse.*

Excommunication: An ancient form of punishing a social deviant by cutting him off from participation in all a community's social and sacred activities. It is even now still quite a powerful means to secure conformity to group norms in rural areas in countries like India.

Exhibitionism: The exposure of one's genitals to an unwitting observer, which provides sexual gratification to the one who exposes himself or herself.

Existential anxiety: An anxiety that largely revolves around the purpose and meaning of life.

Existential philosophy: A philosophical school of though that points to human experience as the main data for understanding human behaviour.

Existential vacuum: A state of despair in an individual in which he/she feels that his/her life is empty of purpose or meaning,

Expectancies: A person's anticipation of future events. This anticipation may be a powerful determinant of present behaviour.

Expectation: (1) An anticipation or prediction of future events that is based on past experiences and present stimuli.

(2) An individual's anticipations that he or she and other people win behave in certain definite ways. In entertaining such expectations, the individual anticipates the nature of interaction in particular situations. Further, his or her expectations and those of the other party are generally shared.

Expedient conformity: A form of conformity in which the individual agrees outwardly with a group's norm although he is in inward disagreement with it.

Experience: This concept refers to those aspects of behaviour that involve personal private feelings, thoughts, dreams, hopes, and fears, as well as the awareness of things that we do, and the things that happen to us, that we can keep to ourselves or share with others,

Experimental design: A plan for collecting and treating the data of a proposed experiment. The design is evolved after preliminary exploration, with the aims of economy, precision, and control, so that appropriate inferences and decisions can be made from the data.

Experimental group: In an experiment, this is the group which is treated in every way the same as the control group except that it is exposed to the independent variable which is manipulated by the experimenter. See *also control group.*

Experimental hypothesis: A testable statement of the relationship between two or more variables.

Experimental method: The method of investigation of natural empirical events that seeks to control the variables involved so as to be able to more precisely define cause and effect relationships. It is most frequently done in a laboratory, but need not be. See *also observational method, variable.*

Experimental neurosis: A breakdown in the efficient functioning of an individual due to his/her inability to distinguish between two conditioned stimuli in a learning situation.

Experimental psychologist: A psychologist whose research interest is in the laboratory study of general psychological principles as revealed in the behaviour of lower organisms and human beings.

Experimental realism: The arrangement of the events of an experiment so that they will seem convincing and have the maximum possible impact on the subjects. This is sometimes accomplished through the use of deception.

Experiment expectancy effects: The undesirable or distorting effects on the outcome and interpretation of an experiment that arise when a researcher's awareness of the hypotheses leads him to subtly vary his behaviour in different experimental conditions, thus unconsciously influencing the results in the predicted direction.

Experimenter effects: The changes or distortions in the results of an experiment that are produced by the experimenter's characteristics or behaviour.

Expiatory punishment: According to Jean Piaget, this concept refers to the belief which .is held by younger children that wrongdoers should suffer a punishment that is painful in proportion to the seriousness of the offense but not necessarily adapted to the nature of the offense. *See also reciprocity.*

Expert power: A form of potential, influence over another person by virtue of the special knowledge or skill that an individual possesses.

Exposure: The first step of observational learning that occurs when an observer encounters modeling cues.

External sanction: A form of social control in which the environment or other persons punish an individual for an offense.

External validity: The extent to which experimental findings can be generalized to other populations, settings, treatments, and so forth.

Extinction: [1] The experimental procedure, following classical or operant conditioning, of presenting the conditioned stimulus without the usual reinforcement. [2] The reduction in response that results from this procedure. *See also reinforcement.*

Extrasensory perception (ESP): A controversial category of experience consisting of perception without the use of the sense organs of stimulation; it includes clairvoyance, parapsychology, recognition, telepathy, psychokinesis.

Extrovert: One of the psychological types that was first proposed by Carl Jung. The extrovert is more preoccupied with social life and the external world than with his or her inward experience. Contrasted with 'introvert.'

Extroversion: A personality trait that is characterized by the enjoyment of other people and activities outside oneself. It is the opposite of introversion.

Figure 13: The structure of the eye and its relationship to the brain

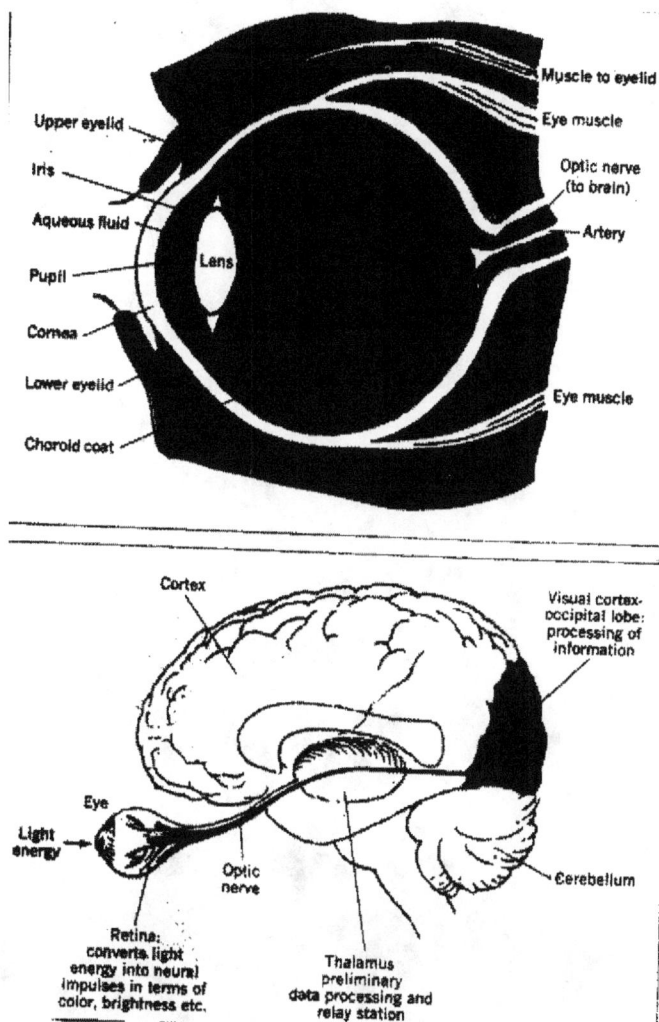

Source: Mednick et al (1975), page 138.

F

Facework: Any behaviour that is designed to repair a particular presentation of self.

Facial vision: The ability, which is most highly developed in blind people, to detect the position of objects by the sense of hearing.

Feet: An observation that has been made (or could be made) repeatedly and consistently by different observers.

Factor analysis: [1] A statistical method which is used in test construction and in interpreting scores from batteries of tests. The method enables the investigator to compute the minimum number of determiners (factors) required to account for the intercorrelations among the scores on the tests making up the battery. [2] A statistical technique that permits a researcher to analyze a large number of interrelationships among the personal qualities of a subject and to abstract the underlying common elements. This procedure has been especially used in *trait* and *type research* in psychology. *See also general factor, special factor.*

Factorial design: A design in which each level of one independent variable is combined with each level of another independent variable (or several others).

Fad: A passing fancy or novelty, interest; the rapid but usually temporary adoption of new habits by a large group of people, such as interest in a new type of dress like laces, bell-bottom trousers, etc.

Fallacy: A mistake in reasoning. Examples include psychological reductionism, sociological reductionism, etc.

Family: A set of persons who are related to each other by marriage, blood, or adoption, that comprises a domestic social group. Family groups represent the bedrocks of all human societies. Membership in a family is based on a combination of biological and cultural factors that vary significantly from society to society. The structure of the family, which consists of the statuses and roles of the family members, is determined culturally. The functions performed by the family also vary a great deal from society to society, but the most common ones include the provision of predictable and inexpensive sexual services for the spouses; the procreation and filliation of children; and the provision of affection for alt family members.

There are several different specific types of families, such as the conjugal, nuclear, extended or compound, patriarchal, matriarchal, single-parent, and joint families.

Family, Equalitarian: The type of family whose members are regarded as equal. The husband, in particular, is not regarded as having more than one wife.

Family, Extended: The type of family organisation which consists of three or more general ions that are affiliated through an extension of the parent-child relationship. As such, it also involves two or more nuclear families. For example, an extended family might include grandparents, their unmarried children, together with the spouses and children of the latter.

Family, Matriarchal: The type of family organisation in which power and authority are rested in the hands of the females, with the eldest female usually wielding the greatest power.

The matriarchal family is usually an extended consanguine (organised In terms of blood relationship) family in which the eldest female is the matriarch. It is doubtful that any society has had a true matriarchal family system: even in societies with matrilineal descent, matrilineal inheritance, and matrilocal residence, power tends to be held by males in the female lineage–usually by the women's brothers. A minority of societies have organised around the female lineage.

Family, Nuclear: The basic unit of family organization, which includes as its members parents and their children, biological or adopted. The nuclear family in which one is the child is his family of orientation; that in which he is the parent is his family of procreation.

Family, Patriarchal: The form of family organisation in which power and authority are rested in the hands of the males, with the eldest male usually wielding the greatest power. The patriarchal family is usually an extended consanguine (organized in terms of blood relationship) family in which the patriarch is .the senior male member. Characteristics associated with the patriarchal family are patrilineal descent, patrilineal inheritance, patrilocal residence, and primogeniture (inheritance by the eldest son). Other characteristics frequently associated with patriarchy are polygamy, double standard of sexual morality, masculine privilege with regard to divorce, low status for women, arranged marriages for children.

Patrilineal families are most frequently associated with hunting, fishing, and agricultural societies, and fade fast with industrialization. Examples of strong patriarchal family systems are the ancient Hebrew, Greek, and Roman families, and other traditional Chinese, Hausa, Fulani,

Yoruba, Benin, and Urhobo families. The modern nuclear family emerged from a modified form of patriarchal family.

Although the ideal of the patriarchal family calls for a father with the ability and personal characteristics to wield absolute power and authority, many fathers have not been able to perform this role.

Vestiges of the patriarchal family system in the modern nuclear family are the beliefs that men should be heads of the household, that fathers should be strong and wise and the custom of women adopting their husband's surnames.

Family, Single-Parent: The type of family organization which is made up of a child or children and one parent who may or may not have been married. The parent may be a father or a mother who is divorced or "widowed or is an adoptive father or a mother who is divorced or widowed, an unmarried mother, or an adoptive mother. Although parents are frequently forced by circumstances into the single-parent family unit. many adults also deliberately choose to be so.

Family therapy: Psychotherapy with the family members as a group rather than treatment of the patient alone. *See also group therapy.*

Fantasy: This concept refers to an ego-defensive mechanism that largely arises from frustration, in which an individual attempts to enhance his/her self-esteem, or to avoid anxiety, by inducing in such vacuous, purposeless, or meaningless practices as day-dreaming, 'wool-gathering' imaginations, building castles in the air, etc. It is used as a personality indicator in projective tests. *See also protective tests.*

Fear: The emotional reaction of strong agitation in the presence of actual or anticipated pain or danger.

Feedback: In psychology, this concept refers to the information or message that is returned to an individual as a consequence of his/her prior behaviour.

Fellatio: The oral stimulation of the male genitalia.

Feminity: The set of ideal behavioural characteristics that are widely regarded to be proper for females in any particular society, For example, in the contemporary multi-ethnic and multi-cultural Nigerian society, many Nigerian mates expect most Nigerian females to be neat, physically attractive, sexually passive buy cooperative, understanding, patient, home-oriented, dependent, and faithful to their better (male) half. On the other hand, most radical Westernized Nigerian females tend to expect that modem Nigerian females should be neat, pretty, independent-minded, sexually-active, career-oriented, but financially dependent upon men.

Feral Child: Literally this concept refers to a wild and untrained child reputedly raised by animals in a totally non-human and non-social environment. The concept is seldom used in social psychology nowadays, largely because of the highly ambiguous and doubtful nature of most of the available accounts of such types of children. Instead, the concept has virtually given way to the concept of *social isolate*, which refers to the different types of individuals whose early childhood was markedly deficient. In "normal" human contacts, thus, rendering them "unsocialized," or "inadequately socialized". Thus, such individuals are both mentally and physically deficient, but, given intensive re-socialization, they can become "normal" human beings again.

Fetishism: The use of an inanimate object or part of the body for-sexual arousal.

Fetus: This term refers to an unborn, developing child, after the third month until birth.

Field experiment: (1) A controlled experiment in a natural setting such as an industrial plant or a school; this contrasts with a laboratory experiment. (2) An experiment that is done in a natural, real-life situation, often without the awareness of the subjects.

Field study: This concept refers to a behaviourial science research that is conducted in a single natural social setting (such as a community, a work group, a club, a neighbourhood, a school), usually over a long period of time. A field study may utilize careful observations or it may also include questionnaires. (Example: a study of leadership practices and productivity in an industrial work group, utilizing observations, interviews with workers, and measurement of productivity).

Field survey: A social research technique to assess the attitudes, beliefs, behaviours, or other characteristics of a population by means of personal interviews with a representative sample of that population. (Example: Determining people's attitudes towards the gradual phasing out of boarding facilities in colleges and universities throughout the country, by interviewing a representative sample of the country's adult population).

Field theory; A basic point of view in general or social psychology, first developed by Kurt Lewin, which proposes that one's social behaviour is a function not only of one's own attitudes, personality, and other intrapersonal factors, but also of one's environment, or "field."

Figure-ground perception: Perceiving a pattern as foreground against a background. Patterns are commonly perceived this way even when the stimuli are ambiguous and the foreground-background relationships are reversible.

Fixation: In psychoanalysis, this concept refers to the arrested development in an individual's personality, through failure to pass beyond one of the earlier stages of psychosexual development or to change the objects of attachment (e.g., fixated at the oral stage, or fixated upon the mother).

Fixed-interval reinforcement schedule: The reinforcement that is administered after a fixed interval of time, regardless of the subject's response rate.

Fixed interval: A reinforcement schedule in which a reward is given according to the time that has elapsed; first response that occurs after a predestinated time interval is rewarded.

Fixed ratio: A reinforcement schedule in which a reward is given after a fixed number of responses have been made.

Flow chart: A diagrammatic representation of the sequence of choices and actions in an activity.

Focal consciousness: That which at any one moment is at the centre of attention. See *also conscious processes.*

"Foot-in-the-door" effect: The case in which previous compliance with a small request makes; it more likely that the person/will comply with a larger (and less desirable) request.

Foot-in-the-door technique: A form of manipulation by graduation, in which one person persuades another to engage in a more extreme act after first convincing him to perform a more moderate act.

Forced compliance: A situation in which a person is compelled .to do something that he doesn't want to do. Forced compliance has been utilized in many experiments to study the cognitive dissonance theory of attitude change.

Formal operations period: This concept refers to the fourth and final stage of cognitive development in Jean Piaget's theory. By about 12 years of age, children are able to solve problems by reasoning at a formal, abstract level.

Formal operational stage: Piaget's fourth stage of cognitive development (age 12 and up) in which a child becomes able to use abstract rules.

Formal social structure: The prescribed structure of a group or social organization. This is the opposite of informal social structure. (Example: The table of organization of a business, social group, institution, or government, indicating titles of position, authority relationships, job descriptions, and so forth).

Forming alternative relations: Establishing a satisfying relation with a person other than P, resulting in reduced dependency on P and a shift towards equalization of the relative social-power of P and O.

Four humours: The four body fluids that were first distinguished and emphasized by the ancient Greek physician Hippocrates. These were: chole or yellow bile; melanchole, or black bile; blood; and phlegm. See *also four temperaments.*

Four temperaments: The four types into which Galen classified all personalities over 1,800 years ago. These were: choleric, melancholic, sanguine, and phlegmatic. Galen associated these types with Hippocrates's four 'humours'. *See also four humours.*

Fovea: The area in the central retina, containing many cones, where vision is most acute.

Fractionation of conflict: A method of resolving intergroup conflict by separating large, all-encompassing issues into smaller, more workable ones (this method was suggested by Roger Fisher). Fractionation is often accomplished by third-party intervention.

Frame of reference: An orientation with which one perceives anything.

Fraternal twins: Twins developed from two ova, fertilized by two sperms. They may be of the same sex, or of opposite sexes.

Free association: A key psychoanalytic technique, in which patients are encouraged to give free rein to their thoughts and feelings, saying whatever comes to mind without censoring anything; with this technique, it is assumed that eventually material that had previously been repressed will come forth for examination by the patient and his analyst.

Free nerve endings: The structures found in the skin that may be important in producing sensations of pain.

Free recall: A memory task in which a subject is given a list of items (usually one at a time) and is later asked to recall them in any order.

Free Love: Living openly with, or having sexual relations with one of the opposite sex without marriage or any continuing obligation. See also Premarital sex.

Frequency distribution: A set of scores that are assembled according to size and grouped info class intervals. *See also class interval, normal distribution.*

Frequency theory; A theory of hearing that assumes that neural impulses arising in the organ of Corti are activated by the basilar membrane of the ear in accordance with the frequency of its vibration rather than with the place of movement. *See also place theory, volley principle.*

Freudian slips: In psychoanalytic theory, these are seemingly accidental acts or words that reveal something of an individual's true hidden feelings or motives.

Frontal lobe: A portion of each cerebral hemisphere in front of the central fissure. *See also occipital lobe, parietal lobe, temporal lobe.*

Frustration: (1) As an event, the thwarting circumstances that block or interfere with goal-directed activity. (2) As a state, the annoyance, confusion, or anger engendered by being thwarted, disappointed, defeated.

Frustration aggression hypothesis: A hypothesis developed in the late 1930s which holds that frustration is the only cause of aggression. Although current research indicates that there may be other causes of aggression, and that frustration may lead to behaviour other than aggression, the theory has generally held up well in research spanning more than forty-five years.

Fugue: A hysterical dissociative reaction in which an individual flees to a new locality, sets up a totally new life, and completely forgets about his previous fife, although he retains his faculties and appears normal to others.

Functional autonomy: (1) The motive force of habits originally adopted to satisfy other motives. (2) The viewpoint that behaviour which has often led to reward may become rewarding in itself, even though it no longer produces the original reward.

Functional distance: The extent to which the physical proximity of two persons' residences, along with the physical layout of the residences, affects their opportunities to interact. Close functional proximity implies frequent opportunity to interact.

Functional fixedness: A difficulty in problem-solving that is caused by a person's inability to view a single object or situation in more than one way,

Functionalist psychology: A school of thought in psychology that focuses upon and emphasizes the adaptive functions of behaviour and consciousness. It was founded by the American psychologist William James, Other prominent contributors include American psychologists James R. Angell and John Dewey.

Functional psychosis: A psychosis of psychogenic origin without clearly defined changes of the central nervous system. See *also organic psychosis, psychosis.*

Function of position: The purpose served by a given position in a group for maintaining the group and enabling it to move towards its goal.

Fundamental attribution error: The tendency to underestimate situational influences on behaviour and assume that some personal characteristic of the individual is responsible; the bias towards dispositional rather than situational attributions. *See also attribution, dispositional Attribution, situational attribution.*

Funnel sequence: Arrangement of questions in an interview with broad, open-ended questions first, then somewhat narrower ones, and finally very narrow and specific questions.

Future shock: A state of psychological disorientation that results from the superimposition of a new culture on an old one; a product of a greatly accelerated rate of change in society.

G

Galvanic skin response (GSR): Changes in electrical conductivity of, or activity in, the skin, detected by a sensitive galvanometer. The reactions are commonly used as an emotional indicator.

Gang: The private, fiercely loyal group of playmates, to which some pre-adolescent children belong.

Ganglia: (sing. ganglion). A collection of nerve cell bodies and synapses, constituting a centre lying outside the brain and spinal cord, as in the sympathetic ganglia. *See also nuclei.*

Gastrointestinal motility: The movements of parts of the digestive tract caused by contraction of smooth muscles; they constitute one form of emotional indicator.

Gender identity: An individuals self-awareness of being male or female.

Gene: The unit of hereditary transmission, which is localized within the chromosomes. Each chromosome contains many genes. Genes are typically in pairs, one member of the pair being found in the chromosome from the father, the other in the corresponding chromosome from the mother. See *also chromosome, dominant gene, recessive gene.*

Genetics: The branch of biology which is concerned with heredity and the means by which hereditary characteristics are transmitted.

General factor (g): (1) A genera) ability underlying test scores, especially in tests of intelligence, as distinct from special abilities that are unique to each test (Spearman). (2) A general ability with which each of the primary factors correlates (Thurstone). *See also factor analysis, special factor. ,*

Generalization: (1) In concept formation problem solving, and transfer of learning, this concept refers to the detection by the learner of a characteristic or principle that is common to a class of objects, events, or problems. (2) In conditioning, the concept refers to the principle that once a conditioned response has been established to a given stimulus, similar stimuli will also evoke that response. *See also discrimination.*

General Psychology: A scientific discipline which studies the various behaviours and experiences of individuals in order to find the laws which govern such individual behaviours and experiences.

Generalization gradient: The strength of a CR as a function of the degree of similarity between a test stimulus and the CS; the greater the similarity between the two, the more the similar stimulus will be able to elicit the conditioned response.

Generalized Other: The third and final stage in the development of self as proposed by the American social psychologist George Herbert Mead. In the process of taking the role of the other, the child, according to Mead, progresses from the stage of taking the role of specific significant others in his environment, generally his parents and immediate peers, to the stage of taking the role of numerous others in society, or, in short, of society in general. The generalized other, then, consists of an organized community of groups or the generalized expectations or appropriate behaviours held in society that are associated with a particular social role. In internalizing his conception of the proper enactment of a social role, the child responds to or internalizes the role expectations and evaluative criteria of diffuse others, and it is these societally ranging attitudes that ultimately become incorporated into the structure of the self.

Generosity error: The error of rating acquaintances more favourably than strangers.

Genital stage: The Freudian developmental stage from age 14 up. It is centred on the development of mature sexuality and love for others.

Genital system: This comprises the reproductive organs and associated glands in humans and other higher vertebrates.

Genotype: The characteristics that an individual has inherited and can pass on to his descendants; an individual's genotype is not necessarily reflected in his phenotype, or external appearance.

Geographical world: This concept refers to the "real world", the world that is largely made up of physical, biological, and chemical phenomena, e.g. hills, valleys, animals, plants, rains, winds, temperatures, etc.

Germ plasm: The chromosomes of sex cells (egg and sperm).

Gestalt: A unified pattern or configuration. Gestalt theory of perception postulates that "the whole is greater than the sum of its parts", since the configuration of pans takes on meaning in its own right. In gestalt therapy groups, presumably the members try to be aware of the total configuration of the group experience.

Gestalt psychology: This is a school of psychology that emphasizes the patterns, organization, and wholeness of human behaviours and experiences.

Glial cells: An important type of cell in the nervous system that provides a support system for the neurons.

Goal: (1) An end state or condition towards which any motivated behaviour sequence is directed, and by which the sequence is completed. (2) Loosely, any incentive. *See also incentive.*

Goal-directed behaviour: The behaviour that is directed towards any object or event towards which an individual strives.

Goals interdependence: A relationship among the members of a group in which one person's movement towards his own goal either facilitates or inhibits another person's movement towards his goal. Positive goal interdependence (or *convergent interests)* leads to *cooperation.* Negative goal interdependence (or *divergent interests)* leads to *competition.* Goals interdependence focuses en the goal rather than the means that is utilized to attain that goal.

Graded potentials: Potential changes of varying sizes that are induced in a neuron's dendrites or cell body by stimulation from synapses from other neurons. When the graded potentials reach a threshold of depolarization an action potential occurs. *See also action potential, depolarization.*

Gradient of texure: If a surface is perceived visually as having substantial texture (hard, soft, smooth, rough, etc.) and if the texture has a noticeable grain, it becomes finer as the surface recedes from the viewing person reproducing a gradient of texture that is important in judgments of slant and of distance. See *also distance cues.*

Gray matter: A set of neutral tissue that is made up primarily of nerve cell bodies.

GRIT (Graduated Reciprocation in Tension Reduction): A method (proposed by Charles Osgood) to reverse the *escalation of conflict between two* parties. Both parties must first recognise *superordinate goal* or *superordinate threat; then* the conflict must be fractionated, and one party must make a graduated series of unilateral concessions, announced dearly in advance, and contingent upon reciprocated concessions.

Goitre: An enlarged thyroid gland.

Gonads: These are the sex glands; they are the testes in the mate and the ovaries in the female. As duct glands, the sex glands are active in mating behaviour, but as endocrine glands, their hormones affect secondary sex characteristics as well as maintaining functional sexual activity. The male hormones are known as androgens, the female hormones as estrogen (syn. sex glands). See *also androgens, endocrine gland, estrogen.*

Group: A collection of individuals who are in inter-dependent relationship with one another. There is a sharing of common norms of behaviour and attitudes. The members of a group usually expect that their continued affiliation will provide a means of obtaining their various desired goals.

Group-centred leadership: A leadership style that is characterized by the use of two forms of *social influence: referent power and informational power.* The group-centred leader wants to both elicit compliance and be accepted by the other members of the group; he permits and encourages the group members to participate fully in decision-making and planning. This style is the opposite of *directive leadership.*

Group cohesion: A pattern of strong relationships and identification among individuals in a group.

Group cohesiveness: The total of a)) of the pressures acting upon the individual members of a group to remain in that group or leave. A group may be characterized as having high cohesiveness, low cohesiveness or negative cohesiveness, (Negative cohesive-ness might arise if the pressures to leave the group were greater than (hose to remain, which could come about if there were barriers to leaving the group).

Group decision: A decision that is arrived at by a group to accept or reject new goals.

Group-decision process: A procedure in which a group is exposed to a persuasive communication or presented with a problem; followed by discussion and a decision on whether to adopt the recommended behaviour or not.

Group discussion: A situation in which all the members of a group sit together and discuss any of the problems facing the group. Each member gives his opinion and participates fully.

Group dynamics: A field of inquiry in social psychology with the aim of advancing knowledge about the nature of groups, and the laws of their development. Its aim is to study the psychological and social forces operating in any group.

Group effects: The influence of a group on an individual, that motivates him to change or not to change.

Group factors: The aptitudes for certain habitual ways of reasoning, or thinking symbolically.

Group locomotion: The movement of a group towards its goal. To facilitate this movement the individual members may need to co-ordinate their beliefs, attitudes, and behaviour, and thus they may experience *interdependence pressures*. Group locomotion may be one source of pressures towards group cohesiveness.

Group norm: A level of performance, pattern of behaviour, or belief, that is formally or informally established as appropriate by a group. An individual member usually experiences pressure to behave in accordance with group norms, and sometimes a group uses positive and negative sanctions to enforce conformity to its norms.

Group solidarity: This refers to a situation in any human group in which there is a community or consensus of interests, feelings, and action or behaviour amongst most of the members of the group so that the group coheres together and the members genuinely feel that they are mutually dependent upon each other.

Group structure: The pattern of differentiation of roles and statuses within a group.

Group test: A text administered to several people at once by a single tester. A college or university examination is usually a group test.

Group therapy: A group discussion or other group activity with a therapeutic purpose participated in by more than one client or patient at a time. See also *psychotherapy*.

Groupthink: A word coined by Irving Janis meaning a "deterioration of mental efficiency, reality testing, and moral judgement (among members of a group) which results from in-group pressures." Janis said that groupthink could more readily be found in highly cohesive groups.

GSR (galvanic skin response): Electrical conductance of the skin which is caused by activity of the sympathetic nervous system.

Guilt feeling: The unpleasant feeling of sinfulness arising from the behaviour or desires that are contrary to one's ethical principles. It involves fear of punishment and self-devaluation.

Gyri: The ridges in the cerebral cortex.

H

Habit: A form of memory in which remembering is shown by the automatic performance of a learned response.

Haetnophillia: An inherited condition, sex-linked to maleness, in which the blood does not clot normally.

Hallucination: A sense experience in the absence of appropriate external stimuli; a misinterpretation of imaginary experiences as actual perceptions. See also *delusion, illusion, schizophrenia.*

Hallucinogens: Psychoactive drugs that usually produce hallucinations. *See also hallucination, LSD, psychoactive drugs.*

Halo effect: Refers to the phenomenon that if one highly desirable trait is noted in an individual, others are likely to be inferred from it. Thus, if someone is physically attractive, it is quite likely that other desirable characteristics, such as friendliness or intelligence, will be attributed to the person.

Haphazard sampling: Sampling without any systematic method and it is, therefore, unrepresentative.

Hashish: The dried resin of the *Cannabis* plant, which produces stronger effects than the dried leaves and stems (which constitute marijuna).

Hawthorne effect: The observation (first noted at the Hawthorn Works of the Western Electric Company) that members of a group will work harder and be more productive if they feel that their group has been singled out as important and that they are participating in a new and special activity.

Hebephrenia: Extremely retrogressive form of schizophrenia, characterized by silliness and childishness.

Mebephrenic schizophrenia: A kind of schizophrenic behaviour in which the individual regresses to an infantile level of behaviour.

Hedonism: The theory that human beings seek pleasure and avoid pain; an extreme form of the theory (in philosophy) is that pleasure or happiness is the highest good.

Helping behaviour: A prosocial behaviour that benefits another person rather than oneself.

Hereditarian: An individual who believes that variations in behaviour are the result of biological differences between individuals that are determined genetically. The hereditarian point of view can be contrasted with that of the advocates of socialization, who argue that learning and experience are the major determinants of behavour.

Heredity: The transmission of traits from one generation to the next through the process of sexual reproduction.

Hermaphrodite: A person who possesses a combination of male and female bodily organs and hormonal patterns, so that the person's sex cannot be clearly defined as entirety female or entirely male.

Heritability: The proportion of the total variability of a trait in a given population that is attributable to genetic differences among individuals within that population.

Heterogeneous groups; A group composed of members with diverse knowledge, skills, and experiences; dissimilar backgrounds; or differing personalities. Heterogeneous groups tend to function more effectively than homogeneous ones, especially when a variety of facts and opinions is required to solve a set of difficult group tasks. On the other hand, the more heterogeneous a group, the more likely that the members will hold contrasting viewpoints. which may lead to group tension and hostility.

Heteronomous stage: An early stage of moral development, in which a child accepts rules as given from authority.

Heterophobia: An individual's pathological fear of having sexual contact with another person of the opposite sex. Psychoanalysis trace this fear back to the events in the individual's early life. According to psychoanalysis and some learning theorists, heterephobia explains homosexuality.

Heterosexuality: The interest in or attachment to a member of the opposite sex; it is the usual adult outcome of a normal psychosexual development.

Hertz (Hz); The wave of frequency of a sound source, or other cyclical phenomena, measured in cycles per second.

Hidden observer: A metaphor to describe the concealed consciousness in hypnosis, inferred to have experiences differing from, but parallel to, the hypnotic consciousness.

Hierarchies of concepts: The relationships among individual concepts. *See also concept.*

Hierarchy: The stratification of people into superordinate versus subordinate positions in any social system [e.g., in a group, organization, community, or society], based on the people's differential possession of combinations of socially valued factors, such as material wealth, educational qualifications, ability, socio-cultural privileges (e.g., royal birth, professional recognition, religious reverence, etc).

Hierarchy of motives: American psychologist Abraham Maslow's way of classifying human motives, ascending from basic biological motives that must be satisfied first to a peak of self-actualization, which is supposedly the highest human motive.

Hierarchy of role obligations: An arrangement of role obligations according to priorities. Those with the highest priority represent the strongest obligations, and should be enacted in preference to those lower in the hierarchy whenever there is a problem of enacting the role.

Figure 14: Maslow's Need Hierarchy

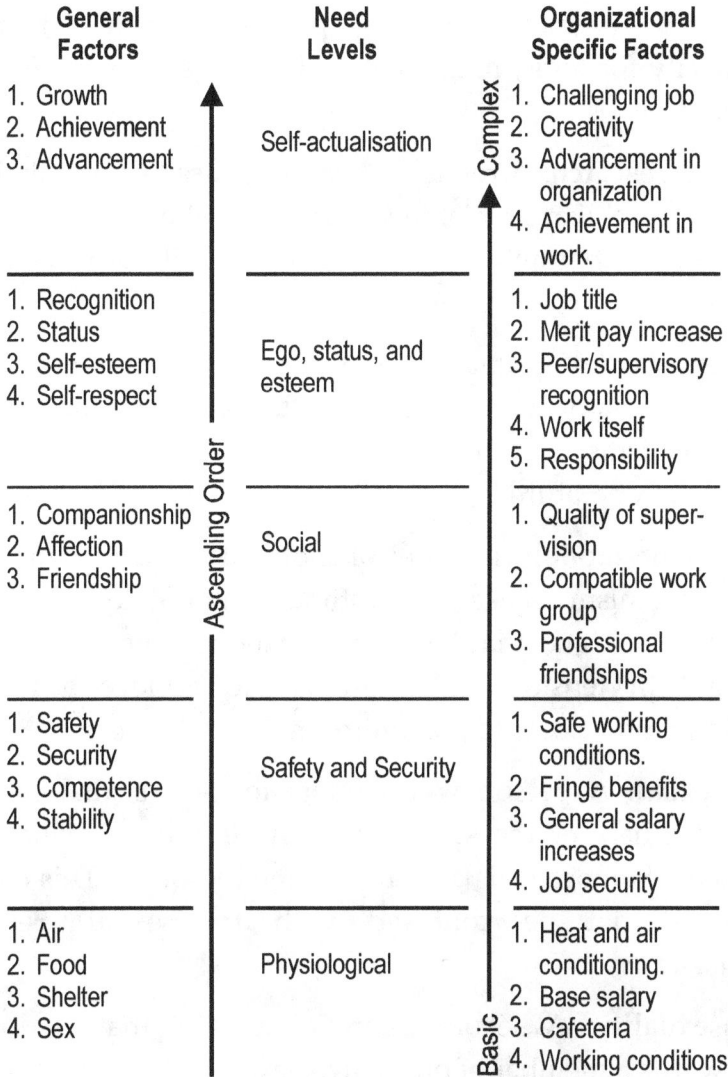

General Factors	Need Levels	Organizational Specific Factors
1. Growth 2. Achievement 3. Advancement	Self-actualisation	1. Challenging job 2. Creativity 3. Advancement in organization 4. Achievement in work.
1. Recognition 2. Status 3. Self-esteem 4. Self-respect	Ego, status, and esteem	1. Job title 2. Merit pay increase 3. Peer/supervisory recognition 4. Work itself 5. Responsibility
1. Companionship 2. Affection 3. Friendship	Social	1. Quality of super-vision 2. Compatible work group 3. Professional friendships
1. Safety 2. Security 3. Competence 4. Stability	Safety and Security	1. Safe working conditions. 2. Fringe benefits 3. General salary increases 4. Job security
1. Air 2. Food 3. Shelter 4. Sex	Physiological	1. Heat and air conditioning. 2. Base salary 3. Cafeteria 4. Working conditions

Ascending Order

Complex → Basic

Source: Andrew D. Szilagyi, Jr. and Mac. J. Wallace, Jr.; *Organizational Behaviour and Performance*. Santa Monica, California: Goodyear Publishing Co., Inc., 1980, page 107.

Higher mental processes: These essentially consist of the various conscious thinking processes, including man's capacity for logic, mathematics, language, imagination, and creativity.

High-risk research: A research technique, used especially in the study of schizophrenia, in which those who have a high probability of becoming abnormal in later life are intensively examined.

Homeostasis: An optimal level of organic function, maintained by regulatory mechanisms known as homeostatic mechanisms; e.g., the mechanisms maintaining a uniform body temperature.

Homeostatic model: *A* model of motivation that assumes that an organism seeks an optimal amount or degree of stimulation and that large discrepancies from the optimum result in tension and a motive to achieve a level of stimulation closer to the optimum.

Homosexual: A person who prefers to have sexual relations with others of the same sex. Can be male or female, but female homosexuals are often termed lesbians. This concept should not be confused with transsexual. See *also transsexual.*

Homosexuality: A sexual desire or activity that is directed towards a member of one's own sex.

Hormones: The chemical substances, secreted internally by the endocrine glands, that affect the workings of the nervous system, end often duplicate the effects of the nervous system.

Hostile aggression: The type of aggression that is primarily intended to harm another person. This contrasts with *instrumental aggression.*

Hostile conflict: The conflict between two or more panics (individuals, groups, or larger social entities) which arises from the fact that one party dislikes or hates the other (an attitude that is probably reciprocated). The primary purpose of a hostile conflict is to harm the opposing party, over and above (often in addition to) the pursuance of disparate extrinsic goals (as in competitive conflict). Hostile conflict thus includes the *hostile aggression* of one party towards the other.

Hue: The dimension of colour from which the major colour names are derived (red. yellow, green, etc.), corresponding to the wavelength of light. *See also brightness, saturation.*

Humanistic psychology: A psychological approach that emphasizes the uniqueness of human beings; it is concerned with subjective experience and human values. It is often referred to as a third force in psychology, in contrast to *behaviourism* and *psychoanalysis*. *See also phenomenology.*

Hunger drive: A drive that is based on food deprivation. *See also drive, specific hunger.*

Hybrid: An offspring of genetically different parents, such as a child who is born by a black and a white parent.

Hyperphagia: Pathological overeating. *See also aphagia.*

Hypnosis: A temporary condition resembling deep steep, in which a person exercises conscious control of his behaviour and feelings according to the suggestions of another person who has hypnotized him.

Hypochondria: A type of neurosis that is characterized by excessive concern with body ailments. This concept is also called *hypo-chondriasis*.

Hypnotic induction: The procedure that is used in establishing hypnosis in a responsive person. It usually involves relaxation and stimulated imagination. *See also hypnosis*.

Hypnotic trance: The dream-like state of heightened suggestibility that is induced in a subject by a hypnotist. See also *post-hypnotic suggestion*.

Hypothalamus: A small but very important structure located just above the brain stem and just below the thalamus. Considered a part of the central core of the brain, it includes centres that govern motivated behaviour such as eating, drinking, sex, and emotions; it also regulates endocrine activity and maintains body homeostasis. *See also lateral hypothalamus. ventromedial hypothalamus.*

Hypothesis (1): A predicted relationship that is derived from a theory. The hypothesis, when tested and confirmed, lends support to the theory.

(2) A proposition that accounts for a set of facts that is subject to verification or proof.

(3) A tentative explanation of a relationship between variables, or a supposition that a relationship may exist. A hypothesis generates some scientific method (such as an experiment) that seeks to confirm or disprove the hypothesis.

Hypothesis testing: Gathering information and testing alternative explanations of some phenomenon.

Hypothetical construct: One form of inferred intermediate mechanism. The construct is conceived of as having properties of its own, other than those specifically required for the explanation; e.g., a drive which is inferred from the behaviour of a deprived organism and is used in the explanation of later behaviour.

Hysteria: The condition of a person who unconsciously converts anxiety into physical symptoms that then become more-or-less independent of the hysteric's control.

Hysterical neurosis: A disorder with a variety of forms that comprise two types: *Conversion reaction:* Paralysis, lack of sensation, sensory disturbances, and insensitivity to pain without organic pathology. *Dissociative reaction:* An alteration in consciousness that is manifested as amnesia, fugue, multiple personality, and somnambulism.

I

Icon: In interpersonal interaction strategy, this concept refers to a linguistic device for confirming a preferred identity; in an attempt to impress others, an individual mentions names of important persons whom he has known, or places that he has been, or refers to certain significant experiences.

Iconic mode: The second mode of representation in American psychologist J. S. Bruner's theory; in which experiences are represented as images that can be manipulated mentally.

Id: In Freud's tripartite division of the personality, the "id" comprises an individual's reservoir of all his or her biological instincts; governed by the pleasure principle and present at birth, it presses for the immediate satisfaction of demands. *See also Ego. Superego.*

Identification: The term "identification" technically refers to the process in which an individual incorporates the behavioural characteristics of his desired models into his personality structure. Identification plays a fundamental and important role in the development of morality, sex-role identity, and personality, and it is the fundamental mechanism of socialization. Identification is basically a lifelong learning process, which involves imitations and emotional attachments to the models (either single persons or social groups).

For the young child the parents are the primary models. Their values, attitudes, and behavioural patterns are echoed in the child's personality as a reflection of societal norms or standards. As the child grows older and becomes more independent, he broadens the scope of his identifications to other significant people and settings.

Motivation and Effects: Two forces motivate identification. The first is the desire to achieve mastery over the environment. (The model is perceived as being powerful, and as a result the individual believes that imitation of the model will bring him power). The second, is the desire to gain the love and practical support of the model by identifying with him. A crucial factor in determining the strength of identification is the degree to which the individual believes he possesses the characteristics of the model. This degree of belief is measured by the kind and amount of social reinforcement received from the environment. The strength of Identification decreases with age, because the individual becomes more able to satisfy his own psychological needs for mastery and love through his own behaviour. When the purpose of Identification is to increase the strength of the individual by taking on the behavioural characteristics of others, it is considered to be a defense mechanism. In this instance identification is operating on the subconscious level.

Identification may produce undesirable behaviour if the Parents, group, or other models present distorted view of societal values. In impoverished environments, desirable models may be scarce, or the individual may be unrealistic in model choice. These situations can be detrimental to the individual's stability. Identification is the primary way in which an individual learns, selects, and incorporates the various social values and norms that he or she likes in society into his or her personality structure.

Identification figures: The adult models (especially parents) whose, behaviours and personality characteristics are copied, partly unconsciously, by a child. *See also identification.*

Identity: In social psychology, the concept of Identity technically refers to the attempt by any person to achieve some expression of uniqueness in any situation which *structures* his behaviour to some considerable extent. Identity does not mean an individual's psychological particularities. But rather, identity simply means what any individual actually strives to be like and also what exactly that he or she has actually made himself or herself to took like. There are two major measures of the identity of any Individual at any particular point in time and place as follows: Firstly, is a person's *virtual self.* It is the aspect of a person's personality which is defined by any situation in which the person finds himself, without necessarily referring to the person's personality characteristics. For example, for a newly recruited soldier in basic training, the virtual self comprises the status and roles that are assigned to him, they dictate what he will do and be *for* all but one or two hours a day: what he will eat, what he will wear, what activities will occupy his time, and even what terms of address he will use in speaking to others. Consequently, the virtual self is often an idealization of what any person is supposed to be given his assigned place in a social stratification. Thus, a doctor is expected to be a highly competent professional, and a mental patient is expected to act in a "crazy" manner, a student is expected to study his or her books, etc. Secondly, is the person's *actual self.* It is the aspect of a person's personality which consists of what could be known about him outside of his assigned place. For example, an undergraduate student with a room in the hostel may actually be a very prosperous landlord, because he has inherited some building from his deceased father or mother.

Identity crisis: This concept refers to a situation in which an individual experiences doubt about who he or she is and the purpose or meaning of his or her life.

Identity formation: The process of achieving adult personality integration, as an outgrowth of earlier identifications and other influences. *See also identification, role confusion.*

Identical twins: *See monozygotic twins:*

Idiosyncrasy credit: The implicit permission that is granted by *a* group to one of its members to be somewhat nonconformist; such permission will depend upon the member's status, prior long-term, pattern of conformity, outstanding contributions to the group, and so forth. (This concept was first presented by American psychologist Edwin Hollander.)

Idiosyncrasy-credit mode): This is American Psychologist Edwin Hollander's model, according to which a leader has the opportunity to deviate more from group norms because he or she has developed "credits" through past efforts in the organization.

Illustrators: The movements in a communication situation which, illustrate what is being communicated verbally.

Illusion: In perception, this concept refers to a misinterpretation of the relationships among presented stimuli, so that what is perceived does not correspond to physical reality; especially, but not exclusively, an optical or visual illusion. *See also delusion, hallucination.*

Illusion of unanimity: The phenomenon in which various members of a group falsely believe that the rest of the group is in unanimous agreement on some issue.

Image: A subjective experience, resembling perception, in the absence of the original stimulus.

Imitation: The observational learning (often called model or social learning), which can occur in the absence of reinforcement or practice and that seems to occur naturally in the primates, including man. Human infants model their parents and others before acquiring verbal skills. Imitation of the same-sex parent is the most common way in which children usually learn what activities, interests, attitudes, emotional expressions, and future work that are most appropriate to their sex.

Implicit personality theories: The assumptions that two or mow traits are related to each other, so that if a person possesses one of them, he or she will also possess the other.

Imitative aggression: The aggression that occurs when one person imitates another person who is aggressive.

Immanent justice: According to Swiss psychologist Jean Piaget, this concept refers to the belief held by younger children that misdeeds will lead naturally to negative consequences, that punishments emanate automatically .from things themselves.

Immediacy behaviour: A behaviour that signals intimacy or psychological closeness, such as making eye contact, adopting close physical proximity, touching, leaning forward, or facing directly.

Implicit theories of personality: The *hypotheses* and *theories* that people hold privately about the traits and attributes of others and themselves.

Impression management: The process by which a person selects and controls his own behaviour as well as the situation in which it is displayed, in order to project a desired image of himself to others.

Imprinting: This is a term that is used by ethologists to refer to a species-specific type of learning that occurs within a limited period of time early in the life of an organism and is relatively unmodified thereafter; e.g., young ducklings learn to follow one adult female (usually the mother) within 11-18 hours after birth. But whatever object they are given to follow at this time they will thereafter continue to follow. See *also ethologist*.

Imputational specialists: The professionals and others whose task is to seek out classify, or diagnose persons as instances of a particular type of individual.

Incentive: [1] A tangible goal object that provides the stimuli that lead to goal activity. [2] Loosely, any *goal. See also goal, negative, incentive, positive incentive.*

Incentive effect: One form of the *halo effect*. If we are well paid for doing something, the positive value of the payment may carry over to our evaluation of that behaviour. In some cases, then, it is hypothesized that if we are well paid to say something, we may eventually believe what we have said. This result differs from what one would expect according to *cognitive dissonance theory.*

Incentive theory: A theory of motivation that emphasizes the importance of negative and positive incentives in determining behaviour; internal drives are not the sole instigators of activity. See *also drive-reduction theory.*

Incidental learning: Casual learning that takes place without incentive or reinforcement.

Independence: The freedom with which an individual may function in a group, derived from his or her position in the communication structure, from the actions of other members, from situational factors, and from the individual's own perceptions and cognitions of the situation.

Independent variable: The variable under experimental control with which the changes studied in an experiment are correlated. In psychological experiments, the independent variable is often a stimulus, responses to which are the dependent variables under investigation. See *also independent variable.*

Individual differences: Relatively persistent dissimilarities in structure or behaviour between persons or members of the same species.

Individual-in-situation: A unit of analysis in which a particular person's behaviour under particular conditions is the focus of study.

Individualistic motive: A condition that leads an individual to optimize personal rewards, without regard to how other participants in the situation fare.

Individualistic reward structure: A reward structure in which goal attainment by one participant has no effect on the probability of goal attainment by others.

Individuation: The culminating state of individual human development as it was defined by the Swiss analytical psychologist Cart G. Jung. This concept refers to the state in which conscious and subconscious pans of the mind are brought into a harmonious relationship, allowing the individuated person to act and reset in a wise, spontaneous, and loving manner. Other psychologists have described a similar, stage of development. For example, the American psychologists A. Maslow calls it "self-actualization", and E. Erikson refers to the stage as one where death is faced with a sense of integrity and compassionate wisdom.

Induced-compliance paradigm: An experimental setting in which a participant is caused to behave in a manner contrary to his attitude.

Induction: A form of parental discipline in which the parent gives explanations or reasons why he or she wants the child to change behaviour, particularly in terms of the consequences of the child's behaviour for the parent or other persons.

Inductive logic: The process of making inferences from some specific observations to a more general rule. Used in constructing a theory on the basis of observed facts.

Industrial psychologist: A type of applied psychologist who is employed in industry to deal with such matters as worker morale and human relations.

Infancy: The period of helplessness and dependency in humans and other organisms; in humans this period is roughly the first two years.

Inferiority complex: This concept which was coined by Alfred Adler, refers to an individual's feeling (which is often unconscious) of inadequacy, unworthiness, lack of competence, and low self-esteem.

Influence: An exercise of power in which a person or group attempts to convince another person or group to behave in accordance with the person or group's preferences. The concept is used particularly in the analysis of political behaviour, when, for instance, a person or group pressures the person(s) in a position of authority to make a decision that is favourable to itself over the preferences of other groups. From the point of view of the influencer, actions are less predictable than if the influencer could control (that is, coerce) the person or group that he is trying to influence. In general, influence is a mild exercise of power and is often difficult to distinguish from persuasion and subtle forms of coercion.

Influencing agent: The person who attempts to influence another person (the target person).

Informal social structure: The structure of a group or social organization that is not formally written down or otherwise.

Informational influence: A process in which an individual accepts information from an outside source as evidence about reality. (Contrasted with normative influence).

Informational power: Social power that stems from the persuasive content of a communication. (Example: A doctor persuades a patient to give up smoking by providing evidence that smoking is closely associated with lung cancer and other serious ailments.)

Information dependence: A form of social dependence in which one person relies on another for information about the environment, its meaning, and the possibilities for action in it. (See *effect dependence*).

Information-processing model: A model based on assumptions regarding the flow of information through a system; usually best realized by a computer programme.

Informed consent: An important ethical principle in research with human subjects, requiring that subjects be given a choice about their participation in research and that they be told beforehand about all the relevant conditions of the research that might make them wish to withdraw.

Ingratiation: A tactic used for impression management, in which the person tries to make others like him or her.

Ingratiation tactics: A set of behaviours for obtaining the support or approval of other persons. Such tactics include giving compliments, behaving in a pleasing manner, and agreeing with or conforming to the expressed opinions of the other person.

Inhibitory synapse: A synapse at which the neurotransmitter changes the membrane permeability of the receiving cell in the direction of the resting potential; i.e., keeps it from firing. *See also excitatory synapse, synapse.*

Initiating structure: A dimension of leadership; the leader's behaviour in identifying the group's goal and moving the group towards its goal.

Innate needs. A lack or deficit within an organism giving rise to activity of the organism to obtain it These are physiological like hunger, thirst, etc.

Inner ear: The internal portion of the ear containing, in addition to the cochlea, the vestibular sacs and the semicircular canals. *See also cochlea, semcircular canals, vestibular sacs.*

Insight: A sudden understanding of the relationships involved in the solving of a problem.

Insight: (1) in problem-solving experiments, this concept refers to the perception of the relationships that lead to a solution. Such a solution can be repeated promptly when the problem is again confronted. (2) In psychotherapy, the concept refers to the discovery by the individuals of dynamic connections between earlier and later events, so that they come to recognize the roots of their conflicts.

Insight therapy: A psychotherapeutic approach that tries to help patients gain greater insight into the causes of their behaviour on the assumption that disordered behaviour is due to repression or other unconscious conflicts.

Insomnia: Inability to sleep under normal conditions.

Instinctive behaviour: An individual's sudden, unpremeditated behaviour, that is presumed to be at least partially pre-programmed, or caused, by genetic factors.

Instinct: The name given to an unlearned, patterned, goal-directed behaviour, which is species-specific, as illustrated by nest-building in birds or by the migration of salmon (syn. species-specific behaviour). *See also ethologist.*

Institutionalization: A relationship that has become socially re-cognized and approved. Shared expectations have emerged recognizing the rightness or legitimacy of the relation. The rights and obligations are shared and enforced not only; by the participants but by other parties as well.

Instrumental aggression: The type of aggression which is used to attain some goal or to defend oneself against a negative act. The primary purpose of instrumental aggression is not to harm another person, as it is with hostile aggression.

Instrumental conditioning: A procedure in which an organism is trained to respond in a specific way in order to obtain a reward or to terminate or prevent the occurrence of an aversive stimulus.

Instrumental learning: A procedure in which an organism must perform a certain response in order to receive a reward or reinforcement. This procedure is to be distinguished from classical conditioning. See *also conditioned stimulus.*

Insulin: The hormone secreted by the pancreas. *See also hormones, insulin shock.*

Insulin shock: A state of coma resulting from reduced blood sugar when insulin is present in excessive amounts. Insulin shock is used as one form of shock therapy in treating mental illness. *See also shock therapy.*

Intellectualization: A defense mechanism whereby a person tries to gain detachment from an emotionally threatening situation by dealing with it in abstract, intellectual terms. *See also defense mechanism.*

Intelligence: An aptitude for original thinking. An ability to solve new problems with facility and ingenuity. A capacity to learn and grasp new concepts and new approaches.

Intelligence: (1) That which a property standardized intelligence test measures. (2) According to Binet, the characteristics of an individual's thought processes that enable the individual to take and maintain a direction without becoming distracted, to adapt means to ends, and to criticize his or her own attempts at problem solving. *See also intelligence quotient, mental age.*

Intelligence quotient (IQ): A scale unit used in reporting intelligence test scores, based on the ratio between mental age and chronological age. The decimal point is omitted, so that the average IQ for children of any one chronological age is set at 100. *See also chronological age, deviation IQ, mental age.*

Interact: To, influence reciprocally: to mutually modify behaviour by the exchange of stimuli.

Interaction: The mutual influence between two or more persons or groups in which the behaviour of either one is the stimulus for the behaviour of the other.

Interactional context: A function of the characteristics of the situation and the actors which determines the role categories to be enacted, the role expectations to be applied, and the range of permissible behaviour.

Interaction process analysis: A procedure developed by American Social Psychologist Robert Freed Bales that can be used to observe and classify the pattern and content of communication in a group, regardless of its history, function, or composition. Using 12 categories, an observer codes the communications of each group member, noting who communicated and the person to whom the message was directed.

Interaction process: The process by which the action of one person causes a change or leads to an action in another person.

Interaction territory: An area around two or more people as they talk, into which passers-by are not welcome. Analogous to a group personal space.

Interdependence: (1) The degree to which the results of one group member's activities are either improved (positive interdependence) or made worse (negative interdependence) with respect to the result of another member's activities, and vice *versa*. Interdependence may be subdivided into *means interdependence* and *goals interdependence*. (2) A dimension of group structure, a pattern of dependence interrelationships among the members of a group. (Example: In an assembly line, each worker is dependent upon the worker who precedes him in the line.)

Interdependence pressures: The pressures on an individual who is in a means interdependent relationship with others to coordinate his behaviour with theirs. A worker on an assembly line will experience interdependence pressures in the form a "push" from the worker who passes the product on to him and a "pull" from the worker who is waiting for the product next.

Interference theory: The hypothesis which states that memory loss occurs because new material displaces the old.

Internal controls: The norms or standards of conduct that one accepts as one's own and which place limits on the expression of various behaviours.

Internalization: The basis of social control. It involves the incorporation of the role behaviour of others as it is perceived by individuals in social interactions. The internalization of norms is responsible for the development of the *super ego* and constitutes the central core of personality. The internalization of a culture (focusing on constraint and cooperation) is the primary aspect of socialization. According to many social psychological interpretations, internalization is the outgrowth of identification. Internalization goes one step further and involves the taking in of total role behaviour.

Value orientations are internalized from emotionally important external agents, starting with the parents and shifting to others. These agents satisfy the individual's most important need – love – using the withdrawal of love as a disciplinary method. The Individual is led to comply with the moral judgement of others and to model his behaviour after theirs. Moral anxiety usually arises when there is a conflict between culturally internalized behaviour and personally preferred but prohibited behaviour. The strength of this anxiety is a factor in deterring violative behaviour.

Internalization occurs in all societies, regardless of their orientation, at least some members of a society will internalize the norms. In all societies there are always some people who internalize few norms and therefore display abnormal behaviour. Generally, the individual learns about the cultural norms, accepts them, and structures his behaviour accordingly.

There are basically two kinds of society. In the first, known as the guilt-oriented society, the individual internalizes the norms of relatively few agents and completely introjects them into his personality (thereby generating internal feelings of guilt). In the second type, known as the shame-oriented society, the individual internalizes the norms of many agents, who remain external as influential forces. No society is either one type or the other exclusively, there is a continuum from those that are shame-oriented (controlled by external forces) to those that are guilt–oriented (controlled, by internal forces). The super ego is a mixture of both types of forces.

Internal sanction: A form of social control in which the individual experiences anxiety, guilt, or shame as a consequence of an act.

Internal validity: (1) The conclusiveness with which the effects of the independent variables are established in a scientific investigation, as opposed to the possibility that some confounding variable(s) may have caused the observed results.

(2) The quality attributed to experiments that have been designed and conducted so that competing explanations of their findings are implausible.

Interneurons: The neurons in the central nervous system that connect afferent with efferent neurons. See *also afferent neuron, efferent neuron.*

Interpersonal congruency: A system state prevailing when the behaviours of P and O imply definitions of self consistent with relevant aspects of P's self concept.

Interpersonal trust: A person's generalized expectancy that promises of other individuals or groups, with regard to the future, can be relied upon.

Interperson system: A set of elements consisting of: (1) an aspect of S's self, (2) S's interpretation of his or her behaviour relevant to that aspect, and (3) his or her beliefs about how another person behaves and feels towards him or her with regard to that aspect.

Interposition: A monocular depth cue; when one object obscures part of another, it is judged to be nearer than the second object.

Interpretation: An important technique in psychoanalysis, in which the analyst points out to the patient where resistances lie and what certain dreams and verbalizations reveal about repressed impulses.

Intimacy: A strong feeling of closeness, warmth, and genuine caring between two people.

Intervening variable: A process inferred to occur between stimulus and response, thus accounting for one response rather than another to the same stimulus. The intervening variable may be inferred without further specification, or it may be given concrete properties and become an object of investigation.

Intervention in an emergency: A helping behaviour that is potentially costly and performed under stress, with little possibility of reward.

Interview: A conversation between an investigator (the interviewer) and a subject (the respondent) used for gathering pertinent data for the subject's benefit (as in a psychotherapeutic interview) or information-gathering (as in a sample survey).

Introjection: The unconscious process in which any individual assimilates other people's attitudes, values, or behaviours into his or her own personality structure. It is generally viewed as *partial identification.*

In psychoanalytic psychology, introjection is regarded as a kind of defense mechanism which is used by any individual to reduce his or her anxiety. A special type of introjection is known as "identification with the aggressor". It refers to the situation in which an individual who is persecuted may defend his or her self by adopting the attitudes and behaviours which are similar to those of his or her persecutor.

Introjection can also be viewed as a normal developmental process which leads an individual to achieving greater personal autonomy and self-fulfillment in life.

Introspection: (1) A specified form of introspection (trained introspection) describing mental content only, without the intrusion of meanings or interpretations. (2) Any form of reporting on subjective (conscious) events or experiences. (3)

Self-examination of one's feelings, thoughts, and visions. *See also phenomenology.*

Introversion: A personality trait that is characterized by shyness and reserve. It is the opposite of extroversion.

Introvert: One of the psychological types that was proposed by Carl Jung, it refers to the individual who, especially in time of emotional stress, tends to withdraw into him or herself and to avoid other people. Contrasted to "extrovert".

Intruding role: A position that generates expectations which are superimposed upon the main role which is being tackled

Intrusion: A violation of interpersonal-distance norms (or some other sign of excessive immediacy) that occurs as two people talk.

Intuition: Immediate knowledge without preliminary reasoning or examination.

Invalid conversion: The fallacy in syllogistic reasoning in which it is assumed that "if X is Y" then "all Y is X.

Invariant: Consistent; following a set sequence without modification.

Investments: Characteristics of an individual or features of his or her past history or background that have become associated with the expectation of a certain level of outcomes. For example, seniority on a job becomes associated with the expectation of additional pay.

Involuntary attention: This concept refers to a situation in which an individual gives his or her attention spontaneously, without his or her prior meditation for it.

Involutional melancholia: A functional psychosis of the climacteric period, characterized by extreme depression

Iris: The coloured band of muscle tissue that surrounds the eye's pupil.

Isolate: In sociometry, this concept refers to a group member who is rarely chosen by other members.

Isolation: In alienation, this concept refers to a kind of detachment in which an individual assigns a low value to goals and beliefs that typically are highly valued in society.

J

James-Lange theory: A classical theory of emotion, named for the two men who independently proposed it. The theory states that a stimulus first leads to bodily responses, and then the awareness of these responses constitutes the experience of emotion. *See also Cannon-Bard theory, cognitive-physiological theory.*

Joint family: A family in which the parents and the sons with their families, live together under one roof, or families of brothers living together; they own the family property jointly. The children build up relationships with all the close relatives.

Justifiability: Excusability; may be interpreted in terms of loci of cause. An action performed because of powerful external pressures is likely to be seen as justifiable.

Justification: The act of thinking of cognitive elements that reduce the uncomfortable dissonance felt after making judgments about persons.

Just noticeable difference (j.n.d.): A barely perceptible physical charge in a stimulus; a measure of difference threshold. The term is used also as a unit for scaling the steps of sensation corresponding to increase in the magnitude of stimulation. See *also difference threshold.*

Juvenile delinquency: Legally prohibited behaviour committed by minors.

"Just-world" phenomenon: The belief that persons get what they deserve in life.

K

Karyotype: A photo of the chromosomes.

Key-word method: A technique for learning the vocabulary of a foreign language via an intermediate key word that is related to the sound of the foreign word and the meaning of the English equivalent. See *also mnemonics.*

Kinesics: The study of gestures.

Kinetic information: The gestures, expressive movements, posture, observable tension or relaxation, and similar items which are used to make judgments about persons.

Kinaesthetic sense: The awareness of body movements, by which one controls co-ordination.

Kinethesis: The muscle, tendon, and joint senses, yielding discrimination of position and movement of parts of the body. *See also equilibratory senses.*

Kinship: A relationship between two or more persons on the basis of recognized common ancestry; it is mainly based on blood relationship.

Klinefelter's syndrome: An abnormal condition of the sex chromosomes [XXY instead of XX or XY]; the individual is physically a male with penis and testicles but has feminine characteristics.

Figure 15: Karyotypes of human female (above) and male (below) chromosome. Note the pair of X chromosomes in the female array, the X and Y chromosomes in the male karyotype.

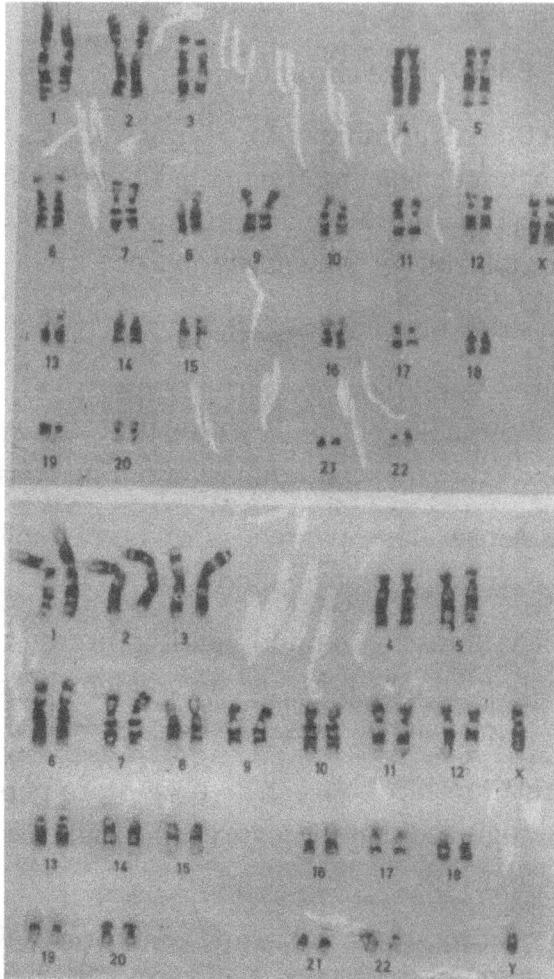

Source: Mednick et al (1975), page 30.

Kluver-Bucy syndrome: That pattern of behaviour including reduced aggressiveness, hypersexuality, and memory impairment that follows surgical destruction of the temporal lobes including the amygdala.

Korsakoff's syndrome: An organic psychosis that is largely caused by alcoholism and vitamin deficiencies, which is marked by the forgetting of recent events.

Koan: This concept refers to any question that is similar to any riddle that is given to Zen monks for the purpose of expanding the respondent's consciousness.

L

Labeling theory: An explanation of deviant behaviour which emphasizes the reaction of other persons (especially those in positions of authority) to the individuals labelled deviant.

Laboratory experiment: A controlled experiment that is carried cut in a laboratory, which is totally different from one's ordinary living and working situation. Most psychological laboratory experiments are performed with undergraduate students in campus laboratories. The laboratory experiment allows maximal control over the relevant variables, but the extent to which the findings can be applied to "real-life" situations has been questioned. This research method contrasts with *field experiment.*

Laissez-faire approach: In child-rearing, this concept refers to the approach in which a child is given almost complete licence to behave in whichever way that he or she likes.

Laissez-faire leadership: One of the three leadership styles that was studied in the classic experiment by American psychologists Lewin, Lippitt, and White. The laissez-faire leader of a group was instructed to act in a friendly, but passive way with the group; not to make suggestions; and not to evaluate individual members or the group itself either positively or negatively.

Language acquisition device (LAD): In Chomsky's theory the innate biological mechanism that governs children's acquisition, understanding, and creative use of language.

Latency: (1) A temporal measure of response, referring to the time delay between the occurrence of the stimulus and the onset of the response. (2) In psychoanalysis, a period in middle childhood, roughly the years from 6-12, when both sexual and aggressive impulses are said to be in a somewhat subdued state, so that the child's attention is directed outward, and his or her curiosity about the environment makes him or her ready to learn. *See also psychosexual development.*

Latency period: In psychoanalytic theory, this is the relatively quiescent or dormant period from about age 5 to 12 when there are no new psychosexual conflicts. Also called Latency stage or phase.

Latent content: In the Freudian method of interpreting dreams, this concept refers to the underlying significance of a dream, e.g., the motives or wishes being expressed by it, as interpreted from the dream's manifest content. See *also interpretation, manifest* content.

Latent hypothalamus (LH): The area of the hypothalamus which is important to the regulation of food intake. Electrical stimulation of this area will make an experimental animal start to eat; destruction of brain tissue here causes an animal to stop eating. See *also hypothalamus, ventromedial hypothalamus.*

Latent learning: Learning that is demonstrated by behaviour at the time of learning but can be shown to have occurred by increasing the reinforcement for such behaviour.

Latent structure: The underlying rules of grammar.

Lateral fissure: A deep fissure at the side of each cerebral hemisphere, below which lies the temporal lobe (syn. fissure of Sylvius).

Law of effect: American Psychologist E. L. Thorndike's principle that successful behaviours will tend to be repeated while unsuccessful ones will tend to fall into disuse.

Law of exercise: The law which states that if any behaviour is repeated it becomes an established tendency.

Law of learning: Statement of (influences that have *been* found to help or hinder learning

Law of reinforcement: The law which states that if any behaviour is rewarded it becomes an established tendency. *See also law of effect.*

Leader: An individual who occupies a key position in a group, influences others in accordance with the rote expectations for that position, and coordinates and directs the group in maintaining itself and working towards its goals. Generally, a leader is a group member who consistently exercises greater influence on the goals and activities of the group than do other members.

Leader-follower relation: The complementary behaviour that occurs between leaders and their followers.

Leadership functions: The services that are provided by a leader and the needs that he fulfills for the group to which he belongs. Leadership functions include: helping the group to establish its goals and define its tasks, maintaining harmony, serving as a group symbol with whom the members can identify, and representing the group in its dealings with other groups or Individuals. Although one or two members generally tend to exercise more leadership than others, the leadership functions may be performed by many different members at various, times.

Leadership style: The characteristic manner in which a leader exercises his or her influence in a group. Although many leadership styles are possible, two seem to be quite common: *directive leadership* and *group-centred leadership.*

Learned helplessness: A condition of apathy or helplessness which is crested experimentally by subjecting an individual to an unavoidable trauma; e.g., shock, heat or cold. Being unable to avoid or escape an aversive situation produces a feeling of helplessness that generalizes to subsequent situations.

Learning: A relatively permanent change in behaviour that occurs as a result of practice. Behaviour changes due to maturation or temporary conditions of an individual (e.g., fatigue, the influence of drugs, adaptation) are not included.

Table 9: Seligman's learned helplessness model of reactive depression

	Learned helplessness in animals	Reactive depression in humans
Manifestations	Passivity in face of stress	Passivity, "paralysis of the will" (Beck, 1970)
	Retardation in learning to deal with stress.	Negative expectations in dealing with stress or challenge, even when performance is adequate; feelings of hopelessness.
	Dissipation of effect with time.	Dissipation with time, although the length of time is very indefinite, ranging from days to years.
	Anorexia (loss of appetite)	Anorexia
	Weight loss	Weight loss
Etiology	Uncontrollable stress – not stress per se but learning that no response reliably reduces aversive stimulation	Inability to control events in life, such as loss of a loved one, physical disease, and failure to act either to relieve suffering or to gain gratification.

Learning curve: A graph drawn to show the time taken by a subject to solve a given problem at successive trials, in which the vertical axis (ordinate) plots a measure of proficiency (amount per unit time, time per unit amount, errors made, etc), while the horizontal axis (abscissa) represents some measure of practice (trails, time, etc).

Children playing and learning in a day-care centre

Learning Theory: An attempt to account for the manner in which the response of an organism is modified as a result of experience. Learning is to be distinguished from remembering, which is not necessary for learning and involves only the recall of previous experience.

Development and Types: An early learning theory was that put forward at the turn of the century by the American psychologist Edward L Thomdike who believed that "learning is connecting". Thorndike's "law of effect" stated that behaviour followed by a reward will tend to be repeated and that behaviour that is not rewarded will tend to fade away. This approach, combined with the tradition deriving from the reflex–conditioning experiments of Ri"3sian Scientist Ivan Pavlov, is now known as conditioning and today dominates learning theory. The foremost contemporary proponent of the theory is the American Psychologist B. F. Skinner, who has attempted to elaborate conditioning theory into a comprehensive psychology of human socialization and behaviour (sometimes known as behaviourism).

Another teaming theory that does not aim to be so comprehensive is that of the Gestalt psychologists. A Gestalt is a pattern of relationships; these patterns may be learned in a moment of sudden insight without any previous experience or stimulus – response association (for example, when one suddenly sees the answer to a riddle or puzzle). Critics of conditioning theory have pointed out that it cannot readily explain the sudden learning that arises from the perception of a Gestalt. In addition, conditioning theory does not provide an adequate account for perceptual teaming that takes place even when there is no reinforcement (for example, the unconscious teaming of a particular route that one has travelled).

Cognitive - developmental psychology, pioneered by the Swiss psychologist Jean Piaget, aims at providing not a theory of learning so much as an account of general intellectual development. It has often been seen as an implicit critique of behaviourism, however. Cognitive – developmental theory stresses the rote of the individual as an active constructor of his own knowledge rather than as a passive organism whose behaviour is explicable only In terms of antecedent conditioning processes.

Table 10: Representative Learning Theories and their Implication for Education

Family of Theories	Classical Exponents of Theories	Modern Exponents of Theories	Theory of Learning	Psychological System of Outlook of Theories	Conception of Man's Nature in Theories	Basis of Transfer of Learning	Emphasis in Teaching
Mental Discipline Theories of Mind Substance	Plato Aristotle	M.J. Adler R.O. Hutchins	Humanistic Mental Discipline	Classicism	*Neutral-Active* mind substance to be developed through exercise	Cultivated mind or intellect	Training of intrinsic mental power
	St. Augustine J. Calvin C. Wolff J. Edwards	Many Christian Fundament-alists	Theistic Mental Discipline	Faculty Psychology	*Bad-active* mind substance continues active until curbed.	Exercised faculties, automatic transfer	Exercise of faculties of the mind
	J.J. Rousseau F. Froebel "Progressiv ists"	P. Goodman J. Holt A.H. Maslow	Natural Unfoldment	Romantic Naturalism or Psychedelic Humanish	*Good-active* natural personality to unfold	Recapitulation of racial history, no transfer is needed.	Negative or permissive education based on feelings.
	J.F. Herbart E.B.	Many teachers	Apperception or Herbart-Herbartianism	Structuralism	*Neutral active* mind composed of active mental or ideas	Growing apperceptive mass	Addition of new mental stress or ideas to a store of old ones in subconscious mind
S – R (Stimulus-Response) Conditioning Theories of Behaviour	E. L. Thorndike	A.I. Gates			*Neutral-passive or reactive* Organism with many potential S-R connections	Identical elements	Promotion of acquisition of desired S-R connection
	J.B. Watson	E.R. Guthrie	Conditioning (Without Reinforcement)	Behaviourism	*Neutral-passive or reactive* Organism with innate reflexive	Conditioned responses or reflexes	Promotion of adhesion of desired responses appropriate stimuli

S-R (Stimulus Response) Conditioning Theories Behaviour	C.H. Hull	R.F. Skinner K.W. Spence R.M. Gagne	Conditioning Through Reinforcement	Reinforcement	*Neutral-passive or reactive* Organism with innate reflexes and needs with their own drive stimuli	Reinforced or conditioned responses plus stimulus and response induction	Successive, systematic change in organism's environment to increase the probability of desired responses
Cognitive Theories of Gestaltists	M. Wertheimer K. Koffka	W. Kohler	Insight	Gestalt Psychology	*Neutral-active* being whose activity follows psychological laws of organisation	Transposition of insight	Promotion of insightful learning
	B.H. Bode B.H. Wheeler	E.E. Bayles	Goal-insight	Configuration-alism	*Neutral-inter-active* purposive individual in sequential relationships with his environment	Tested insights	Aid students to developing high quality insights
	Kurt Lewin E.C. Tolman J. Dewey G.W. Allport A. Ames A.W. Combs H. Canril R. May	R.G. Barker M.L. Bigge J.S. Brunner D. Snygg M. Deutch S. Kock H.F. Wright	Cognitive Field	Field Psychology or Positive Relativism	*Neutral-inter-active* purposive person in simultaneous mutual interaction with his psychological environment, including other people.	Continuity of life-spaces, experience, or insight	Help students to restructure their life-spaces; gain new insights into their own contemporaneous situations.

Source: Dr. Iro Eweka, University of Benin, Benin City.

Least preferred co-worker (LPC): A measure of a leader's attitude towards the group member whom he considers the worst co-worker. This measure was used by American Psychologist F. Fiedler in developing his contingency model of leader effectiveness. A low LPC score, which indicates the leader's personal rejection of the worst co-worker, characterizes a directive leader; a high LPC score, which indicates that a leader is favourably disposed towards a poor co-worker, characterizes a group-centred leader.

Left hemisphere: The left cerebral hemisphere. Controls the right side of the body and, for most people, speech and other logical, sequential activities (syn. major hemisphere). *See also cerebral hemisphere, corpus callosum, right hemisphere, split-brain subject.*

Legitimacy: The social perception of actions and attitudes as being in accordance with socially recognized principles, laws, or social norms.

Legitimacy (of a role expectation): The recognition by actors that their role partners are justified in holding a particular expectation.

Legitimacy of leadership: A condition in which group members accept an individual as their leader and share his acceptance with each other.

Legitimacy (in a relationship): The recognition by the parties to a relationship and by outside parties that a relationship based on shared agreement concerning patterns of exchange has been developed. *See also institutionalization.*

Legitimate power: Social power that arises when one person accepts an influencing agent's right to influence him and thereby feels an obligation to comply. Legitimate power can be due to acceptance of a formal structure (a worker accepts the legitimate power of his supervisor); formal obligation (the right of a person who has done a favour to expect one in return); and the legitimate power of those in need who cannot ordinarily expect help from those in power.

Lens: The transparent, flexible eye tissue that focuses light on the retina.

Lesbian: A female homosexual.

LH: See *lateral hypothalamus*.

Level of aspiration: This concept refers to an individual's personal standard of achievement in life.

Libido: In psychoanalytic theory, this concept refers to the psychic energy of the sexual instincts which is built up and released through the erogenous zones of the body.

Lie detector: See *polygraph, voice stress analyser*.

Light adaptation: The decreased sensitivity of the eye to light when the subject has been continuously exposed to high levels of illumination. *See also dark adaptation.*

Likert-type scale: A type of attitude scale that poses statements and asks the respondent to indicate how much he or she agrees or disagrees with each statement.

Limbic system: The set of structures (amygdala, hippocampus and septum) in and around the midbrain, which form a functional unit that regulates motivational-emotional types of behaviour such as waking and sleeping, excitement and quiescence, feeding and mating. *(See page 113)*

Linear perspective: A monocular depths cue; parallel tines coverage in the distance producing a perception of depth.

Linear programme: A teaching programme in which the student progresses along a fixed track from one instructional frame to the next. After responding to a frame, the student moves to the next frame regardless of whether his or her answer is correct.

See *also branching programme, CAL.*

Linguistic group: A group which speaks the same language, a group with one mother tongue.

Linguistic relativity hypothesis: The proposition that one's thought processes, the way one perceives the world, are related to one's language.

Lithium carbonate: A compound based on lithium, an element related to sodium. Has been successful in treating manic-depressive psychoses.

Live modeling: The example of the behaviour which is provided by the persons to whom we are directly exposed. See also *modeling cues, symbolic modeling.*

Lloyd Morgan's Canon: The warning by a nineteenth-century English biologist, not to read human qualities into animal subjects.

Lobotomy: An operation in which the connexions between the prefrontal lobes and the more primitive parts of the brain are surgically severed, to diminish violent excitement brought on by feelings of great guilt and hate.

Lobes (frontal, parietal, temporal, and occipital): Distinct areas in the cerebral cortex.

Localized functions: The various behaviours that are controlled by known areas of the brain; e.g., vision is localized in the occipital lobes. *See also projection area.*

Location constancy: The tendency to perceive the place at which a resting object is located as remaining the same even though the relationship to the observer has changed. See *also object constancy.*

Locus of cause: The place where an act originates. The locus of cause is viewed as internal if the act seems to originate in the actor and as external if it seems to originate in compelling circumstances.

Locus of control: In attribution theory, the locus of control is either external, in which the cause of an action is attributed to outside forces and beyond the control of the individual, or internal, willed by the individual and under his control.

Logo-therapy: A form of psychotherapy that is associated with Victor Frankl. The main purpose of this method of logo-therapy is to help the individual patient to find meaning in his/her existence. Logo is the search for the relevant meanings that govern an individual's life. In using this method of psycho-therapy the psychologist presumes that the individual's mental illness occurred because his/her search for his/her life's meaning was thwarted.

Longitudinal study: A research method that studies an individual through time, taking measurements at periodic intervals. *See also case history.*

Long-term memory: The enduring retention of information in an organized or consolidated form. *See also short-term memory.*

Looking-Class Self: This concept was coined by the American Social Psychologist Charles Norton Cooley, to refer to the process whereby an individual comes to know or define himself through the process of internalizing his perceptions of how he thinks that other people around him, especially his *significant others,* perceive him. He comes to adopt or accept as his own those evaluations, definitions and judgements of himself that he believes he sees "reflected" in the faces of others in his social environment, it is, therefore, the individual's conception of the responses of others towards him, rather than the actual responses of others that is the essential element in the process of self-development.

The process is especially important in the early years of a child. The resultant self, then, is a social product involving three components: the actual responses of others towards an individual; the related perceived responses of others towards the individual; and the individual's internalization of these perceived responses. In this final step (i.e. *internalization)* the individual comes to define and distinguish himself, or to create a self that is congruent with those social definitions and judgments of him made by the significant others in his social environment.

Loudness: An intensity dimension of hearing correlated with the amplitude of the sound waves that constitute the stimulus. Greater amplitudes yield greater loudnesses. *See also pitch, timbre.*

LPC: Least preferred co-worker.

LSD: See *lysergic acid derivatives.*

LSD (d-lysergic acid diethylamide): A drug that was synthesized in 1938 and discovered to be a hallucinogen in 1943; it is derived from lysergic acid, the principal constituent of the alkaloids of ergot, a grain fungus that centuries ago produced epidemics of spasmodic ergotism, a nervous disorder that is sometimes marked by psychotic symptoms.

Lymphatic system: The system that controls various internal body functions; it consists of the lymph nodes and intestinal lymphoid masses.

Lysergic acid derivatives: Chemical substances derived from lysergic acid, the most important of which is LSD. When taken by a normal person, it produces symptoms similar in some respects to those of schizophrenia. *See also schizophrenia.*

M

Machiavellianism: The degree to which an individual' is motivated to manipulate and does manipulate other persons to gain his or her own ends. A personality test for measuring this trait is called the Mach V.

Marginal consciousness: That which at any one moment is at the fringe of attention. *See also conscious processes.*

Major hemisphere: *See left hemisphere.*

Maladaptive: Characteristic of a response which makes it inappropriate in dealing with stress.

Melancholic: Depressed. One of Galen's four temperaments.

Mania: Psychotic excitement.

Manic-depressive psychosis: A psychosis characterized by mood swings from the normal in the direction either of excitement and elevation (manic phase) or of fatigue, despondency and sadness (depressive phase). Many patients do not show the whole cycle. *See also affective disorder.*

Manifest content: The remembered content of a dream, the characters, and their actions, as distinguished from the inferred latent content. *See also latent content.*

Manipulation: An indirect form of social influence, in which an influencing agent succeeds in changing another person's belief, attitudes, emotion, or behaviour by first changing some other aspect of the person or his environment. (Example: A parent can influence a child to eat some cereal that the child does not especially like by serving it in the child's favorite bowl, which has a picture of Goldilocks and the three bears on the bottom). *See also Ecological manipulation.*

Mantra: *See Transcendental Meditation.*

Marijuana: The dried leaves of the hemp plant; also known as hashish, "pot," or "grass." Hashish is actually an extract of the plant material and, hence, is usually stronger than marijuana. Intake may enhance sensory experiences and produce a state of euphoria.

Marker: A device used to signal occupancy or possession of a territory.

Marriage: The legal matrimonial union between a man and a woman, which is entered into according to the marriage law and/or custom of some social system (e.g. a community, ethnic group, religion, or society). It forms the initial and basic social framework of the domestic social group called the family. Types of marriages include monogamy, polygynous-polygamy and polyandrous polygamy.

Marriage, Arranged: The pairing of marriage partners by parsons other than themselves. The arrangements may completely exclude the participation of those to be married in the choice of spouses, or the prospective mates may be consulted–with varying degrees of consideration for their opinions–by the marriage arrangers. In arranged marriages, parents (or other family members) play an important role in selecting the spouses. Usually, marriages are arranged on the basis of financial, religious, political, or ethnic considerations.

Marriage Counseling: The counseling to help with marital problems. It can use many approaches, including behaviouristic, psychoanalytic, case-history, transactionalist, and eclectic methods. Counselors work with individual spouses, the couple or even the family as a whole. They handle marital and premarital problems. Their main task is to help the couple to arrive at some "rational" understanding of and solution to their marital problems. The marriage counselor is not necessarily committed to "saving the marriage". He hopes to discover what is best for all parties concerned. *See also Sex therapy.*

Marriage, Group: The marriage among two or more women and two or more men at the same time. Early Anthropologists such as Frazer, Morgan and Briffault, speculated extensively about the possibility of group marriage for early man but there's little evidence to support them. George P. Murdock found no evidence of it as a cultural norm. The practice of wife exchange by the Commanche Indians of North America is not the same as group marriage because specific husband–wife relationships are still recognised and endured.

In modern times, group marriage has appeared in some communes to provide sexual variety, to satisfy different mates' needs, to help with work, and also to counter capitalistic attitudes of personal possessiveness. However, the common form of marriage in communes is monogamous. Group marriage is more common in the United States of America than in all other countries of the world. Group marriage is very rare, if at all it ever exists in Nigeria.

Marriage, Legal: A marriage that is properly contracted according to the marriage law and/or custom of any society.

Marriage, Mixed: A marriage between persons belonging to different social backgrounds – such as tribes, races, religions, nations and socio-economic classes – whose members normally disapprove at least to some extent, of marriage to members of the other group. In such marriages, two types of problems may arise. One involves the attitudes of the marriage partners themselves and is, therefore, amenable to solution by their own actions; the other involves the attitudes of outsiders, including the couple's families and the local community, and is therefore not easily controllable by the couple involved. Some of the problems confronting mixed -- marriage couples may arise because of cultural differences regarding such matters as child-rearing practices, marital-role expectations, and marital-authority patterns. For example, a partner coming from a social group that places high value on an egalitarian authority pattern may encounter considerable difficulty in a marriage to a spouse whose cultural background places high value on a strong husband as the authority pattern.

Marriage, Trial: A socially sanctioned form of marriage in which one man and one woman are united to each other at one time. This marriage can be terminated by death, divorce, or annulment after which another marriage can take place. Monogamy is the only form of marriage that is accepted as legal in all Western societies, such as the U.S.A., Britain, West Germany, etc. It is also the most commonly practised form of marriage throughout the whole world. It implies the most intimate and mutually beneficial sharing of sexual privileges, common residence, companionship, and the filliation of children between the spouses.

Marriage, Polygamous: A marriage that is still on an experimental basis. In some traditional societies, trial marriages are used to determine whether the wife is able to bear a child. If she becomes pregnant the couple is officially married.

In the contemporary Western societies, trial marriages are advocated to help reduce the increase in divorce. Such relationships would provide a means for the partners to know one another (sexually and inter-personally) in a relatively formal way but without children, complicated divorce proceedings, or alimony, if the marriage does not work out. This plan differs from simple "living together" in that the state sanctions trial marriage, but does not sanction ordinary, loose "living together" of a male and a female.

Masking: Giving the appearance of experiencing a certain feeling in order to conceal one's true feelings.

Masochism: A pathological desire to inflict pain on oneself or to suffer pain at the hands of others, in order to obtain sexual pleasure. See *also sadism.*

Mass media: The newspapers, magazines, motion pictures, the radio and the television in which there is mass production and mass distribution of information. A large number of people in the country and throughout the world can be influenced by the massages sent through the mass media.

Master status: A classification which dominates the evaluation of a person. Each individual has many statuses, but master statuses (e.g., status as a criminal or a mental patient) have a compelling effect on how one is evaluated.

Maternal drive: The drive, particularly in animals, induced in the female through bearing and nursing young, leading to nest-building, retrieving, and other forms of care. See *also drive.*

Mathematical model: A model of a phenomenon formulated in mathematical terms. See also *mode.*

Maturation: A genetically programmed growth process in the individual in which certain behaviours, such as crawling, walking, and talking emerge in orderly manner at certain fixed times in the individual's development. It is relatively independent of experience and wide variations in the environment, although it may require a normal experience and environment.

Matrix representation: A method of representing patterns of interpersonal and intergroup relationship, used especially by social exchange theorists. The various behaviour options available to one party are listed along the horizontal dimension, and the options available to the other are listed along the vertical dimension. The intersecting squares show the costs and rewards for each of the parties, according to the combination of behaviour options. Matrix representation has also been utilized for other analyses of social structure, including sociometric, interdependence and communication. In these analyses, the members of the group are listed along the horizontal and vertical dimensions, and the relationship (for example, positive, negative, or neutral) is shown in the intersecting squares.

Maya: This concept, which is mainly used in Zen psychology, refers to the notion that much of conventional wisdom is an illusion and unreliable for most practical, positive pursuits.

Maze: A network of paths through which it is difficult to find the way to a goal.

Mean: The arithmetical average; the sum of all scores divided by their number. See *also measure of central tendency.*

Means interdependence: A relationship between members of a group in which the means used by one person to reach his own goal are positively or negatively affected by the means used by another person to reach his goal. Compare *goals interdependence*. The goals of the two members may be common or different (Example of negative means interdependence: Two men who are in a workshop, one building a radio and the other an air conditioner, must share one Phillips-head screw-driver. Example of positive means interdependence: Two men who are working in a carpentery shop, one building a door and the other a boat, must both use the power saw to complete the project, but each needs the assistance of the other in order to operate it).

Measure: To quantify a variable, using a continuous numerical scale. Examples of scales include nominal, ordinal, interval, and ratio scales.

Measure of central tendency: A value representative of a frequency distribution, around which other values are dispersed; e.g., the mean, median, or mode of a distribution of scores. *See also mean median, mode.*

Measure of variation: A measure of the dispersion or spread of scores in a frequency distribution; e.g., the range, or the standard deviation. See *also range, standard deviation.*

Mechanical aptitude quotient: A number that measures the relative rank of a person's mechanical aptitude. Obtained by dividing mechanical aptitude age by chronological age, and multiplying by 100. Abbreviated to M.A.Q.

Mechanisms: The various kinds of habits that people acquire in attempts to satisfy their motives.

Median: The statistical term for the item in the exact middle of a list, when the. items are listed in order of increasing magnitude. *See also measure of central tendency.*

Memory: The present knowledge of a past experience.

Memory trace: The inferred change in the nervous system that persists between the time something is learned and the time it is recalled.

Memory span: The number of items (digits, letters, words) that can be reproduced in order after a single presentation; usually 7 – 2. *See also chunk, short-term memory.*

Menarche: The first menstrual period, indicative of sexual maturation in a girl. *See also menstruation.*

Menopause: The stopping of the periodic menstrual flow in women, usually between the ages of forty and fifty, sometimes attended by mild personality disturbances.

Menstruation: The approximately monthly discharge from the uterus. See *also menarche.*

Mental age (MA): A scale unit proposed by Binet for use in intelligence testing. If an intelligence test is properly standardized, a representative group of children of age 6 should earn an average mental age of 6, those of age 7, a mental age of 7, etc. A child whose MA is above his or her chronological age (CA) is advanced; one whose MA lags behind is retarded. *See also chronological age, intelligence quotient.*

Mental faculty: This concept refers to the view that an individual's mind contains certain in-born abilities, such as memory, will, and concentration.

Mental imagery: The mental pictures that are used as an aid to memory. Not the same as eidetic imagery. See *also eidetic imagery.*

Mentally defective: A descriptive term applied to a mentally subnormal individual whose deficiency is based on some sort of brain damage or organic defect See *also mentally retarded.*

Mentally gifted: An individual with an unusually high level of intelligence, commonly an IQ of 140 or above.

Mental retardation: Subnormal intellectual development.

Mentally retarded: A mentally subnormal individual whose problems lie in a learning disability with no evident organic damage. *See also mentally defective.*

Mentally subnormal: An individual whose intelligence is below that necessary for adjustment to ordinary schooling; the more intelligent among the subnormal are classified as educable in special classes, the next level as trainable, while the lowest group is classified as more severely retarded (syn., but now obsolete, feeble minded). See *also mentally defective, mentally retarded.*

Mental maturity: A stage in life when a person stops showing the previously continuous improvements in his ability to answer the general questions asked on intelligence tests. Reached somewhere between the ages of fourteen and eighteen.

Mental rotation: The notion that a mental image of an object can be rotated in the mind in a fashion analogous to rotating the real object.

Mesomorph: The second of three types of physique in Sheldon's type theory. It refers to the prominence of bone and muscle, as in the typical athlete. *See also ectomorph, endomorph, type theory.*

Metabolism: All of the chemical processes in the cells of the body, including the conversion of food to energy, the storing of energy, the using of energy, the repair of tissues, and the disposing of wastes.

Method of loci: An aid to serial memory. Verbal material is transformed into mental images, which are then located at successive positions along a visualized route, such as an imagined walk through the house or down a familiar street.

Minor hemisphere: *See right hemisphere.*

Mixed-motive situation: A game like situation in which both co-operation and competition are part of the process of negotiation.

Mixed-motive relationship: A relationship in which the participants have both cooperative and competitive tendencies; both convergent interests and divergent interests exist simultaneously.

Modal Personality: The predominant type of personality which can be found among a majority of the individual members of any one human group, organization, community, or society. Thus, for example, the modal personality of most Nigerians is the typical or characteristic way in which most adult Nigerian men and women behave in their every-day lives. It is the type of behaviour which Nigerian journalist and magazine publisher Peter Enahoro attempted to portray in his once very popular small book. *How to be a Nigerian.*

Mode: The most frequent score in a distribution, or the class interval in which the greatest number of cases fall. *See also measure of central tendency.*

Model: (1) Miniature systems are often constructed according to a logical, mathematical, or physical model. That is, the principles according to which data are organized and made understandable parallel to those of the model; e.g., the piano keyboard is a model for the feedback principle of cybernetic. (2) In behaviour therapy, a person who models or performs behaviours that the therapist wishes the patient to imitate.

Modeling: A term which is used mainly by psychologists to describe the process of imitation. It is also known as learning by observation. Modeling is considered a very important aspect of socialization. Using it, a child learns what types of behaviour are appropriate and approved by parents and the society as a whole. The person (or thing) whose behaviour the chila imitates is called the model. Various characteristics of models increase the likelihood that children will imitate them. Three of the most important are a high degree of nurturance displayed by the model towards the child, power to reward others including the child, and a high frequency of interaction between the child and the model. All these characterize parents and thus give them a very significant role in the socialization process.

Moderator variable: A variable that links two other variables or affects the influence of one or the other.

Monochromatism: Total colour blindness, the visual system being achromatic. A rare disorder. *See also dischromatism, trichromatism.*

Monozygotic (MZ) twins: Twins developed from a single egg-They are always of the same sex and commonly much alike in appearance, although some characteristics may be in mirror image; e.g., one right-handed, the other left-handed (syn. identical twins.) See *also dizygotic twins.*

Moral Behaviour Versus Moral Judgement: The first of these two concepts, *moral behaviour,* refers generally to all of the desirable ways of behaviour that are prescribed by a society for the well-being of its people. Moral behaviour, which is obviously more important during the first years of life than moral judgement -basically develops in two ways - (1) direct parental training with consequential reinforcers enforcing what the correct behaviour is in specific situations, and (2) identification of the child with "admirable" people (especially the parents) end the resulting indirect adoption of both their desirable and undesirable behavioural patterns.

The second of these two concepts, *moral judgement,* is the subjective evaluation of the moral behaviour of one person by another person. The American psychologist Lawrence Kohlberg studied extensively the development of moral judgement in relation to, or in the context of three primary levels of moral development. The first, or *pre-conventional* level concerns itself with an awareness of what is culturally right or wrong in terms of physical or hedonistic consequences. The second, or *conventional* level involves conformity to group or family expectations and maintenance of the social order. The last, or *post-conventional* level, is concerned with self-defined ethnical principles, the relativism of values and consensual rules. According to Kohlberg, the quality of moral judgement is reflective of the level of moral development achieved (and therefore of the way the social structure is internalized).

The comparison of moral behaviour and moral judgement is basically the comparison of the relationship between moral thoughts or evaluations and moral action. Both are concerned with the welfare of society, and there is an overlap between the two concepts. A person's judgement may or may not correspond to the person's moral behaviour. The position taken by Kohlberg and others is that moral judgement is the outgrowth of a person s behavioural interaction with the social environment. However, it should not be assumed that because a person can evaluate other people's behaviour, he can, therefore, also evaluate and control his own behaviour.

Moral entrepreneurs: The individuals who take it upon themselves to fight against a particular condition, or form of behaviour, that they perceive as being a threat to society's values. They are instrumental in creating new classes of deviant persons.

Moral independence: According to Piaget, this is the second stage in moral development, in which the child comes to believe in the modification of rules to fit the needs of the situation. Moral judgment: As studied by Piaget, Kohlberg, and others, this concept refers to a subject's beliefs regarding good and bad behaviour in certain situations.

Table 11: Classification of moral judgment into levels and stages of development

Level	Basis of Moral Judgement	Stage of Development	Sample Responses of Moral Dilemma, "The Drug Robbery"
I Pre-conventional Morality	Moral value resides in awareness of rules of "good" and "bad" but is interpreted in terms of physical actions and reward and punishment.	Stage 1: Obedience and punishment. Obedience and punishment orientation. Egocentric deference to superior power or authority, or avoiding trouble.	"He was sad to steal because he will get caught and punished."
		Stage 2: Naïve Instrumental Hedonism. Naively egoistic orientation. Right action is that instrumentally satisfying the self's needs and occasionally others'. Awareness of relativism of value to each actor's needs and	"He should steal the drug because he needs his wife to live so she could take care of his house for him."

		perspective. Naïve egalitarianism and orientation to exchange and reciprocity.	
II Conventional Morality	Moral value resides in performing good or right roles, in maintaining the conventional order by conforming to the expectancies of others and social standards.	Stage 3: Approval seeking, Good-boy Orientation. Orientation to approval and to pleasing and helping others. Conformity to stereotypical images of majority.	"If he truly loves his wife he will and should steal the drug for her."
		Stage 4: Maintenance of Authority. Orientation to "doing duty" and to showing respect for authority and maintaining the given social order for its own sake. Regard for learned expectations of others.	"He shouldn't steal because it's against the law. If people lived by their private rules there would be chaos."
III Post-Conventional Morality	Moral value resides in conformity to shared standards, rights or duties. However, this includes a recognition that disobedience of conventional standards may, under certain circumstances, be moral and ethical.	Stage 5: Social Contract. Contractual, legalistic orientation. Recognition of an arbitrary element or starting point in rules or expectations for the sake of agreement. Duty defined in terms of contract, general avoidance of violation of the will or rights of others, and majority will and welfare.	"As a general rule, the law should be obeyed. However, under certain circumstances, stealing is justified as in this case, since saving a life is more important than property rights."
		Stage 6: Principles of Conscience. Conscience or principle orientation. Orientation not only to actually ordained social rules but to principles of choice involving appeal to logical universality and consistency. Orientation to conscience as a directing agent and to mutual respect and trust.	"Justice, love, and the right to life are the highest human values and must be satisfied before all other values."

Source: Mednick et al (1975), page 423.

Morpheme: The smallest meaningful unit in the structure of a language, be it a word, base, or affix; e.g., man, strange ing, pro. *See also phoneme.*

Motion parallax: This term means a cue to depth perception that involves apparent motion of objects as the head shifts laterally in the visual field.

Motivation: The conditions (including material, coercive and normative or symbolic ones) which arouse and maintain an individual in engaging in some line of behaviour that might lead him/her to accomplish some goal, including satisfying his/her needs, wants, and/or drives. *See also incentive.*

Motive: Any condition of an organism that affects its readiness to start on or continue in a sequence of behaviour.

Motive to avoid success: A hypothesized personality trait. People who score high on this trait are believed to avoid success out of fear of negative consequences.

Motor area: A projection area in the brain lying in front of the central fissure. Electrical stimulation Commonly results in movement, or motor responses. *See also somatosensery area.*

Mutation: Any heritable sudden alteration of the genes or chromosomes of an organism, that permanently and often radically alters the gene structure that an individual can pass on.

Multimodal distribution: A distribution curve with more than one mode. See *also mode.*

Multiple personalities: An extreme form of dissociation in which an individual's personality is split into separate personalities often alternating with each other. The memories of one of the split-off personalities commonly are not accessible to the other.

Muscular dystrophy: A crippling disease in which the kinaesthetic sense, though not the intellect, is impaired.

Mutual need gratification: A form of complementarity in which each member of a dyad has an inner urge which is expressed in behaviour that is rewarding to the other member.

Myelin sheath: The fatty sheath surrounding certain nerve fibers known as myelinated fibers. Impulses travel faster and with less energy expenditure in myelinated fibers than in unmyelinated fibers.

Myxoedma: A sluggish condition due to an insufficiency of the thyroid-gland hormone thyroxin.

Mnemonics: A system for improving memory often involving a set of symbols that can substitute for the material to be remembered; e.g., in attempting to remember a number sequence, one may translate the sequence into letters of the alphabet that in turn approximate words that are easily remembered.

N

Nature: This concept refers to the hereditary, or genetic, qualities which parents pass on to their offspring.

Nanometer (nm): A billionth of a meter. Wavelength of light is measured in nanometers.

Narcissism: Self-love in psychoanalytic theory, this means the normal expression of pregenital development.

Narcolepsy: A sleep disturbance characterized by an uncontrollable tendency to fall asleep for brief periods at inopportune time.

Nativism: The view that behaviour is innately determined. See *also empiricism.*

Natural experiment: A research method similar to the controlled experiment, except that the researcher does not manipulate the independent variable himself; he takes advantage of a natural occurrence that manipulates the variable for him. (Example: In testing the hypothesis that fearful events increase people's tendencies to affiliate, the researcher might compare those who live in a community that had experienced an earthquake with those .who live in a comparable one that had not, and examine the closeness of family life before and after the event).

Naturalistic observation: Unselective observation and recording of typical behaviour in natural settings; it is a favourite method of anthropologists.

Nature-nurture issue: The problem of determining the relative importance of heredity (nature) and the result of upbringing in the particular environment (nurture) on mature ability.

Need: A physical state involving any lack or deficit within an organism. *See also motive, drive.*

Need for nurturance: An inner urge to give help and support to other persons.

Negative transfer: A situation in which previous learning interferes with new learning. See *also positive transfer.*

Need for succorance: An inner urge to receive emotional support and help from other persons.

Negative goals interdependence: *See Goals interdependence and Interdependence.*

Negative incentive: An object or circumstance away from which behaviour is directed when the object or circumstance is perceived or anticipated. See also *positive incentive.*

Negative influence: Social influence in which a person changes his attitudes or behaviour in a direction that differs from the one desired by the influencing agent. This is the opposite of positive influence.

Negative reference group: A group used by an individual as *a* standard to deviate from.

Negative referent power: A condition where an individual is influenced to behave in a manner opposite to that of the power figure.

Negative reinforcement: Reinforcing a response by the removal of an aversive stimulus. See *also negative reinforcer.*

Negative reinforcer: Any stimulus that/when removed following a response, increases the probability of the response. Loud noise, electric shock, and extreme heat or cold classify as negative rein-forcers. *See also punishment.*

Negative sanctions: Actions by other persons that negatively reinforce or punish an individual.

Negativism: A type of defiant behaviour in which there is active refusal to carry out requests. Common in early childhood but met occasionally at all ages (syn. negativistic behaviour).

Neurosis (pl. neuroses): An emotional disturbance that is characterized by an individual's inability to cope with anxieties and conflicts and develops abnormal symptoms, such as a strained or exaggerated reliance on mechanisms of defence. The disturbance is not so severe as to produce a profound personality derangement, as with psychotic reactions (syn. psychoneurosis). *See also anxiety reaction, conversion reaction, neurotic depression, obsessive-compulsive reaction, phobia.*

Nerve: A bundle of elongated axons belonging to hundreds or thousands of neurons, possibly both afferent neurons. Connects portions of the nervous system to other portions and to receptors and effectors. *See also axon, neuron.*

Nerve cell: *See neuron.*

Neurasthenia: A neurotic condition whose predominant symptom is continuous fatigue.

Neuron: The nerve cell; the unit of a synaptic nervous system.

New brain: The most complex, most recently evolved part of the human brain. Controls thinking and deliberate actions.

Neurotic depression: A neurosis characterized by continuing sadness and dejection that is out of proportion to any precipitating event; distinguished from psychotic depression in that reality perception is not grossly impaired. *See also affective disorder, neurosis, psychosis.*

Figure 16: Schematic diagram of a neuron.

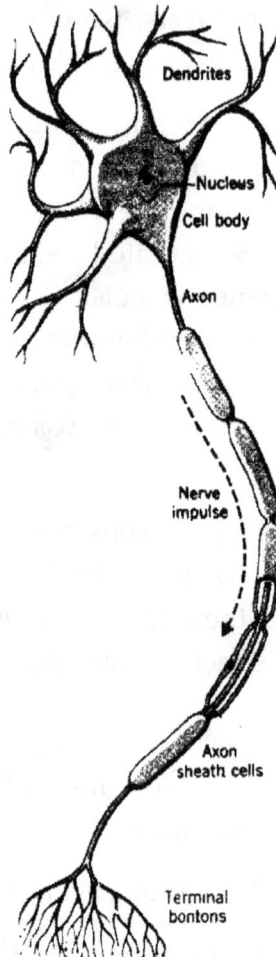

Source: Libert and Neale (1977), page 28.

Neurotic paradox: Refers to the tendency of neurotics to cling to defensive patterns that are self-defeating. See *also neurosis.*

Neurotransmitter: A chemical involved in the transmission of nerve impulses across the synapse from one neuron to another. Usually released from small vesicles in the terminal button of the axon in response to the action potential; diffuses across synapse to influence electrical activity in another neuron. *See also dopamine, epinephrine, norepinephrine. seretenin.*

Neutralization: One of the rules for displaying emotion, in which an agitated person tries to appear unperturbed.

Neutralization, techniques of: Elaboration of various ideas, beliefs, and feelings to deny responsibility for one's actions, or to defend or to justify them.

Night blindness: An inability to see properly at night, due to a deficiency of visual purple in the red cells of the retina.

Nonconscious processes: Those forms of unconscious processes that are never accessible to consciousness; e.g., control of salt concentration in the blood. *See also conscious processes, unconscious processes.*

Noncontingent reinforcement: Reinforcement not contingent on a specific response.

Nonmanipulative method: The so-called correlational method of science.

Nonreactive measure: A type of measurement that does not change the phenomenon being measured.

Non-voluntary group: A group which arises because of birth as in the case of a caste group, a communal group, a linguistic group etc. *See also Voluntary group.*

Noradrenalin: *See norepinephrine.*

Norepinephrine: One of the hormones secreted by the adrenal medulla. Its action is in some, but not all, respects similar to that of epinephrine (syn. noradrenalin). See *also adrenal gland, epinephrine.*

Norm: An average, common, or standard performance under specified conditions; e.g., the average achievement test score of 9-year-old children or the average birth weight of male children. See *also test standardization.*

Normal curve: The plotted form of the normal distribution.

Normal distribution: A group of test scores distributed in such a way that most of them are somewhere in the middle of the range, with fewer and fewer scores as either extreme is approached.

Normal distribution: The standard symmetrical bell-shaped frequency distribution, whose properties are commonly used in making statistical inferences from measures derived from samples. *See also normal curve, skewed distribution.*

Normal-smith: A type of individual who sees good in everyone and believes that all persons are capable of change. The term comes from the function of the normal-smith in eliminating deviant behaviour.

Normative influence: A process in which an individual conforms to the expectation of another person or a group because of a desire to maintain the relationship. (Contrasted with informational influence).

Normative judgements: Judgements shared by a group which are believed by members of the group to be appropriate or expected.

Normative-reeducative strategy: A strategy of planned change, which assumes that before trying to change a person or group, the cultural or normative factors (such as the past history of the person or group) must be taken into account.

Norm of altruism: The widely shared idea that a person in need is entitled to receive help. (Compare norm of social responsibility).

Norm of fairness or justice: The idea that in a social exchange where each party receives something from the other, the amount received by each party should be in accord with his contribution.

Norm of reciprocity: The idea that when an individual does a favour for another person, the other person is obligated to do something in return.

Norm of social responsibility: The generally accepted idea that an individual should help other persons in need. (Compare norm of altruism).

Norm-sending processes: The operations by which norms ere communicated and enforced.

Norms, Social: A norm is the shared expectation of a social group or society. The concept assumes a relationship between the perceptions of these shared expectations by members of the social group and the extent to which the norm influences behaviour. To the degree, then, to which human behaviour is influenced by the normative content of the culture of one's society, such behaviour is influenced by the normative content of the culture of one's society, such behaviour might be explained in terms of the collective expectation as perceived, shared, and enforced by the group. However, normative variations exist even in a relatively stable culture. These variations are due to the generalized nature of norms relative to specific social situations and to the variations in their perceptions and interpretations by individuals, Furthermore, in plural societies like Nigeria, whose social structure manifests many socio-cultural variations, ambiguities and variations concerning the meaning of social norms are to be expected.

Norms are external to the individual to the extent that normative definitions exist in the social reality defined by a particular culture, which may pre-exist his or her being. There is a hierarchy of such normative definitions of "right and wrong". These are traditionally identified as *folkways, mores,* and *laws.* In other words, folkways, mores, and laws are various classes of norms.

Nuclei (sing. nucleus): A collection of nerve cell bodies grouped together in the brain or spinal cord. *See also ganglia.*

Null hypothesis: A statistical hypothesis that any difference observed among treatment conditions occurs by chance and does not reflect a true difference. Rejection of the null hypothesis means that we believe the treatment conditions are actually having an effect.

Nurturance: A motive or related behaviour directed towards caring for and providing aid and comfort to another.

Nurture: This refers to the effects of learning and of the social and physical opportunities provided by environments to organisms.

Nyctophobia: An irrational fear of the dark, e.g. a dark night.

O

Object constancy: The tendency to see objects as relatively unchanged under widely altered conditions of illumination, distance, and position. *See also brightness constancy, colour constancy, location constancy, shape constancy, size constancy.*

Object permanence: A term used by Piaget to refer to a child's realization that an object continues to exist even though it is hidden from view. *See also sensorimotor stage.*

Object size: The size of an object as determined from measurement at its surface When size constancy holds, the observer perceives a distant object as being near its object size. *See also retinal size*

Objective: Factual; independent of personal bias.

Objectivity: Openness to observation by many observers; hence, a display of consensual agreement, a factual nature.

Obscenity: That which is considered to be offensive to the mass populace, and hence which should be proscribed. Recent definitions have limited obscenity to offensive sexual materials.

Observational method: Studying events as they occur in nature, without experimental control of variables; e.g., studying the nest-building of birds or observing children's behaviour in a play situation. *See also experimental method.*

Obsession: A persistent, unwelcome, intrusive thought, often suggesting an aggressive or sexual act, sometimes to the exclusion of everything else. See *also compulsion, obsessive-compulsive reaction.*

Obsessive-compulsive reaction: A neurosis taking one of three forms: (1) recurrent thoughts; often disturbing and unwelcome (obsessions); (2) irresistible urges to repeat stereotyped or ritualistic acts (compulsions); (3) both of these in combination.

Occipital lobe: A portion of the cerebral hemisphere, behind the parietal and temporal lobes. *See also frontal lobe, parietal lobe, temporal lobe.*

Oedipal stage: In psychoanalysis, an alternative designation of the phallic-stage of psychosexual development, because it is at this stage that the Oedipus complex arises. *See also Oedipus, psychosexual development.*

Oedipus conflict: The attraction of the child towards (he parent of the other sex, accompanied by envy and hostility towards the parent of the same sex. A part of the phallic stage of personality development, according to Freud.

Oedipal complex: The repressed desire of a male child to have sexual union with his mother. In Freudian theory, this takes the form of a triadic drama between both parents and the child, who overcomes this complex by identifying with and imitating the father (and the male sex role), since this is the only way he can resolve the sexual rivalry with his seemingly omnipotent father. This idea was first discovered and named by Freud after the legendary Greek hero who was said to have unknowingly killed his father and married his mother.

Office landscaping (Burolandschaft): A German innovation in office design in which office workers are separated not by walls, but by office furniture, plants, bookcases, and other movable articles.

Old brain: More primivite part of the human brain. Controls automatic actions, both inborn and acquired, and contains the site of feelings and sensations.

Olfactory: Of the sense of smell.

Olfactory epithelium: The portion of specialized skin within the nasal cavity that contains the receptors for the sense of smell.

Open-ended question: One that the respondent answers in his own words.

Operant behaviour: Behaviour defined by the stimulus to which it leads rather than by the stimulus that elicits it; e.g., behaviour leading to reward (syn. emitted behaviour, instrumental behaviour). See *also respondent behaviour.*

Operant conditioning: The strengthening of an operant response by presenting *a* reinforcing stimulus if, and only if, the response occurs (syn. instrumental conditioning, reward learning). *See also classical conditioning.*

Operant earning: A kind of conditioning of particular interest to B.F. Skinner. It contrasts to classical conditioning in that the behaviour is emitted by the organism rather than elicited by stimuli.

Operational definition: Definition of a concept by specifying the procedures or operations by which it is measured.

Organismic variables: Measurable characteristics of an organism that influence behaviour.

Opinion: A judgment held as true, arrived at by some intellectual effort though not necessarily based on evidence sufficient for proof. It is a view or an estimate on a particular problem or issue.

Opinion leaders: A fairly well-informed member of a sub-group (farmer, factory worker, etc.) to whom the other members go in order to learn about the situation or the issue that is confronting the group. See *also two-step flow of information.*

Opinion poll: A method by which the opinion of individuals regarding some issue is collected using an interview schedule on a specified sample of the group.

Opponent-process theory: The theory that human colour vision depends on 3 pairs of opposing processes: white-black, yellow-blue, and red-green. *See also Young-Helmholtz theory.*

Opportunity constraints: The blocking career and other paths ordinarily open to everyone but denied to deviant individuals.

Optic nerve: The pathway of light stimuli from the eye to the brain.

Oral behaviour: Behaviour deriving from an infant's need to suck or, more generally, to be fed through the mouth.

Oral stage: In psychoanalysis, the first stage of psychosexual development, in which pleasure is derived from the lips and mouth, as in sucking at the mother's breast. *See also psychosexual development.*

Oral gratification: Pleasure obtained by biting, sucking, or chewing.

Organic psychosis: A psychosis, such as senile dementia, caused by disease, injury, drugs, or other definable structural changes of the central nervous system. See *also functional psychosis, psychosis.*

Orgasm: This term refers to the ecstatic condition which males and females experience either separately or simultaneously as the height of pleasure during sexual activity. It is also called a "climax" because it is brief in duration and brings about rapid relief from sexual tension.

Organism: In biology, any form of plant or animal life. In psychology, the word is used to refer to the living individual animal, whether human or sub-human.

Organ language: Colloquial and slang phrases that express the truths of psychosomatic medicine, such as 'It gripes me,' 'It breaks my heart,' and 'I haven't the guts for it.'

Organ of Certi: In the ear, the actual receptor for hearing, lying on the basilar membrane in the cochlea and containing the hair cells where the fibers of the auditory nerve originate. *See also brailer membrane, cochlea.*

Orientation (towards role obligations): An actor's preferred attitude towards certain expectations, particularly when faced with role strain. Three possible orientations are: (1) a moral orientation, which favours doing the legitimate thing, (2) an expedient orientation, which favours doing what will be rewarded and not punished, and (3) a moral-expedient orientation, a compromise attitude which takes both morality and expediency into account.

Orienting reflex: (1) A nonspecific response to change in stimulation involving depression of cortical alpha rhythm, galvanic skin response, nupillary dilation, and complex vasometer responses (a term introduced by Russian psychologists). (2) Head or body movements that orient an organism's receptors to those parts of the environment in which stimulus changes are occurring

Osmoreceptors: Hypothesized cells in the hypothalamus that respond to dehydration by stimulating the release of ADH by the pituitary gland, which, in turn, signals the kidneys to reabsorb water back into the bloodstream. *See* also *anti-diuretic hormone, volumetric receptors.*

Overgeneralization: In psychology, this term refers to any situation in which an individual inappropriately responds in the same way to similar stimuli.

Other-oriented: In personal involvements, seeing the other person as an entity separate from the self.

Otoliths: *"Ear* stones." *See also vestibular sacs.*

Outcome: In exchange theory, this term refers to the net effect of carrying out an activity; it is expressed in terms of rewards less costs.

Outside density: Density within neighbourhoods, outside of dwellings.

Ovarian hormones: *See estrogen.*

Ovet-intensification: A display role, involving the expression of more emotion than one feels.

Overtone: A higher frequency tone, a multiple of the fundamental frequency, that occurs when a tone is sounded by a musical instrument. See *also timbre*

Overt responses: The responses that are readily observable, like crying or laughing.

Overextension: The tendency of a child, in learning a language, to apply a new word too widely; eg., to call all animals "doggie."

Overlearning: Repeating one's practice and study beyond the point of bare mastery.

P

Paired-associate learning: The learning of stimulus-response pairs, as in the acquisition of a foreign language vocabulary. When the first member of a pair (the stimulus) is presented, the subject's task is to give the second member (the response).

Pancreas: A bodily organ situated near the stomach. As a duct gland it secretes pancreatic juice into the intestines, but some specialized cells function as an endocrine gland, secreting the hormone insulin into the bloodstream. *See also endocrine gland.*

Panic: A temporary attack of intense fear.

Paradigm: A broad method by which science progresses. A paradigm includes laws and theories; it poses problems for science to solve.

Paralanguage: Nonverbal vocalizations. These include the inflection and emphasis of verbal statements as well as other nonverbal vocalizations such as a laugh, a sign, or a moan, all of which frequently convey some meaning.

Parallel model explanation: An attempt by Leventhal to explain the persuasive effects of communications which arouse fear. The model proposes two parallel and independent reactions: (1) to control the fears aroused by the threat and (2) to cope with the danger. The two reactions have different consequences for attitude change.

Parallel processing: A theoretical interpretation of information processing in which several sources of information are all-processed simultaneously. *See also serial processing.*

Parameter: Any of the constants in a function that defines the form of the curve. It ordinarily differs when experimental conditions or subjects are changed.

Parametric study: An experiment in which three or more values of the independent variable are used.

Paranoia: Functional psychosis marked by extreme suspiciousness of the motives of others, and fixed delusions of grandeur or persecution.

Paranoid schizophrenia: A schizophrenic reaction in which the patient has delusions of persecution. *See also schizophrenia.*

Parapsychology: A subfield of psychology that studies such paranormal phenomena as extrasensory perception and psychokinesis. *See also clairvoyance, extrasensory perception, pre-cognition. psychokinesis, telepathy.*

Parasite: An animal that lives on another without making any useful and fitting return.

Parasympathetic division: A division of the autonomic nervous system, the nerve fibers of which originate in the cranial and sacral portions of the spinal cord. Active in relaxed or quiescent slates of the body and to some extent antagonistic to the sympathetic division. *See also sympathetic division.*

Parathyroid gland: The endocrine glands adjacent to the thyroid gland in the neck, whose hormones regulate calcium metabolism, thus maintaining the normal excitability of the nervous system. Parathyroid inadequacy leads to tetany. *See also endocrine gland.*

Paresis: An organic psychosis caused by syphilitic damage to the brain.

Parietal lobe: A portion of the cerebral hemisphere, behind the central fissure and between the frontal and occipital lobes. *See also frontal lobe, occipital lobe, temporal lobe.*

Partial reinforcement: Reinforcing a given response only some proportion of the times it occurs (syn. intermittent reinforcement) *See also reinforcement, reinforcement schedule.*

Partial withdrawal: Activity reducing O's dependence on P and resulting in a shift towards equalization of the relative social power of P. and O.

Participant observation: An observation method in which the observer becomes a member of a group being observed and participates in its activities but tries not to influence the activities himself.

Participatory leader: A leader who seeks to evoke the maximum involvement and participation of every member in the group activities and in the determination of group objectives. *See also Democratic leader.*

Particularistic orientation: The tendency to behave towards other persons in terms of their unique characteristics of their special relationship to oneself rather than in terms of some abstract category (e. g. honesty or morality). *See also universalistic orientation.*

Pecking order: A dominance hierarchy This term is derived from the observation that chickens seem to follow a stable pattern that gives certain chickens the ability to peck others and not be pecked in return. Typically, the dominant chicken in the pecking order, a, will be able to peck all of the others (and not be pecked in return); b, and so forth. Similar pecking orders, including both aggressive behaviour and influence, have been observed in nursery-school playgrounds, boys gangs, and industrial hierarchies.

Peer: A person of equal or similar rank, status, age, class, race, and so forth. A peer or peer group may serve as a basis for social comparison and have referent power over a given individual.

Peer groups: The group of persons of the same age. During later childhood and adolescence, the ideals and social norms of a person are greatly influenced by the individuals of the same age.

Table 12: The sensory – perceptual systems

System	Mode of Attention	Receptive Units	Sense	Stimuli	Information Obtained
Visual	Looking	Rods and cones	Vision	Light	Information about the shape and size of objects, motion, pattern, colour
Auditory	Listening	Basilar membrane in cochlea	Audition	Sound (air vibration)	Frequency, pitch, location of objects.
Haptic	Touching	A variety of specialized receptors embedded in the skin.	Touch	Skin contact with objects	Information about shape and texture
	Touching for passive registration)	A variety of specialized receptors in the skin	Temperature	Temperature changes	Air or object temperature
	Locomotion or body movement	Specialized receptors in deep muscles and joints	Kinaesthetic sense (body and limb movement)	Muscles stretching, joint movement, skin pressure	Location and movement of body and limbs

	Passive registration	Free nerve endings	Pain	Intense stimuli, pressure, breaks in skin	Degree of injury or damage to body
Chemical Senses	Smelling	Odor receptors in nasal passages	Smell	Chemicals in air	Odor
	Tasting	Taste buds on tongue	Taste	Chemicals in solution	Taste, chemical value of material
Equilibriu m	Body balance	Semicircul ar canals in inner ear	Vestibular sense (body balance)	Body and head movement	Direction of motion, balance of body

Source: Mednick et al (1975), page 150.

Perception: This term refers to the process by which an individual selects, organizes, and interprets sense input. Perception is the process of becoming aware of objects, qualities, or relations by way of the sense organs. While sensory content is always present in perception, what is perceived is influenced by the individual's set and prior experience, personal and social influences, so that perception is more than a passive registration of stimuli impinging on the sense organs. *See also subliminal perception.*

Percept: The end result of the perceptual process; that which the individual perceives.

Perceptual: Pertaining to those aspects of the external world which are taken in and processed by an organism and on which a discriminative response becomes contingent.

Perceptual patterning: The tendency to perceive stimuli according to principles such as proximity, similarity, continuity, and closure. Emphasized by Gestalt psychologists. *See also figure ground perception. Gestalt psychology.*

Performance: Overt behaviour, as distinguished from knowledge or information not translated into action. The distinction is important in theories of learning.

Peripheral nervous system: The part of the nervous system outside the brain and spinal cord; it includes the autonomic nervous system and the somatic nervous system. *See also autonomic nervous system, somatic nervous system.*

Persistence of vision: The time lag, of one-sixteen of a second, between the removal of a stimulus and the fading away of its after-image.

Personal involvement: The way in which observers bring themselves into a description of another person.

Personality: The individual characteristics and ways of behaving that, in their organization or patterning, account for an individual's unique adjustments to his or her total environment (syn, individuality).

Personality assessment: (1) General, appraisal of personality by any method. (2) More specifically, personality appraisal through complex observations and judgments, usually based in part on behaviour in contrived situations.

Personality disorders: Ingrained, habitual, and rigid defects in an individual's personality, including sexual deviation, alcoholism, and various forms of addiction, that severely limit the individual's adaptive potential; often society sees the behaviour as maladaptive while the individual does not (syn. character disorders).

Personality dynamics: Theories of personality that stress that personality dynamics are concerned with the interactive aspects of behaviour (as in conflict resolution), with value hierarchies, with the permeability of boundaries between differentiated aspects of personality, etc. Contrasted with developmental theories, though not incompatible with them.

Personality inventory: An inventory for self-appraisal, consisting of many statements or questions about personal characteristics and behaviour that the person judges to apply or not to apply to him or her. *See also protective test.*

Personality psychologist: A psychologist whose area of interest focuses on classifying individuals and studying the differences between them. This specialty overlaps both developmental and social psychologists to some extent. See *also developmental psychologist, social psychologist.*

Personality Structure: The dynamic organizational and organized framework which encompasses the sum total of all of any one individual's personality traits, which include all of his or her beliefs, attitudes, values, habits, needs, ideals, expectations, skills, knowledge, motives, interests, feelings, and behaviour. Personality structure as an organized framework develops as a response to biogenetic needs, cultural transmission of values, and the processes of socialization and the development of "self" or "ego". It represents a generally organized coherent interrelated system. In dynamic terms, an individual's personality structure serves to interpret and organize reality and respond to and act towards all of the several different external and internal exigencies which an individual encounters in his or her everyday life.

Table 13: Personality structure according to the psychoanalytic perspective

Structure	Functioning Principle	Mode of Operation
Id The instincts; source of psychic energy; biological substratum of personality	*Pleasure Principle* Seeks to gratify instinctual drives immediately	*Primary Process* Direct motor-discharge of energy or drive, e.g., dreams, wish fulfilment.
Ego Developed from the id; reality-oriented; judging; executive.	*Reality Principle* "Executive function", i.e., moderates demands of instinctual impulses and demands of external reality.	*Secondary Process* Differentiates objective from subjective reality; relies on past experience; judges
Superego Developed from the ego; represents introjection of parental moral standards and values	*Moral Evaluation* Judges rights and wrong, "good" and "bad".	*Conscience* Source of moral judgement *Ego Ideal* Image of person child would like to become.

Source: Richard H. Price (1978), page 41.

Personality Traits: Any one relatively distinctive aspect, quality, attribute, element, or characteristic of any individual's personality structure - *e.g.*, cognition, skill, value, belief, etc. Any individual's set of personality traits represent that individual's typical behavioural patterns, elements, characteristics, or attributes. That is, the totality of any individual's personality traits represent all of the various observable ways and manners in which the individual actually thinks, feels, and behaves in all the different social contexts or forums in his or her everyday existence - these include: his or her aspirations, ideals, motives or motivations, values, interests, needs, beliefs, habits, knowledge or cognition, skills or roles, feelings, and concrete deeds or behaviours.

All of the different behavioural traits or elements which make up the sum total of any one individual's entire or complete personality structure may be classified under three categories, as follows; (1) the psychological core, (2) the typical responses, and (3) the role - related behaviours. These three categories represent the three major sub-systems which make up the entire or complete structure or system of each individual's basic personality.

Figure 17: A representation of the components of personality within the social environment.

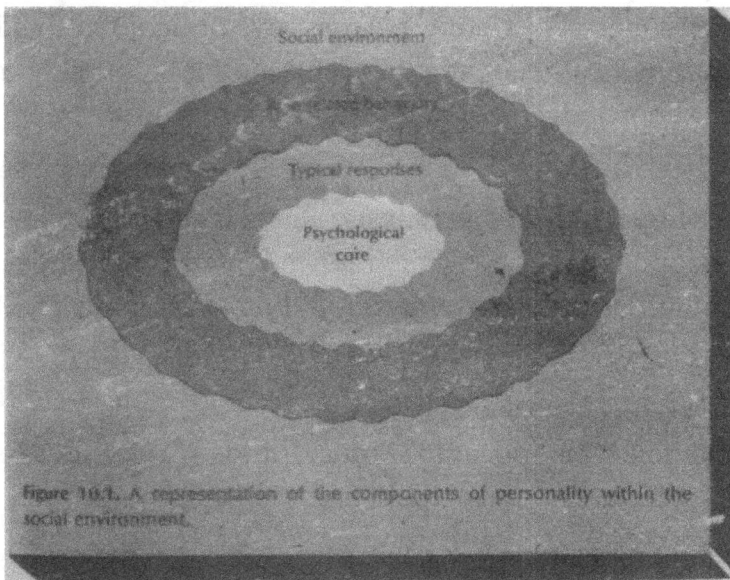

Figure 10.1. A representation of the components of personality within the social environment.

Source: Edwin P. Hollander (1976), page 331.

Personal space: An area around a person's body inside which other people are not welcome; the zone of interpersonal distance "too close for comfort."

Personal-space invasion: A violation of interpersonal-distance norms in which another person approaches to an uncomfortably close distance in uncrowded conditions, without attempting to initiate conversation. It usually results in signs of discomfort and eventual flight.

Personal stereotype: The attributes which an individual personally believes should be assigned to a category of persons.

Personification: The pretence of regarding something that is not human as a person.

Person perception: The process by which impressions, opinions and feelings about other persons are formed. On this basis, we try to assess the intentions and motives of other persons. Our knowledge of and expectation about others are determined in part by the impressions we form of them.

Phallic stage: In psychoanalysis, that stage of psychosexual development in which gratification is associated with stimulation of the sex organs and the sexual attachment is to the parent of the opposite sex. *See also Oedipal stage, psychosexual development.*

Phenomenon: The appearance of any thing (object, idea, etc) in the mind and human experience.

Phenomenological approach: A point of view in social psychology stating that the environment *as a* person perceives it is an important influence on behaviour.

Phenomenological method: A scientific research method that is also used in psychology which requires that a subject's experiences should be reported as they were observed without analysis, interpretation, or embellishment.

Phenomenology: The art of making an unembellished report on conscious experience, as by a child, as contrasted with the use of trained introspection. Emphasis is on the individual's subjective experience and his subjective view of a situation. *See also humanistic psychology, introspection.*

Phenotype: In genetics, the characteristics that are displayed by an individual organism, e.g., eye colour or intelligence, as distinct from those traits that one may carry genetically but not display. *See also genotype.*

Philosophies of human nature: Expectations that people possess certain qualities and will behave in certain ways.

Phiphenomenon: Stroboscopic motion in its simpler form. Commonly produced by successively turning on and off two separated stationary light sources; as the first is turned off and the second turned on, the subject perceives a spot of light moving from the position of the first to that of the second. *See also stroboscopic motion.*

Phlegmatic: Calm. One of Galen's four temperaments.

Phobia: Phobia is a morbid fear of some object or situation. People fear things that pose a threat or danger to them. It is only when fear is abnormally strong and without apparent logical basis that it is called a phobia. Phobia is associated with neurotic person, such a person often realizes that his fears are unreasonable, but he is never the less unable to control them. A phobia could be an intense, paralyzing fear of something, anything, in the absence of any real obvious danger.

Phobias are disorders, which are closely linked to anxiety over things/situations, which many other people will find bearable.

The word phobia is from the Greek word "Phobos" which means, "fear". It is a pathological fear of a specific object or situation. In psychiatry such (phobic) reactions are classed as a single form of neurosis.

All humans have a certain level of fear of objects or things that pose a threat or danger to them. It is only when the degree of fear is abnormally strong without an apparent logical basis that it is called Phobia.

There are many different types of phobias. Examples are as follows:-

Acrophobia (also called *Altophobia*): The fear of height; the people who cannot stand on high places like story buildings, mountaintops, and hill, or climb a tree. Most of the people suffering from this phobia are children.

Aerophobia: Fear of flying objects e.g. airplanes.

Agoraphobia: A marked fear of being alone, or being in public places from which escape might be difficult. People suffering from this type of phobia avoid such things as elevators, tunnels and crowds' especially crowed stores or busy streets. Most of the agoraphobics are women.

Ailurophobia: Fear of cats.

Androphobia: Fear of men.

Anglophobia: Fear of English, English things and people.

Anthrophobia: Fear of people.

Antophobia: Fear of being alone.

Argophobia: Fear of pain.

Astraphobia: Fear of lightening, thunder, storms.

Autophobia: Fear of being alone.

Bathophobia: Fear of depths, e.g. depths of swimming pools, rivers, seas, lakes, oceans.

Biblophobia: Fear of books.

Blackphobia (also called *Negrophobia*): Fear of black people.

Brontophobia: Fear of storms involving thunder and lightening.

Claustrophobia: This is when people fear closed places, small rooms, closets, elevators, alleys, and subways. They do not like going to dark places.

Counterphobia: Fear of facing or countering a dangerous threat or challenge.

Cynophobia: These people suffer from fear of dogs. They do not like seeing dogs; they can even collapse at the sight of a dog or when a dog barks. They see dogs as something that has connection with evil.

Demonophobia: Fear of demons and devilish things or spirits.

Demophobia: Fear of being in a crowd.

Disease Phobia (also called *Pathophobia*): Fear of having a disease, even with the absence of any symptoms.

Electrophobia: Fear of electricity.

Enythrophobia: Fear of blushing.

Equinophobia: Fear or dislike of horses.

Ergophobia: Fear of work

Gephrogophobia: Fear of crossing water, like rivers, lakes, etc.

Gynophobia: Fear of women.

Hematophobia: The people that suffer from this phobia are scared of blood. They cannot stand the sight of blood. They cannot slaughter anything that has blood. They cannot even treat somebody that has a bloody injury.

Heterophobia: Fear of having sexual contact with another person of the opposite sex.

Homilophobia: Fear of sermons, especially long ones.

Homophobia: Fear of blood.

Hydrophobia: Fear of water, e.g. rivers, streams, lakes, ponds, water falls etc.

Kakoraphobia: Fear of failure

Lalophobia: This is the fear of speaking for a long time.

Melissophobia: Fear of bees.

Metalophobia: Fear of metallic objects.

Microphobia: Fear of small things e.g. ants.

Musophobia: Fear of mice.

Mysophobia: Fear of being poisoned, the people who display this trait fear to eat outside their homes for fear of being poisoned.

Necrophobia: Fear of dead bodies.

Nightmare Phobia: Fear of bad dreams at night (horror dreams, nightmares)

Nosophobia: Fear of diseases.

Nyctophobia: Fear of darkness.

Ochlophobia: Fear of being in the midst of crowds.

Ophidophobia: Fear of going near places like forests or zoo where snakes can be found.

Panthophobia: Fear of everything.

Pasthenophobia: Fear of virgins.

Phobophobia: Fear of fear or alarm,

Photophobia: Fear of light.

Photophobia: Hatred of noise.

Posttraumatic Phobia: Fear of the re-occurrence of some past painful experiences e.g. fire, flood, close encounter with dangerous animals, horrors of military combat, etc

Pyrophobia (also known as *Parophobia*): Fear of fire.

Rupophobia (also known as *Mysophobia*): Fear of dirty environment or dirt generally.

School Phobia: The people that suffer from this phobia do not like school; they can develop a headache or even fall sick when they are reminded of school. They cannot stand the sight of school environment.

Simple Phobia: This is a general type of phobia, which includes when people are afraid of snakes that they cannot go to a zoo, walk through a field, or even look at pictures of snakes without trembling. It also includes such fear as those of darkness, infections and even running water. However, there are sub-divisions or specific types of simple phobias, as we shall show subsequently.

Sitophobia: Dislike or fear of food.

Social Phobias: These are fears generally connected with the presence of other people, e.g. fear of public speaking. These people do not like speaking in public places. This begins during adolescence, when an individual is experiencing growing awareness of his or her interactions with other people.

Speedphobia: Fear of high speed while traveling or moving from one location to another.

Taphephobia: Fear of being buried alive.

Terriphobia: Fear of horror.

Thanatophobia: Fear of death

Tocophobia: Fear of childbirth.

Troublephobia: Fear of falling into trouble.

Vehicle Phobia: They that suffer from this phobia do not like the sight of vehicles; they cannot enter cars, trains, planes, and ships. They are always scared of any form of moving vehicle; they cannot even stand or get close to vehicles. They might feel dizzy.

Weaponphobia: Fear of harmful weapons like guns, knives, scissors, bombs etc.

Zenophobia (also spelt *Xenophobia*) (and also known as *Strangophobia*): This refers to intense dislike of strangers, the people who also do not like seeing foreigners. They feel uncomfortable when they see foreigners, people they are not familiar with. There is disorderliness when strangers are around them. Fear of being in an unfamiliar place, of unidentified sounds, and fear of unknown/unidentified/ strange movements.

Zoophobia: Fear of animals e.g. snakes.

Phoneme: Serves to distinguish different utterance from one another. *See also morpheme.*

Physical reality: That which is believed to be true base on the direct evidence of one's senses. (Contrasted with social reality).

Physiological limit of learning: The upper limit of a person's ability to learn and remember.

Physiological motive: A motive based on an evident bodily need, such as the need for food or water.

Physiological psychologist: A psychologist concerned with the relationship between physiological functions and behaviour.

Physiology: That branch of biology concerned primarily with the functioning of organ systems within the body.

Pitch: A qualitative dimension of hearing correlated with the frequency of the sound waves that constitute the stimulus. Higher frequencies yield higher pitches. *See also loudness, timbre.*

Pituitary gland: An endocrine gland joined to the brain just below the hypothalamus. It consists of two parts, the anterior pituitary and the posterior pituitary. The anterior pituitary is the more important part because its secretions influence growth, sexual development, and metabolism of the endocrine glands (syn. hypophysis). See *also endocrine gland.*

Placebo: A harmless, powerless imitation medicine – for example, a sugar pill – given to an hysteric such as members of the control in an experiment, with the suggestion that it is a potent remedy. It's mostly used in studies on drug effects.

Place theory: A theory of hearing that associates pitch with the place on the basilar membrane where activation occurs. See *also frequency theory, volley principle.*

Plateau: A period during the learning process in which no progress seems to be made. Symbolized by a straight line segment in the graph of the learning curve.

Pleasure principle: The tendency, according to Freud, to satisfy the id impulses. See *also reality principle.*

Pluralistic ignorance (1) A phenomenon in which various members of a group or social unit share the same false impression of what the group norm is, and, while disagreeing with it, tend to behave publicly in accordance with it. (Example: In the classic Hans Christian Anderson tale. The Emperor's Clothes, all of the adult citizens fought that everyone else believed that the emperor was wearing beautiful new clothes; therefore, no one spoke up to say that the emperor was naked, for fear of being treated as a deviant). (2) The tendency for persons in a group to mislead each other about a situation; e.g., to define an emergency as a nonemergency because others are remaining calm and are not taking action.

Polygenic traits: Characteristics determined by many sets of genes; e.g., intelligence, height, emotional stability.

Polygraph: (1) A machine that measures simultaneously several physiological responses that accompany emotion; e.g., heart and respiration rate, blood pressure, and GSR. Commonly known as a "lie detector" because of its use in determining the guilt of a subject through responses while answering questions. *See also voice stress analyzer.* (2) A machine, often called the 'lie detector', sensitive enough to detect and draw a graph of the slight changes in blood pressure, pulse rate, breathing rate, and skin electricity that "usually accompany the telling of lies.

Population: (1) The total universe of all possible cases from which a sample is selected. The usual statistical formulas for making inferences from samples apply when the population is appreciably larger than the sample, e.g., 5 to 10 times larger than the sample. (2) In statistics, a population is the statistics universe of any group, from whom a sampling can be drawn and analyzed in order to generalize to the entire group. *See also sample.*

Population density: The number of persons (or other animals) per unit of space, for example the number of persons per acre.

Pornography: Written, oral, or visual materials that are considered to be sexually stimulating.

Position: A location within the differentiated structure of a group. The person who occupies that position is expected to fulfill a particular role and is accorded the degree of status considered appropriate for that position. A position also tends to have a specified function for the group. (Examples: Leader, follower, supervisor, father, mother child, policeman, arbitrator, joker).

Positive goals interdependence: See *goals interdependence and interdependence.*

Positive incentive: An objector circumstance towards which behaviour is directed when the object or circumstance is perceived or anticipated. See *also negative incentive.*

Positive influence: Social influence in which a person changes his attitudes or behaviour in the direction desired by the influencing agent or in such a way that the person becomes more similar to the agent. This is the opposite of negative influence.

Positive means interdependence: *See interdependence and means interdependence.*

Positive reinforcement: Reinforcing *a* response by the presentation of a positive stimulus. *See also positive reinforcer.*

Positive reinforcer: Any stimulus that, when applied following a response, increases the probability of the response (syn. reward), See *also negative reinforcer.*

Positive sanctions: Actions by other persons that gratify or reinforce an individual's behaviour.

Positive transfer: A situation where learning is made easier due to something learned earlier.

Postfigurative culture: A culture in which children learn primarily from their elders.

Post-hypnotic amnesia: A particular form of post hypnotic suggestion in which the hypnotized person forgets what has happened during the hypnosis until signalled to remember. *See also post-hypnotic suggestion.*

Post-hypnotic suggestion: A suggestion made to a hypnotized person that he or she will perform in a prescribed way (commonly to a prearranged signal) when no longer hypnotized. The activity is usually carried out without the subject's awareness of its origin. *See also hypnosis.*

Potlatch: A ceremony that was onto common among Northwest American Indians, particularly the Kwakiutl, in which the participants vied with one another to give increasingly expensive gifts that were then destroyed to demonstrate that the recipient had no need for the gifts. This is an example of a runaway norm.

Power and toughness: Preoccupation with the dominance-submission, strong-weak, leader-follower dimension; identification with power figures; a characteristic of the authoritarian personality syndrome.

Power assertion: A form of parental discipline in which the parent, by virtue of his or her power over the child, punishes the child either physically or by deprivation.

Power-coercive strategy: A strategy that uses either violent or non-violent pressures (e.g. lobbying, petitions, strikes, riots, and so on) to bring about social change.

Power of the powerless: A form of legitimate power based on the concept that those who are helpless and in need have a right to expect assistance from those who are in a position to help them.

Pre-apology: A preface to remarks, designed to prevent other persons from questioning one's expertise or accuracy.

Pre-cognition: A claimed form of extra sensory perception in which a future event is perceived in advance. *See also clairvoyance, extrasensory perception, telepathy.*

Preconscious processes: In psychoanalysis, a term for memories that are available but not now conscious. *See also conscious processes, nonconscious process, unconscious processes.*

Prefigurative culture: A culture in which adults learn from their children.

Prejudice: A prejudgment that something or someone is good or bad on the basis of little or no evidence; an attitude that is firmly fixed, not open to free and rational discussion, and resistant to change.

Pre-operational stage: Piaget's second stage of cognitive development (age 2-7 years). The child can think in terms symbols but does not yet comprehend certain rules or operations, such as the principles of conservation. See *also conservation.*

Pre-tests and post-tests: An integral part of the strategy of the experimental method, in which a group is tested, exposed to the independent variable, and then re-tested. If the independent variable has had an effect, there will be a change in score on the post-test.

Primary abilities: The abilities, discovered by factor analysis, that underlie intelligence test performance. *See also factor analysis*

Primary colours: See *colour mixture primaries, psychological primaries.*

Primary dimensions of personality: The dimensions of personality which statistical tests have shown to have low correlations with each other, so that each dimension is separate and distinct in meaning from the others.

Primary drives: These refer to the physiological needs which man shares with animals – hunger, thirst, pain avoidance, fatigue, sleep, sex, etc. They are drives that are very essential for survival and that must be dealt with before other drives.

Primary effect: (1) In memory experiments, the tendency for initial words in a list to be recalled more readily than later words. (2) In studies of impression formation or attitude change, the tendency for initial information to carry more weight than information received later. This is the opposite of recency effect. *See also recency effect.*

Primary environment: A place where a person spends a relatively large amount of time, relates to others on a personal basis, and performs a wide range of personally important activities. In such settings, the experience of crowding may be relatively difficult to resolve (Stokols, 1974).

Primary group: Any small, intimate group in which members are highly dependent on each other for the satisfaction of their emotional needs (e.g., nuclear family, friendship groups, small, groups dealing with enduring stresses and problems).

Primary process thinking: In psychoanalytic theory, this concept refers to the form of thinking used by the id, characterized by-irrational attempts to satisfy needs without consideration of reality. *See also id, secondary process thinking.*

Primary reinforcement: Reinforcements that satisfy the biological drives of an organism such as hunger and thirst.

Primary sex characteristics: The structural or physiological characteristics that make possible sexual union and reproduction. *See also secondary sex characteristics.*

Primary territory: An area that an individual or group owns and controls on a relatively permanent basis. Such areas are central to the everyday lives of the occupants (Altman, 1975)

Principle of equity: The idea that the more one puts into an activity, as compared with the input of another person, the more one should get in return.

Prisoner's Dilemma game: This is a paradigm for the study of mixed-motive relationships and is taken from a hypothetical situation in which each of two suspects in a crime is confronted with the dilemma of whether to implicate his partner (and thus receive more favourable treatment) or remain silent (thus assuring his partner of more favourable treatment, but subjecting himself to punishment). It is of interest because the best individual choice leads to the worst joint result. Thus, a player's strategy is determined in part by the degree of trust he has for his partner.

Private dependent influence: The socially dependent influence in which the maintenance of an individual's changed position does not require the influencing agent to be aware that any change has occurred. Expert power, legitimate power, and referent power lead to private dependent influence. This is the opposite of public dependent influence. (Example: A student who solves a problem according to his teacher's instructions because he believes that the teacher probably knows the best way will continue to relate his charge to the teacher, but he will not care whether the teacher knows about it).

Privacy: The selective control over access by others to oneself or one's group. Includes control over inputs from others and transmission of information to others (Attman, 1975).

Private stereotype: *See personal stereotype.*

Proactive interference: The interference of earlier (earning with the learning and recall of new material. *See also retroactive interference.*

Probability sampling: Sampling done in such a way that every member of the population has a known probability (usually an equal probability) of being included.

Probe: (1) An optional follow-up question designed to obtain a complete answer in an interview. (2) In studies of memory, the concept refers to a digit or other item from a list to be remembered that is presented as a cue to the subject; e.g., the subject could be asked to give the next digit in the list.

Progestin: A female hormone that regulates ovulation and menstruation.

Progesterone: A female sex hormone produced by the ovaries; it helps prepare the uterus for pregnancy and the breasts for lactation.

Programme: (1) A plan for the solution of a problem; often used interchangeably with "routine" to specify the precise sequence of instructions enabling a computer to solve a problem. (2) In connection with teaching, the concept refers to a set of materials arranged so as to maximize the learning process. The programme can be presented in book form as well as in a form suitable for use with a computer.

Programmed social interaction: A technique commonly utilized in simulation experiments whereby a subject interacts with either an assistant (whom he assumes to be another subject) or a computer. The programmed behaviour, by assistant or computer, follows a predetermined script, which may remain the same or vary according to the subject's responses. Thus, in a simulated bargaining study, the assistant or computer can match the offer made by the subject, make a counter offer that is higher or lower than the one made by the subject, or follow a more complex bargaining strategy – as predetermined by the experimenter. The programmed behaviour may constitute the independent variable and the subject's behaviour the dependent variable.

Projection: A defence mechanism by which people protect themselves from awareness of their own undesirable traits by attributing these traits excessively to others. *See also defense mechanism.*

Projection area: A place in the cerebral cortex where a function is localized; e.g., the visual projection area is in the occipital lobes.

Projective test: A personality test in which subjects reveal ("project") themselves through imaginative productions. The projective test gives much more free possibilities of response than the fixed alternative personality inventory. Examples of projective tests are the Rorschach Test (ink blots to be interpreted) and the Thematic Apperception Test (pictures that elicit stories). *See also personality inventory.*

Projectivity: The disposition to believe that wild and dangerous things go on in the world; the projection outward of unconscious emotional responses. A characteristic of the authoritarian personality syndrome.

Prolactin: A pituitary hormone associated with the secretion of milk. *See also hormones.*

Propaganda: The presentation to the public of facts, arguments and opinions so organized as to induce conclusions favourable to the interests of the group conducting the propaganda.

Propinquity: Nearness; closeness in regard to space.

Proposition: A sentence or component of sentence that asserts something, the predicate, about somebody (or something), the subject. As sentences can be broken down into propositions.

Prostitution: The sale of sexual services usually engaged in by women.

Prosocial behaviour: The behaviour that has positive social consequences, that improves the physical or psychological well-being of another person or persons.

Proxemics: The study of interpersonal proximity and spatial behaviour; it includes the study of crowding and territoriality.

Psi: The special ability said to be possessed by a subject who performs successfully in experiment on extrasensory perception and psychokinesis. *See also extrasensory perception, psychokinesis.*

Psychedelic drugs: An alternate name for "consciousness expanding" drugs. See also *hallucinogens. LSD, psychotomimetic drugs.*

Psychiatric nurse: A nurse specially trained to deal with patients suffering from mental disorders. See *also psychiatrist.*

Psychiatric social worker: A social worker trained to work with patients and their families on problems of mental health and illness, usually in close relationship with psychiatrists and clinical psychologists. *See also psychiatrist, clinical psychologist.*

Psychiatrist: A medical doctor specializing in the treatment and prevention of mental disorders both mild and severe. *See also psychoanalyst, clinical psychologist.*

Psychiatry: A specialized branch of medicine that is concerned with mental health and mental illness. See also *psychiatrist, psychoanalyst.*

Psychoactive drugs: Drugs that affect one's behaviour and consciousness. See also *depressants, hallucinogens, LSD, psychedelic drugs, stimulants, tranquilliser.*

Psychoanalysis: (1) The method developed by Sigmund Freud and extended by his followers for treating neuroses. (2) The system of psychological theory growing out of experiences with the psychoanalytic method. Psychoanalytic theory emphasizes the Importance of unconscious mental processes in both normal and abnormal behaviours.

Psychoanalyst: A psychotherapist, usually trained as a psychiatrist, who uses methods related to those originally proposed by Freud for treating neuroses and other mental disorders. See *also clinical psychologist, psychiatrist.*

Psychodrama: A specialized technique of psychotherapy in which patients act out, usually before an audience of other patients, the roles, situations, and fantasies relevant to their personal problems.

Psychogenic: Caused by psychological factors (e.g., emotional conflict, faulty habits) rather than by disease, injury, or other sorhatic cause; functional rather than organic.

Psychograph: A diagram, prepared from rating scales, that shows how a person rates in each of several traits. Also known as a 'personality profile'. *See also trait profile.*

Psychokinesis (PK): A claimed form of mental operation said to affect a material body or an energy system without any evidence of more usual contact or energy transfer; e.g affecting, the number that comes up in the throw of dice by a machine through wishing for that number. See also *extrasensory perception.*

Psycholinguistics: The study of the psychological aspects of language and its acquisition.

Psychological motive: A motive that is primarily learned rather than based on biological needs.

Psychological primaries: The hues that appear to be pure i.e., not composed of other hues. Most authorities choose a particular red, yellow, green, and blue, (The red-green and blue-yellow pairs chosen in this way are not complementary colours). *See also colour-mixture primaries*

Psychology: The science that studies individuals behaviour, experiences, and mental processes.

Psychometrician: A psychologist who specializes in giving and interpreting psychological tests.

Psychopathic personality: A type of personality disorder marked by impulsivity inability to abide by the customs and laws of society, and lack of anxiety or guilt regarding behaviour (syn. antisocial personality).

Psychopathology: The general term for deviant or abnormal behaviour in which psychological factors are thought to play a role. See *also individual disorders e.g. psychosis.*

Psychopharmacology: The study of the effects of drugs on behaviour.

Psychophysical function: A curve relating the likelihood of a response to the intensity of the presented stimulus.

Psychophysics: A name used by Fechner for the science of the relationship between mental processes and the physical world. Now usually restricted to the study of the sensory consequences of controlled physical stimulation.

Psychosexual development: In psychoanalysis, the theory that development takes place through stages (oral, anal, phallic. latent, genital), each stage characterized by a zone of pleasurable stimulation and appropriate objects of sexual attachment, culminating in normal heterosexual mating. *See* *also anal stage, genital stage, latency state, oral stage, phallic stage, psychosocial stages.*

Table 14: The major psychosexual stages

Stage of Psychosexual Development	Erogenous Zone	Prototypical Activity	Later Personality
Oral Stage (0-2 yrs.)	Mouth	Sucking; incorporation; biting	Oral-incorporative; "sucker"; aggressive; oral-sadistic
Anal Stage (2-3 yrs.)	Anal sphincter	Urge for elimination; strict toilet training rewarded	Anal-retentive or expulsive; productive; creative
Phallic (4-5 yrs.)	Genital organs	Masturbation; autoerotic activity; castration fear; penis envy	Oedipus complex; Electra complex; later relations with men and women

Source: Richard H. Price (1978), page 37.

Psychosis (pi. Psychoses): Mental illness in which the individual shows severe change or disorganization of personality, often accompanied by agitation or depression, delusions, hallucinations; commonly requires hospitalisation. *See also functional psychosis, organic psychosis.*

Psychosomatic medicine: The branch of medical science and applied psychology that attempts to detect and cure those ailments whose physical symptoms express emotional stresses.

Psychosocial stages: A modification by Erik Erikson of the psychoanalytic theory of psychosexual development, giving more attention to the social and environmental problems associated with the various stages of development and adding some adult stages beyond genital maturing. *See also psychosexual development.*

Psychosomatic illnesses: Physical illnesses that are in part due to psychological and emotional stresses, (syn. psycho-physiological disorder).

Psychosurgery: A form of biological therapy for abnormal behaviour. Involves destroying selected areas of the brain, most often the nerve fibers connecting the frontal lobes to the limbic system and/or the hypothalamus.

Psychotherapy: This concept refers to the psychological therapeutic techniques that are used by clinical psychologists and psychiatrists to treat people with emotional and behavioural problems.

Puberty: The period of attaining sexual maturity, usually beginning in girls between the ages of nine and eighteen, in boys between the ages of eleven and eighteen.

Public: A group that includes individuals outside the family caste, creed and other such in-groups.

Public commitment: In coercive persuasion settings, the confession of wrong thinking and profession of "proper" attitudes.

Public dependent influence: Socially dependent influence in which the maintenance of an individual's changed position depends upon his belief that the change will be noticed or brought to the attention of the influencing agent. Reward power and coercive power lead to public dependent influence. (Example: A student follows his teacher's instructions in working on a problem, but only because he is afraid that the teacher will notice what he is doing, and because his course grade is dependent upon following the instructions).

Public opinion: The opinion of a significant portion of a population towards a given issue.

Public stereotype: The adjectives an individual thinks would be attributed to a person category by the general public.

Public territory: A space in a public place that is temporarily used by an individual or group (for example, a bench, cafeteria table, or bus seat)

Punishment: A procedure used to decrease the strength of a response by presenting an aversive stimulus whenever the response occurs. Note that such a stimulus when applied would be a punisher; when removed it would act as a negative reinforcer, reinforcing whatever led to its removal. This is the mechanism of escape learning. *See also escape learning, negative reinforcer.*

Punishment: An imposition of an aversive or negative stimulus upon an organism as a consequence of its having engaged in an unacceptable behaviour.

Pupillary reflex: Involuntary contraction of the pupil of the eye, caused by a sudden increase in the amount of light entering the eye.

Purkinje phenomenon: The change in a person's ability to distinguish colours as the day fades into night. Warm colours darken, while cool colours lighten.

Push and pull: A form of interdependence pressure on a worker in an assembly line.

Q

Quasi-Experimental research: Social research in which the investigator does not have full experimental control over the independent variable, but does have extensive control over how, when, and for whom the dependent variable is measured.

Quickening: The first movement of the foetus in the womb.

Quota sampling: Sampling done by assigning each interviewer a quota of respondents who are in specified categories of a classification system (usually using several dimensions such as urban-rural, sex, age, and so on). The total sample has the same proportion of people in each category as does the population, but it still is not completely representative because of probable bias in the interviewers' choices of respondents.

R

Race: A population that is geographically contiguous and whose members breed together.

Racism: This comprises any prejudicial and discriminatory attitude, action and/or institutional condition which the members of any racial group inflict upon the members of any other racial group largely because of their racial differences. Racism not only has the component of antagonism within it, but also is an attempt to relegate the affected group to a lower status.

Radical behaviourism: An extreme form of behaviourism, identified with B. F. Skinner, in which all learned behaviour change is accounted for in terms of contingencies of reinforcement.

Randomization: (1) A statistical technique in laboratory experimentation that is used to control for sources of extraneous variation by randomly assigning subjects to experimental conditions. Through randomization, the researcher attempts to guarantee that subjects with special or unusual attributes are no more likely to appear in one experimental condition than another. (2) In the experimental method, this concept refers to the assigning of subjects to the experimental or the control group on the basis of chance to insure the elimination of any selective factor that would introduce bias.

Random sampling: A form of probability sampling that involves a completely random selection from a list that enumerates the whole population.

Range: The variation of scores in a frequency distribution from the lowest to the highest. The value grows larger as the number of cases increases, hence it should be used with extreme caution. *See also measure of variation.*

Rank correlation (p): A correlation computed from ranked data. The coefficient is designated by the small Greek letter rho (p) to distinguish it from the product-moment correlation (r), of which it is an approximation. *See also coefficient of correlation.*

Rapid Eye Movements (REMs): Eye movements that usually occur during dreaming and that can be measured by attaching small electrodes laterally to and above the subject's eye. These register changes in electrical activity associated with movements of the eyeball in its socket.

Rapport: (1) A comfortable relationship between the subject and the tester, ensuring co-operation in replying to test questions. (2) A similar relationship between therapist and patient. (3) A special relationship of hypnotic subject to hypnotist.

Rational approach: Reaching conclusions by reasoning or speculating about wants rather than actively collecting data. Contrasted with the empirical approach.

Rating scale: A device by which raters can record their judgments of others (or of themselves) on the traits defined by the scale.

Rationalization: A defense mechanism in which the individual distorts perception and thought to find plausible but false reasons to justify failures or questionable behaviours. *See also defense mechanism.*

Rationalize: To give socially acceptable reasons for some act whose true motive is embarrassing.

Reactance: A form of negative influence that comes about when someone is afraid that his freedom and individuality may be threatened by the attempt to influence him.

Reaction formation: A defense mechanism in which a person denies a disapproved motive through giving exaggerated expression to its opposite. See *also defence mechanism.*

Reaction range: The range of potential intellectual ability specified by a person's genes. According to this concept, the effects of an enriched, average, or a deprived environment will be to change the person's IQ, but only within his or her genetically specified reaction range.

Reaction time: The time between the presentation of a stimulus and the occurrence of a response. *See also latency.*

Reaction to transgression: The emotional reaction to actions that violate some norm or moral code.

Reactive measure: A measurement of a variable whose characteristics may be changed by the very act of measuring it.

Reactivity: The degree to which the very process of measuring a variable may bias the resulting score. Asking a job candidate to describe his qualifications to an interviewer may constitute a reactive measure, whereas inspecting his dossier does not.

Reality principle: The action of the ego, according to Freud, as it tries to cope with the realities of on environment. *See also pleasure principle.*

Reality therapy: According to William Glasser, this is an approach to psychotherapy in which the therapist attempts to guide a patient directly towards a practical (reality-oriented) path in life.

Real similarity: The correspondence between a perceiver's own personal characteristics and those of a person whom he or she is judging or describing (the criterion data).

Reasoning: The form of thinking in which possible solutionist problems are tried out symbolically.

Rebellion: An organised, armed resistance to established government.

Recall: Producing from memory the correct element with a minimum of external cues.

Recall method: A method of testing learning in which the learner is required to produce the correct response from his or her memory with a minimum of external cues.

Receiver-operating-characteristic curve (ROC curve): The function relating the probability of hits and false alarms for a fixed signal level in a detection task. Factors influencing response bias may cause hits arid false alarms to vary, but their variation is constrained to the ROC curve. *See also signal detection task.*

Recency effect: (1) In memory experiments, this is the tendency for the last words in a list to be recalled more readily than other listed words. (2) In studies of impression formation or attitude change, the concept refers to the tendency for later information to carry more weight than earlier information. This is the opposite of *primacy effect. See also primacy effect.*

Receptor: A specialized portion of the body sensitive to particular kinds of stimuli and connected to nerves composed of afferent neurons; e.g., the retina of the eye. Used more loosely, the organ containing these sensitive portions; e.g., the eye or ear. *See also afferent neuron, effector.*

Recitation: A method of study that combines reciting, repeating, and self-quizzing.

Recessive gene: A member of a gene pair that determines the characteristic trait or appearance of the individual only if the other member of the pair is recessive. If the other member of the pair is dominant, the effect of the recessive gene is masked. See *also dominant gene.*

Recessive trait: A trait that will not be expressed in any individual in whom its gene is paired with a corresponding dominant gene.

Reciprocal: In person perception, seeing a mutual two-way relationship between oneself and another person.

Reciprocal effects: The mutual action and reaction between persons participating in social relations.

Reciprocity: According to Piaget, a belief held by older children that punishment should be logically related to the offence so that the rule breaker all understand the implications of his or her misconduct. *See also expiatory punishment.*

Reciprocity norm: A norm or standard of behaviour that says that people should help those who have helped them and refrain from injuring those who have helped them.

Recognition: A method of measuring retention where the subject is asked to pick from a number of examples the items that were previously learnt.

Reconditioning: Teaching a subject to make a response directly opposite to an undesirable conditioned response.

Red-green colour blindness: The commonest form of colour blindness, a variety of dichromatism. In the two subvarieties, red-blindness and green-blindness, both red and green vision are lacking, but achromatic bands are seen at different parts of the spectrum. See *also colour blindness, dichromatism.*

Reference Groups: This concept was probably originated by the American behavioural scientist Herbert Hyman to indicate any social group which is used by an individual as a standard for evaluating his behaviour. The group can consist of mutually interacting individuals (a family or club) or of larger aggregates of non-interacting persons (a social class). The individual does not necessarily have to tie a member of the group to use it as a referent, although he usually is.

Reference groups serve two main functions. They are normative in that they let an individual know what kinds of behaviour and attitudes are appropriate for him or her and they are evaluative in that they enable an individual to compare himself or herself with others in order to reach a relatively objective or judicious appraisal of his or her attitudes, behaviours, abilities, or the like.

There are many bases upon which a person may choose his or her reference groups. Among the most frequently cited are the similarity between the individual and members of a group; the frequency of interaction with members of a group, and the desirable characteristics of a group, such as prestige, the display of acts of bravery, courage, achievement, and the like.

Referent power: Social power that arises when the person who is being influenced identifies with the influencing agent, perceives some communality or wants to form a unit with him. (Example: Adolescents often look to their peers in deciding what type of clothes to wear; a young man may adopt the hairstyle of his favourite sports hero).

Reflex act: An unlearned automatic, muscular response to a stimulus.

Refractory phase: The period of temporary inactivity in a neuron after it has fired once.

Registration: This term refers to the receptive processing in which information is processed but not perceived. *See also perception, subliminal perception.*

Regression: A defense mechanism that involves an escape from stress or threat but reverting to more primitive or infantile behaviours and solutions. See also *retrogression.*

Rehearsal: The process of recycling information in short-term memory. The process facilitates the short-term recall of information and its transfer to long-term memory. See *also dual-memory theory.*

Reincarnation: The belief in rebirth; i.e. that a person has lived before.

Reinforcement: (1) In classical conditioning, the experimental procedure of following the conditioned stimulus by the unconditioned stimulus. (2) In operant conditioning, the analogous procedure of following the occurrence of the operant response by the reinforcing stimulus. (3) The process that increases the strength of conditioning as a result of these arrangements. See *also classical conditioning, extinction, negative reinforcement, operant conditioning, partial reinforcement, positive reinforcement.*

Reinforcing stimulus: (1) In classical conditioning, the unconditioned stimulus. (2) In operant conditioning, the stimulus that reinforces the operant (typically, a reward (syn. reinforcer). *See also negative reinforcer, positive reinforcer.*

Reinforcement hypothesis: A hypothesis derived from teaming theory stating that individuals tend to repeat any behaviour that has been rewarded and avoid any behaviour that has been punished.

Reinforcement schedule: A well-defined procedure for reinforcing a given response only some proportion of the time it occurs. *See also partial reinforcement.*

Reinforcement theory: A theory that emphasizes that behaviour is determined by the rewards or punishments given in response to it.

Relationship statement: Statements that specify how objects and events regularly vary together or else that indicate how changes in one object or event accompany, precede, or follow changes in another object or event.

Releaser: A term used by ethologists for a stimulus that sets off a cycle of instinctive behaviour. *See also ethologist, instinct.*

Relative deprivation: One's perceived state in relation to the perceived stale of others or in relation to unfulfilled expectations.

Re-learning: A measure of retention based on the difference between the original learning and the re-learning time.

Reliability: (1) The self-consistency of a test as a measuring instrument. Reliability is measured by a coefficient of correlation between scores on two halves of a test, alternate forms of the test, or retests with the same test; a high correlation signifies high consistency of scores for the population tested. (2) Consistency of measurement. Stability of scores over time. equivalence of scows on two forms of a test, and similarity of two raters scoring of the same behaviour are examples of three different kinds of reliability. *See also validity.*

Representativeness: Similarity of a sample to the population from which it is drawn – an essential characteristic of scientific sampling.

Representative sample: A small group of individuate selected so that they represent all relevant characteristics of the population being studied.

Repression: (1) A defence mechanism in which an impulse or memory that might provoke feelings of guilt is denied, and 'shoved away' from awareness and pushed into the unconscious part of personality. (2) A theory of forgetting. *See also defense mechanism, suppression.*

Reproduction: The form of memory in which accurate copies or quotations can be made.

Research methods: These comprise the various standard, objective, and replicable scientific procedures and techniques which psychologists and other scientists use for collecting, processing, collating, and presenting empirical data for use in scientific analysis. There are *eight* major scientific research methods that are commonly used in modern psychology, as follows: (1) archival, (2) survey, (3) field study, (4) natural experiment, (5) quasi-experiment, (6) field-experiment, (7) simulation and (8) laboratory experiment research methods.

Resistance: In psychoanalysis, a blocking of free association; a psychological barrier against bringing unconscious impulses to the level of awareness. Resistance is part of the process of maintaining repression. See *also interpretation, repression.*

Resistance to change: Any innovation or departure from the prevailing practice or belief will induce strong resistance. Generally people will oppose the change either because of inertia or dread of the new or fear of loss of existing privileges, etc.

Resistance to temptation: Suppression of a behaviour that would have a high incidence if it were not for the influence of a prohibition or norm.

Resource: In social power, a property or conditional state of an individual – a possession, an attribute of appearance or personality, a position held, or a certain way of behaving – which enables him or her to modify the rewards and costs experienced by another person.

Respondent behaviour: A type of behaviour corresponding to reflex action, in that it is largely under the control of, and predictable from, a stimulus (syn. elicited behaviour). *See also operant behaviour.*

Respondent conditioning: It is the classical conditioning discovered by Pavlov. An experimental method in which a conditioned stimulus and an unconditioned stimulus are paired. (*See conditioned stimulus: instrumental learning*).

Response: (1) The behavioural result of stimulation in the form of a movement or glandular secretion. (2) Sometimes, any activity of an organism, including central responses (such as an image or fantasy), regardless of whether the stimulus is identified and whether an identifiable movement occurs. (3) Products of an organism's activity, such as word types per minute.

Response evocation: In congruency theory, behaving so as to evoke congruent responses from other persons.

Response sets: Systematic ways of answering questions that are not directly related to the content of the question but related to the form or the social characteristics of the alternative answers. Common types of response sets are social desirability and acquiescence.

Responsibility: The amount of personal volition involved in a particular set When the cause of an act is seen as external, the individual is seen as having minimal responsibility for it. When the cause of the act is seen as internal, the actor is seen as having responsibility for the act.

Resting potential: The electrical potential across the nerve cell membrane when it is in its resting state (i.e., not responding to other neurons), the inside of the cell membrane is slightly more negative than die outside. *See also action potential.*

Reticular system: A system of ill-defined nerve paths and connections within the brain stem, lying outside the well-defined nerve pathways, and important as an arousal mechanism.

Retina: The light-sensitive, back layer of the eye, on which images of objects are projected. It contains two kinds of receiving cells, namely, rods and cones.

Retinal image: The image projected onto the retina by an object in the visual field.

Retinal size: The size of the retinal image of an object; retinal size decreases in direct proportion to the object's distance See also *object size.*

Retroactive inhibition: The interference by later learning in earlier learning.

Retroactive interference: The interference in recall of something earlier learned by something subsequently learned. See also *proactive interference.*

Retrograde amnesia: The inability to recall events that occurred during a period of time immediately prior to a shock or functional disturbance, although the memory for earlier events remains relatively unimpaired. *See also anterograde amnesia.*

Retrogression: A retreat by a person of a certain age level to an adjustive mechanism more appropriate to a lower age level called 'regression' by psychoanalysis

Revolution: A sudden, sweeping change in societal structure, generally associated with large-scale violence.

Reward: (1) A synonym for positive reinforcement. (2) In exchange theory, any activity by an individual that contributes to the gratification of another person's needs.

Reward power: Social power that comes from the influencing agent's ability to mediate rewards or benefits for the person who is being influenced (the target person), and where it is clear that the agent will reward the person only if he complies with the request. Impersonal reward power refers to a reward of some impersonal commodity such as money, a good grade in a course, a recommendation for promotion; personal reward power uses approval, love, and acceptance as commodities.

Ribonucleic acid (RNA): Complex molecules that control cellular functions; theorized by some to be the chemical mediator of memory.

Right hemisphere: The right cerebral hemisphere. Control the left side of the body and, for most people, spatial and patterned activities (syn. minor hemisphere). *See also cerebral hemisphere, corpus callosum, left hemisphere, split-brain subject.*

Risky shift: The tendency for people in groups, under certain circumstances, to make more risky and les, conservative decisions than they would as lone individuals. When it occurs, the risky shift may be an instance of a *runaway norm. See also runaway norm.*

Rites of passage: The ceremonial recognition given to important status passages (movements from one role category to another).

Role: A pattern of behaviour that characterizes and is expected of a person who occupies a certain position in a group or social organization. (Example: The behaviours expected of a person who is identified as a father, mother, man, woman, teacher, student, and so forth). *See also social role.*

Role bargaining: Same as *role negotiation.* See role negotiation.

Role behaviours: The acts of a person in a role category that are relevant to expectations for that role.

Rote category: A grouping of persons whose behaviour is subject to similar expectations.

Role conflict: The situation that arises when a person simultaneously occupies two roles that have conflicting demands. (Example: A woman who is married and has young children may experience a role conflict if she also has a job as a travelling sales person – the demands of these two roles are not complementary).

Role confusion: A stage of development said by Erikson to characterize many adolescents (and others) in which various identifications have not been harmonized and integrated See *also identification, identity formation.*

Role differentiation: The development and assumption by group members of specialized functions.

Role expectation: The expected behaviour of a person occupying a particular position in a group with a specific function.

Role identity: The views that individuals have of themselves as actors in a particular position

Role learning: Learning to behave, feel, and see the world in s manner similar to that of other persons who are in the same role category.

Role negotiation: (Also known as *role bargaining*). This is the process by which an actor and his or her role partners work out to their mutual satisfaction how each will behave in particular encounters and situations, and decide on what the genera) character of their relationship will be. Usually this process is less explicit and more subtle and indirect than ordinary negotiation; the partners may be unaware that they are negotiating.

Role obligations: The behaviours expected of role partners because of the positions they occupy in relation to each other. *(See also role fights, which are the complements of role obligations.)*

Role partner: An actor occupying a role category which specifies particular behaviours towards actors in related role categories.

Role player: An individual in a role category or position. (Also referred to as an actor.)

Role playing: A method for teaching attitudes and behaviours important to interpersonal relations by having the subject assume a part in a spontaneous play, whether in psychotherapy or in leadership training. *See also psychodrama.*

Role rights: Privileges expected of role partners because of the positions they occupy in relation to each other. *(See also role obligations, which are the complements of role rights.)*

Role strains: The difficulties in attempting to enact a role.

Romantic Love: A relationship between two persons based on personal preference and intense social-psychological identification and involvement. Romantic lovers tend to see only the best traits in one another, to be physically and emotionally attracted to one another, and to evaluate one another uncritically. Thus, the components of romantic love are idealization, physical attraction, and sympathetic understanding. As a widespread phenomenon, romantic love is said to have begun in the Middle Ages.

Rorschach test: A projective test of personality in which the subject is asked to tell what he 'sees' in each one often ink-blots.

Rumour: Communicating rapidly unverified assertions and statements about people and events.

Runsway norm: A social norm in which the desired level of behaviour, altitude, or performance exceeds that of the group as a whole, The risky shift phenomenon may be a special instance of a runaway norm.

Role Learning: The kind of learning in which what is to be learned is essentially meaningless in and of itself, and where much repetition is required to accomplish mastery of the learning process.

S

Saccule: *See vestibular sacs.*

Sadism: A pathological motive that leads to inflicting pain on another person. *See also masochism.*

Safety needs: According to Abraham Maslow, these are the needs that are centred around the human requirement for an orderly and predictable world. They include the needs for stability and security.

Sample: A small group of individuals selected by a researcher from a population and measured on some variable in order to infer characteristics of the population. If selection is random, an unbiased sample results; if selection is nonrandom, the sample is biased and unrepresentative. See *also population.*

Sampling: The process by which a subset from a large population is obtained to serve as a basis for inferring certain characteristics of the population as a whole.

Sampling errors: (1) The variation in a distribution of scores, or of statistics derived from them to be attributed to the fact that measurements are made on a variable sample from a larger population. Thus sampling errors persist even though all measurements are accurate. See also sample. (2) The inevitable margin of error in estimating the characteristics of a population from a data on the characteristics of sample.

Sample survey: This term refers to the scientific research method in which the investigator defines a group, or "population", of interest (e.g. university students, senior civil servants, single girls or women, etc), then selects a sample from the population and collects some data for each subject in the sample (e.g. attitude towards free education, official working hours, the use of the female private part for drug and currency trafficking, etc) in order to describe the population.

Sanctions: Rewards for conforming to social norms or punishments for not conforming.

Sanguine: Cheerful. One of Galen's four temperaments.

Satori: This term refers to a sort of unique experience which is purported by students of Zen philosophy to be beyond conventional experience, and in which conventional categories of perception are useless.

Saturation: The dimension of colour that describes its purity; if highly saturated it appears to be pure hue and free of gray but if of low saturation it appears to have a great deal of gray mixed with it. *See also brightness, hue.*

Scaling: Converting raw data into types of scores more readily interpreted; e.g., into ranks, centiles, standard scores.

Scapegoat: A form of displaced aggression in which an innocent but helpless victim is blamed or punished as the source of the scapegoater's frustration. *See also displaced aggression.*

Scapgoating: The displacement of hostility upon less powerful groups or individuals when the source of frustration is not available for attack or not attackable for other reasons.

Schema (pi. schemata): A hypothetical structure stored in memory that preserves and organizes information about some event or concept. *See also cognitive map.*

Schizoid: Having some characteristics that resemble schizophrenia but are less severe. Occurs with higher frequency in families of schizophrenics and thus tends to support a genetic basis for schizophrenia. *See also schizophrenia.*

Schizophrenia: A functional psychotic disorder in which there is a lack of harmony or split between aspects of personality functioning, especially between emotion and behaviour. Symptoms may include autism, hallucinations, and delusions. *See also paranoid schizophrenia, psychosis.*

School psychologist: A professional psychologist employed by a school or school system, with responsibility for testing, guidance, research, etc. *See also educational psychologist.*

Scientific laws: Hypotheses that are confirmed by repeated research.

Secondary deviance: A term used to refer to the proposition that so-called "deviants" in society may be mal-adjusted as a result of the way society treats people in their condition, rather than as a result of the condition itself.

Secondary deviation: The social processes that bring about changes in individuals and in their relationships with others as a consequence of their having initially been defined as deviant.

Secondary environment: A place where a person spends little time, relates to others on an impersonal basis, and performs relatively unimportant activities (Stokols, 1974).

Secondary motives: The motives which arise as a result of experience, social pressure and aspiration. They are based on the primary drives. See *also primary drives.*

Secondary process thinking: In psychoanalytic theory, the form of Thinking used by the ego, characterized by realistic and logical attempts to satisfy needs. See *also ego, primary process thinking*.

Secondary reinforcer: A reinforcer which has derived its reinforcing properties from being associated with one or more primary reinforcers – e.g. in experiments monkeys have teamed to work for poker chips which could later be exchanged for food. The poker chips were the secondary reinforcers which could be exchanged for the primary reinforcer of food.

Secondary sex characteristics: The physical features distinguishing the mature male from the mature female, apart from the reproductive organs. In humans, the deeper voice of the male and the growth of the beard are illustrative. *See also primary sex characteristics.*

Secondary territory: A physical area often claimed by a person or group, even though it is recognized that others may occupy that area at times.

Self-actualization: According to Abraham Maslow, this is the highest of man's needs. It consists of developing one's own true self and fulfilling one's potentialities.

Self-appointed mindguards: Members of a group who take it upon themselves to urge conformity on any member who deviates. According to Irving Janis, self-appointed mindguards are especially likely to contribute to the groupthink process.

Selective avoidance: A process by which individuals refrain from exposing themselves to communications that are dissonant with their attitudes.

Selective breeding: A method of studying genetic influences by mating animals that display certain traits and selecting for breeding from among their offspring those that express the trait. If the trait is primarily determined by heredity, continued selection for a number of generations will produce a strain that breeds true for that trait.

Selective evaluation: A process in which individuals maximize congruency or minimize incongruency by altering their estimation of self, behaviour, or the other person in a positive or negative direction.

Selective exposure: The process by which individuals choose to notice communications that are consonant with their attitudes and choose not to notice communication that are dissonant with them.

Selective interaction: A process in which individuals choose to be involved with those persons who behave congruently towards them and avoid involvement with those who behave incongruently towards them.

Self: See *self-concept.*

Self-awareness: The state of being an observer of the self as actor.

Self-commitment: Making a judgement or decision in a manner that makes one feel obligated to carry out the act.

Self-concept: The subjective and reflective representation in consciousness of an individual to himself, including his thoughts, impulses and actions. The individual as he sees himself. The nature of the self helps to determine the organization of the individual's wants and goals; the defence of the self may become one of his major concerns.

Self-consciousness: A form of heightened self-awareness when an individual is especially concerned about reactions of others to him or her.

Self-disclosure: The process of revealing oneself to others fully and honestly.

Self-enhancement, need for: The idea that individuals have an urge to behave so as to receive positive evaluations from others and to evaluate themselves positively.

Self-esteem: A pension's assessment of his own value, competence, or adequacy.

Self-estrangement: In alienation, a lack of intrinsic satisfaction in one's activities.

Self-fulfilling prophecy: Descriptive of a process in which a person's belief about what he expects to happen can cause him to act in such a way as to create the conditions by which his expectations may come about.

Self-image: The way in which an individual perceives himself or herself.

Self-perception: An individual's awareness of him or herself; it differs from self-consciousness, because it may take the form of objective self-appraisal. See *also self-consciousness*.

Self -perception theory: An extension of attribution theory, advanced by Daryl Bem, stating that individuals make inferences about their own beliefs and attitudes by observing their own behaviour and the context in which it occurs. Bem suggests that self-attribution analysis may explain dissonance reduction in a forced compliance situation.

Self-persuasion: The process by which individuals opinions change so that they are consistent with their behaviour.

Self-presentation: Acting so as to guide and control the impressions that other persons form of oneself.

Self-regulation: In behaviour therapy, monitoring one's own behaviour and using techniques such as self-reinforcement or controlling stimulus conditions to modify maladaptive behaviour. *See also behaviour therapy.*

Semantic concepts: Concepts with one-word names that refer to things that occur frequently and thus allow us to think and communicate efficiently. Used as one major category of long-term memory coding. *See also concept.*

Semantic conditioning: A form of classical conditioning in which semantic concepts are used as the conditioned stimuli and generalization occurs through semantic similarities.

Semantic differential: A method for using rating scales and factor analysis in studying the connotative meanings of words. *See also connotative meaning, denotative meaning.*

Semantic differential scale: A scale developed by Osgood, based on the finding that people describe most personality traits along three dimensions: evaluative (good – bad), potency (strong – weak), and activity (active – passive).

Semantic Differential Technique: The technique of measuring the subjective meaning of words developed by Osgood. Any word or concept may be located on three dimensions: evaluation (good - bad), potency (strong – weak) and activity (active – passive)

Semicircular canals: Three curved tubular canals, in three planes, which form part of the labyrinth of the inner ear and are concerned with equilibrium and motion. *See also equilibratory senses.*

Senile dementia: An organic psychosis caused by the degeneration and disappearance of nerve cells in the brains of old people.

Sensation: The relationship between physical stimuli such as light and sound waves and the effects on sense organs such as eyes and ears. *See also absolute threshold; hearing; psycho-physics; vision.*

Sense organ: A specialized part of the body, selectively sensitive to some types of change in its environment but not to others. For example, the eye.

Sensitivity group: *See encounter group.*

Sensitivity training: A method by which normal persons gain feedback about their inter-personal skills and their effectiveness in groups.

Sensorimotor stage: Piaget's first stage of cognitive development (birth – 2 years) during which the infant discovers relationships between sensations and motor behaviour. *See also object permanence.*

Sensory adaptation: The reduction in sensitivity that occurs with prolonged stimulation and the increase in sensitivity that occurs with lack of stimulation, most noted in vision, smell, taste, and temperature sensitivity. *See also dark adaptation, light adaptation.*

Separation: A situation in which a husband and wife live apart, generally as a prelude to divorce. Under separation the couple remain legally man and wife, and they cannot marry other people until a divorce is finalised. In a voluntary separation both parties agree to live apart without litigation; a separation agreement can be blown up by the couple's lawyers, but the husband cannot be jailed for violation of payment of agreement. In a legal separation one spouse brings litigation against the other. The innocent party is awarded support, and violations of the support payments can result in a jail sentence.

Septal area: A portion of the brain deep in the central part between the lateral ventricles, that when stimulated electrically (in the rat, at least) appears to yield a state akin to pleasure.

Serial memory search: Comparing a test stimulus in sequence to each item in short-term memory. See *also short-term memory.*

Serial processing: A theoretical interpretation of information processing in which several sources of information are processed in a serial order; only one source being attended to at a time. See also *parallel processing.*

Serotonin: A neurotransmitter found in the midbrain and believed to play a role in psychosis, particularly in depression. See *also neurotransmitter.*

Set: A temporary but often recurrent state of an organism which orients it towards certain stimuli in a selective way. Thus the set makes for the readiness of the organism to make a certain response.

Sexism: A discriminative attitude that implies that the male is superior to the female and has certain sexual rights (that vary from one culture to another) that the female does not have. In addition, this prejudice also implies that as children, women, are likewise in need of guidance and protection by men.

Sex-linkage: The association of certain physical trait with the mate or female sex of a person. For instance, colour blindness.

Sex-linked trait: A trait determined by a gene transmitted on the same chromosomes that determine sex; e.g., red-green colour blindness. *See also X, Y chromosome.*

Sex-role socialization: The process by which an individual learns the roles that society has defined as appropriate for men and for women and adopts those behaviours that are consistent with his or her own gender.

Sex-role standards: The behaviours that a society considers appropriate for the individual because of his or her sex.

Sex Therapy: Treatment for sexual dysfunction in marriage. The methods used for the treatment vary significantly according to the professional training and expertise of the therapist. Some of the well established and widely used methods include the one developed by the two Americans, Doctors William H. Masters and Virginia Johnson, reported in their books *Human Sexual Response* (1966), and *Human Sexual Inadequacy* (1971). In a two-week-long treatment session Masters and Johnson concentrate on treating a couple's marriage rather than their psychological problems. Through a series of lengthy discussions between the couple and the therapists, the therapists gain enough Information to plan an adequate system of treatment. The treatment centres on removing the couple's libido – depressing and confidence – depressing anxieties in the belief that sexual function is never actually destroyed completely. Operant conditioning and desensitizing exercises are prescribed for the couple and are carried out in privacy. The Masters and Johnson Reproductive Biology Research Foundation in St. Louis, U.S.A., claims an 82 per cent success rate in treating sexual problems. Sex therapy teams trained at their foundation are now practising at various locations throughout the United States and other countries. *See also* Marriage Counselling.

Sex-typed: Referring to actions that are consistent with a society's norms regarding male and female behaviours.

Shading of behaviour: Modifying operant behaviour by reinforcing only those variations in response that deviate in a direction desired by the experimenter; the whole population of responses thus reinforced then drifts in the desired direction (Skinner) (syn. method of approximations).

Shape constancy: The tendency to see a familiar object as of the same shape regardless of the viewing angle. *See also object constancy.*

Shock: An extreme degree of emotion in which the agitated person is incoherent and behaves either deliriously or stuporously.

Shock therapy: A form of treatment of mental illness, especially in the relief of depression. See *also electroshock therapy, insulin shock.*

Short-term memory (STM): The assumption that certain components of the memory system have limited capacity and will maintain information for only a brief period of time. The definition varies somewhat from theory to theory. See *also long-term memory.*

Sibling: One of one's brothers or sisters.

Sibling rivalry: Jealousy between siblings, often based on their competition for parental affection.

Signal detectability theory; A theory of the sensory and decision processes involved in psychophysical judgments, with special reference to the problem of detecting weak signals in noise. *See also signal detecting task.*

Signal detection task: A procedure whereby the subject must judge on each trial whether or not a weak signal was emboddied in a noise background. Saying "yes" when the signal was presented is called a hit and saying "yes" when the signal was not presented is called a false alarm. *See also receiver-operating-characteristic curve.*

Significance (statistical): The statistical probability (p) that a given numerical finding could have occurred by chance alone; the lower the probability of chance occurrence, the greater the significance of the finding.

Significant Others: This concept refers to those other people who are most important for an individual in determining his attitudes, beliefs and behaviours. Most people value the opinion of certain people above those of others and use those opinions to shape their behaviours. At a party the perceived opinion of an admired member of the opposite sex may have special importance; at work, the opinion of an employer or respected senior colleague may be taken with special seriousness.

Significant others may determine an individual's behaviour by example, indirect statement or direct advice. Most typically, they exert their influence through what the individual believes they are thinking, or would think about his behaviour. His or her projection of what he or she believes their judgement would be, guides his or her actions.

The American behavioural scientist Erving Goffman has argued that the term "significant others" is perhaps misleading In that most behavioural scientists use it to imply that a restricted group (e.g, the family) has special influence in shaping a person's behaviour. Goffman's point is that everyone with whom an individual comes into any contact influences him or her to some extent.

Until more is learned about exactly what shapes behaviour, the notion of significant others should be used with considerable care. Like other concepts, it can become a bit of naive jargon that blinds analysts from more fundamental determinants of social action.

Silent speech: The inaudible movements of the larynx during silent reading.

Similarity hypothesis: The hypothesis that two or more persons will tend to be attracted to each other to the extent that they have similar traits, needs and other characteristics. See *also complementarity hypothesis.*

Single-blind control: A control procedure in which the subjects are uninformed about the real purpose of the study or which treatment group they are in.

Size constancy: The tendency for objects to be seen as their correct size regardless of their distance or the size of the retinal image. *See also object constancy.*

Simple cell: A cell in the visual cortex that responds to a bar of light or straight edge of a particular orientation and location in the visual field. See *also complex cell.*

Simple differentiating item: In the description of persons, a level of descriptions that refers to the individuals described but does not provide much information about them as people. Simple differentiating items, behaviour items denoting specific acts but implying a disposition or trait, global dispositions or categories, expressions of liking or disliking, and role category items.

Simulation: The creation in an experimental laboratory of a social situation that is analogous in its basic elements (though not necessarily in specifics) to a situation in the real world. Behavioural and social scientists have attempted to simulate prisons, international conflict, urban communities, factories, and other social organizations. Simulation is often achieved by means of programmed social interaction using computers or assistants.

Simultaneous conditioning: A classical conditioning procedure in which the CS begins a fraction of a second before the onset of the US and continues with it until the response occurs. See *also delayed conditioning, trace conditioning.*

Situated identities, theory of: A theory proposing that for each social situation, there is a certain pattern of behaviour that conveys an identity that is appropriate for that setting.

Situational attribution: Attributing a person's actions to factors in the situation or environment, as opposed to internal attitudes and motives. See *also dispositional attribution.*

Situational demands: The expectations imposed upon an actor by the nature of the circumstances. These include not only role expectations, but also any special features of the situation that generate expectations.

Situational personality characteristics: The traits of an individual which are temporary or which occur only under certain conditions (e.g., anxiety about failing at the time of taking a test). Often such characteristics are created experimentally to determine their effects on individuals in combination with other conditions.

Skewed distribution: In statistics, a frequency distribution that is not symmetrical. It is named for the direction in which the tail lies; e.g., if there are many small incomes and a few large ones, the distribution is skewed in the direction of the large incomes. *See also frequency distribution, symmetrical distribution.*

Skinner box: A chamber for animals used to study operant conditioning.

Steeper effect: (1) A positive influence exerted by a communication that is designed to change an attitude or opinion, but whose effect cannot be seen immediately. (Example: A man is given a very persuasive sales message from an encyclopaedia salesman, who argues for the advantages of having a good encyclopaedia at home. The man refuses to place an order. He is not going to be taken in by a slick sales pitch from someone who simply wants to earn money from him. Sometime later, however, the man sees an encyclopaedia on sale in a store and decides to purchase it. It is possible that the sleeper effect was due to the negative dependent influence of the salesman (the man's rejection of the communication), which was dissipated over time, while the positive influence of the content of the communication (which was socially independent) was more stable. (2) The phenomenon in which the negative source of a message is forgotten over time but the actual message is remembered.

Small family norm: With the improvement in standard of living in the industrial society the aim of each family will be to have only two or three children. This new norm is set up because of the decrease in mortality rate and the increase in the standard and cost of living.

Small group: Groups with a small number of members so that each one can make a critical difference to the group.

Smooth muscle: The type of muscle found in the digestive organs, blood vessels, and other internal organs. Controlled via the autonomic nervous system. See also *cardiac muscle, striate muscle*

Social accommodation: A normative process consisting of conforming behaviour resulting from a desire to maintain positive relations with liked people.

Social change: Variations or modifications in any aspect of social process, pattern or form. Sometimes social change is deliberately initiated by some individuals or groups. This involves learning the new and unlearning the old. Hence the resistance for social change. *See also resistance to change.*

Social class: A grouping of persons who share common values, interests, income level, and educational level.

Social comparison: (1) The process of evaluating one's inputs and outcomes in relation to those obtained by other persons in order to see whether they are equitable. (2) The general process by which an individual evaluates his own opinions, attitudes, beliefs, emotions, or behaviours by referring to those of others. Festinger developed a social comparison theory for the purpose of studying group effects on opinions and abilities; the theory was later extended to emotions.

Social-comparison theory: A theory, developed by Festinger, that proposes that we use other people as sources for comparison, so that we can evaluate our own attitudes and abilities.

Social contagion: The spread of a behaviour, attitude, or emotional state among the members of a group or social organization in a manner resembling the spread of a contagious disease.

Social development: Initiating changes in the society so that there is improvement in the living conditions and the well-being of the members of the society. Definite goals are set up.

Social density: The number of persons in an area, which determines the amount of space per person and the potential number of interaction partners.

Social-desirability bias: A response set to answer questions about oneself in the socially approved manner.

Social distance: A person's acceptable degree of closeness (physically, socially, or psychologically) in regard to members of an ethnic, racial, or religious group.

Social distance scale: The scale developed by Bogardus to measure the reserve or constraint in social interaction, between individuals belonging to different groups.

Social-emotional leader: An individual who helps to boost group morale and to release tension when things are difficult.

Social exchange theory: A theory that analyzes interpersonal and group interaction in terms of interdependence. The process of interaction is examined according to the individual's inputs (or costs) and the rewards and/or punishments he anticipates and receives in the social relationship.

Social facilitation: The process by which a person works faster and turns out more when he is working with others than when he is working alone. The sight and sound of others doing the same thing increases the output of each person.

Social heritage: The body of social customs, folkways, thoughtways (or ideologies) and culture achievements which have been received by social transmission from previous generations.

Social indicator: A statistic of direct normative interest, which facilitates concise, comprehensive, and balanced judgments about the condition or major aspects of a society.

Social influence: A change in one person – in his beliefs, attitudes, behaviour, emotions, and so forth – that is due to the behaviour, or simply the presence of another person.

Social influence: An hypothesized cause of the bystander effect; a process by which a person in a group is less likely than a person who is alone to interpret an event as a situation calling for helping behaviour.

Social inhibition: A decrease in the activity or productivity of one person that can be attributed to the actions of one or more other persons who are performing a parallel activity. See *also social facilitation.*

Socialization: The social process in which socialization agents (parents, peer-groups, schools, occupational organizations, mass media, etc) teach the expected and required social attitudes and behavioural patterns to children and strangers, who in turn learn and acquire their own distinctive attitudes and behavioural orientations, that enable them to adapt adequately to their society.

Figure 18: The major components in the socialization framework

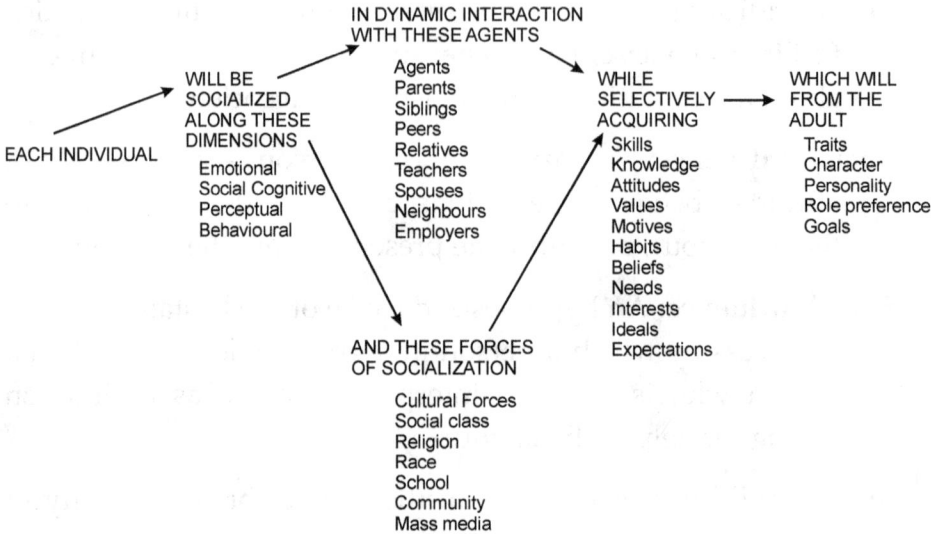

IN DYNAMIC INTERACTION
WITH THESE AGENTS

EACH INDIVIDUAL

WILL BE
SOCIALIZED
ALONG THESE
DIMENSIONS
Emotional
Social Cognitive
Perceptual
Behavioural

Agents
Parents
Siblings
Peers
Relatives
Teachers
Spouses
Neighbours
Employers

WHILE
SELECTIVELY
ACQUIRING
Skills
Knowledge
Attitudes
Values
Motives
Habits
Beliefs
Needs
Interests
Ideals
Expectations

WHICH WILL
FROM THE
ADULT
Traits
Character
Personality
Role preference
Goals

AND THESE FORCES
OF SOCIALIZATION

Cultural Forces
Social class
Religion
Race
School
Community
Mass media

Source: Severy et al (1976), page 144.

Table 15: Two modes of socialization.

Repressive socialization	Participatory socialization
Punishing wrong behaviour	Rewarding good behaviour
Material rewards and punishments	Symbolic rewards and punishments
Obedience of child	Autonomy of child
Nonverbal communication	Verbal communication
Communication as command	Communication as interaction
Parent-centered socialization	Child-centered socialization
Child's discernment of parent's wishes	Parent's discernment of child's needs
Family as significant other	Family as generalized other

Source: L. Broom and P. Selznick (1973), page 100.

Socially dependent influence: Social influence in which the person who has changed continues to relate his new behaviour, belief, or attitude to the influencing agent. This is the opposite of socially independent influence. (Example: A doctor who wishes his patient to give up smoking can rely on his expertise – "You'll have to take my word for it, since I have studied these things and know what is best for you". The patient who accepts the influence continues to relate it to the doctor – "I stopped smoking, but only because my doctor asked me to do so".

Social independent influence: Socially influence in which the person who has changed stops relating his new behaviour, belief, or attitude to the influencing agent. This is the opposite of socially dependent influence. (Example: If a mathematics teacher explains the logic behind solving a problem in a particular manner and the student understands the explanation, then the influenced change will no longer be socially dependent upon the teacher. It will, however, depend upon other cognitions – the student's previous knowledge about mathematics and its logic, his under-standing of the symbols used and the concepts involved, and so forth).

Social learning: The process by which a person learns social roles, self-concept, etc. Such learning takes place through processes such as imitation, identification, etc.

Social learning theory: A theory that proposes that learning is not only by reinforcement but by observation, imitation, and modeling. An individual can learn a new response by watching it being performed by another person.

Social motive: A set of behaviours that have a common goal as their object.

Social motivation: The motivations that are learned in the process of growing up and living in a society.

Social movement: The occasional concerted efforts which the members of any social group make to change or maintain any aspect of society.

Social norm: An expectation shared by group members which specifies behaviour that is considered appropriate for a given situation.

Social norms: A group or community's unwritten rules that govern its members' behaviours, attitudes, and beliefs.

Social organization: The organization of a society into sub-groups. In modem societies these sub-groups are based on age, sex, occupations, residence, property, etc. The Indian social organization includes in addition to the above sub-groups based on caste, creed and language.

Social perception: The perception of social objects, qualities, relations or events.

Social power: Potential social influence. The ability of one person or group to influence another. French and Raven have listed six major bases of social power: coercion, reward, legitimacy, expertise, reference, and information.

Social pressures: Coercion on the part of a group to make individuals conform to the standards of the group.

Social psychologist: A psychologist who studies social interaction and the ways in which individuals influence one another.

Social psychology: A discipline that attempts to understand, explain, and predict how the thoughts, feelings, and actions of individuals are influenced by the perceived, imagined, or implied thoughts, feelings, and actions of others.

Social reality: Perception of the attitudes and opinions of other people as a major resource for checking opinions or beliefs. (Contrast with physical reality).

Social reality: A belief about to be true. A need for social reality will produce pressures towards uniformity in a group, especially when it is not possible to check physical reality. (Example: If I am not sure why the price of oil has gone up, I may look to my associates to see what explanation they accept).

Social-responsibility norm: A norm or standard of behaviour that dictates that people should help persons who are dependent or in need of help.

Social role: A social role consists of a category of persons and the expectations for their behaviour. (Also referred to as role).

Social science: A general term for all the sciences which are concerned with human affairs – history, economics, government, law, education, psychology, sociology and anthropology. The last three are called Behaviour Sciences since they collect their facts on the basis of the observation of actual behaviour of human beings in contrast to the other social sciences which depend on documents, etc.

Social status: A situation in which relationships with other persons are involved.

Social structure: The network of relationships among individuals and groups in a society.

Social structure, group: The pattern of relationships that various members of a group establish with one another. Among the most prominent dimensions of social structure are: evaluation (or sociometric), interdependence, influence, status, role, and communication (or communication network). Social structure may be sub-divided into formal and informal structure.

Social system: A set of interlocking social roles (e.g., the roles in a family).

Social tensions: An emotional state resulting from conflict between groups over a considerable period of time; violent clashes between groups arise when there are social tensions.

Socio-emotional group: A group whose members view the purpose of the group as satisfying certain social and emotional needs (for example, friendship, prestige, self-understanding), rather than as accomplishing some task (as in a task-oriented group).

Socio-emotional specialist: A particular group role, whose occupant assumes responsibility for maintaining harmony and good feelings in the group, thereby reducing interpersonal conflict. (This observation was made by Bales). This is the opposite of a task specialist.

Sociofugal space: An arrangement of space that keeps people apart.

Sociology: (1) The behavioural or social science which deals with group life and social organization in literate societies. See *also behaviour sciences.* (2) The scientific study of the structure and functions of social groups, organizations, and institutions. (3) The science of the nature, origin, and development of human social groups and community life.

Sociometric analysis: An analysis of a group's sociometric structure in terms of the pattern of interpersonal attraction and rejection among its members. This is typically carried out by means of a sociometric questionnaire, in which each member is asked to indicate whom he likes and whom he dislikes in the group. This analysis may be done informally by observing the members' likes and dislikes or by examining other indications of socio-metric choice.

Sociometric method: An index of group cohesiveness that requires each member of the group to indicate the names of individuals he likes to participate with him in some activity. This technique was developed by Moreno.

Sociometric structure (or evaluative structure; effective structure): The pattern of inter-personal attraction and rejection among the members of a group.

Sociometry: (1) A measure of group cohesion developed by American social psychologist Jacob L. Moreno. Each individual indicates which members of the group he likes best. By comparing the frequencies, it is possible to construct a sociogram, a diagram that shows one form of group structure.   (2) A method of studying structures based on affection or attraction. The basic data collected consist of choices of the most preferred (and sometimes the (east preferred) members of the group made, by each individual member. The choices are then tallied and patterns discernable in them are identified.

Sociopetal space: An arrangement of space that brings people together.

Somatic nerves: The nerves that carry information from the sense organs to the CNS, and from the CNS to muscles that control body movements.

Somatic nervous system: A division of the peripheral nervous system consisting of nerves that connect the brain and spinal cord with the sen receptors, muscles, and body surface. *See also autonomic nervous system, peripheral nervous system.*

Figure 19: Three sociometric patterns

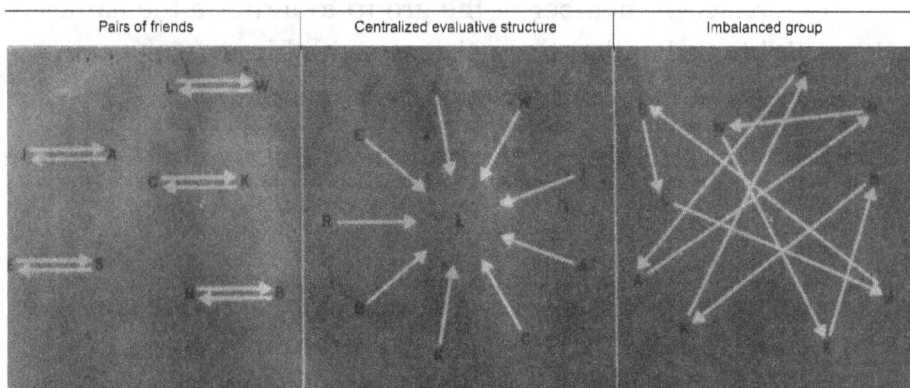

Pairs of friends	Centralized evaluative structure	Imbalanced group

Source: Raven Rubin (1976), page 253.

Somatosensory area: An area in the parietal lobe of the brain that registers Sensory experiences, such as heat, cold, touch, and pain. Also called body-sense area. *See also* motor *area.*

Somnambulism: A dissociation in which the individual tries to carry out in his sleep acts which he unconsciously desires. Also called 'sleep-walking'.

Spatial density; In research on crowding, the effect of variation in the size of a room with a constant-sized group.

Special factor(s): A specialized ability underlying test scores, especially in tests of intelligence; e.g., a special ability in mathematics, as distinct from general intelligence. *See also factor analysis, general factor.*

Specific hunger: Hunger for a specific food incentive, such as a craving for sweets. See *also hunger drive.*

Specimen record: A relatively complete, nonselective, sequential, narrative description of an individual's behaviour, usually over a period of several hours.

Spindle: An EEG characteristic of stage-2 sleep, consisting of short, bursts of rhythmical responses of 13-16 Hz; slightly higher than alpha. See *also electroencephalogram.*

Split-brain subject: A person who has had an operation that served the corpus callosum, thus separating the functions of the two cerebral hemispheres. *See also cerebral hemispheres, corpus callosum.*

Spontaneous recovery: The return of a response after extinction trials to almost full strength without further reinforcement.

Spontaneous remission: Recovery from an illness or improvement without treatment.

S-R psychology: *See stimulus-response psychology.*

Stabilized retinal image: The image of an object on the retina when special techniques are used to counteract the minute movements of the eyeball that occur in normal vision. When an image is thus stabilized it quickly disappears, suggesting that the changes in stimulation of retinal cells, provided by the eye movements are necessary for vision.

Stages of development: The developmental periods, usually following a progressive sequence, that appear to represent qualitative changes in either the structure or the function of an organism (e;g. Freud's psychosexual stages, Piaget's cognitive stages).

Standard deviation: The square root of the mean of the squares of the amount by which each case departs from the mean of all the cases (syn. root mean square deviation). *See also measure of variation, standard error, standard score.*

Standard error: The standard deviation of the sampling distribution of a mean and of certain other derived statistics. It can be interpreted is any other standard deviation. See *also standard deviation.*

Standardized test: A test that has been given to a large representative sample of a population so that one subject's scores can be compared to the whole population. *See also Creativity tests; Intelligence tests; Personality assessment.*

Standard score: A score that has been converted to a scale of measurement with a mean of 0 and a standard deviation of 1.0, based on A distribution of scores used in calibration.

State-dependent learning: Learning that occurs during a particular biological state, e.g., while drugged; so that it can only be demonstrated, or is most effective, when the person is put in the same late again.

State of congruency: A condition in which the behaviours of P and 0 imply a definition of self that is consistent with relevant aspects of P's self-concept.

State of egocentrism: The assumption by a child that other persons view events in the same way that he or she does.

State of equity: A condition in which the ratio of inputs and out-comes of individuals is equal to that of the persons with whom they compare themselves.

State of realism: A condition in which children confuse objective and subjective reality (e.g., they think of their dreams as actually occurring).

Statistical inference: A statement about a population or populations based on statistical measures derived from samples. See *also descriptive statistics.*

Statistical methods: Methods dealing with the collection, classification, analysis and interpretation of masses of numerical date.

Statistical significance: The trustworthiness of an obtained statistical measure as a statement about reality; e.g., the probability that the population mean falls within the limits determined from a sample. The expression refers to the reliability of the statistical finding and not to its importance.

Statistical test: A mathematical procedure for determining the significance of a numerical finding – that is, the likelihood that it is a dependable finding that would occur regularly if repeated observations were made under the same conditions. The significance of the finding is stated in terms of a p value.

Status: The social position of an individual, indicating his relative Standing compared to that of others in the same group.

Status congruence: A condition in which all the status attributes of a person rank higher than, equal to, or lower than the corresponding attributes of another person. *(See status).*

Status conversion processes: A series of changes that lead to status congruence. Individuals behave so that other persons will judge them similarly on the various dimensions of status. *(See status)*

Status envy: Jealousy of a person who occupies a powerful and coveted position. Status envy has been proposed as one of the sources of identification with a role.

Status passage: Change from one role category to another during the course of an individual's life.

Status structure: The pattern formed by the statuses of positions in a group. *(See status).*

Statue-symbol: An attribute which initially has no intrinsic value but which through regular association with a particular level of worth comes to be seen as indicative of that level.

Stereoscopic vision: (1) The binocular perception of depth and distance of an object owing to the overlapping fields of the two eyes. (2) The equivalent effect when slightly unlike pictures are presented individually to each eye in a stereoscope. *See also distance cues.*

Stereotype: A preconceived idea about the characteristics of some grouping of people; it is often oversimplified, rigid, and uncomplimentary. Once a person is identified with that group, his own individuality tends to be overlooked, and the characteristics of the group are attributed to him with little qualification. (Example: According to common stereotypes, Igbos are sometimes viewed as ambitious and clannish; blades as athletic and musical; professors as absentminded and impractical).

Stereotyping: A sociocultural phenomenon in which people identify a category of persons, agree in attributing sets of traits or characteristics to the category of persons, and attribute the characteristics to any person belonging to the category.

Steroids: Complex chemical substances, some of which are prominent in the secretions of the adrenal cortex and may be related to some forms of mental illness. *See also adrenal gland.*

Stimulants: Psychoactive drugs that increase arousal. *See also amphetamines, depressants, hallucinogens.*

Stimulus: (pi. stimuli): (1) Some specific physical energy impinging on a receptor sensitive to that kind of energy. (2) Any objectively describable situation or event (whether outside or inside the organism) that is the occasion for an organism's response. *See also response.*

Stimulus generalization: The process in which, after a person learns to make a certain response to a certain stimulus, other similar but previously ineffective stimuli wilt also elicit that response.

Stimulus or target person: The individual who is the object of a persuasive attempt.

Stimulus-response (S-R) psychology: A psychological view that all behaviour is in response to stimuli and that the appropriate tasks of psychological science are those identifying stimuli, the responses correlated with them, and the processes intervening between stimulus and response.

Stratified random sampling: A form of probability sampling that involves dividing the population into several categories (strata) on one or more dimensions (for example, region of the country, rural or urban residence) and then selecting respondents randomly from each category. This is a representative sample because the selection of respondents is random (in contrast to a quota sample, In which it is not).

Stress: Any force which physically and/or psychologically strains the coping mechanisms of an organism.

Striate muscle: Striped muscle; the characteristic muscles controlling the skeleton, as in the arms and legs. Activated by the somatic, as opposed to the autonomic, nervous system. *See also cardiac muscle, smooth muscle.*

Stroboscopic motion: An illusion of motion resulting from the successive presentation of discrete stimulus patterns arranged in a progression corresponding to movement; e.g., motion pictures. *See also phiphenomenon.*

Structural information: Relatively unmodifiable elements, such as physiognomy and body build or type, which are used to make judgments about persons.

Structuralists: A school of psychologists who claimed that complex mental experiences were really 'structures' built up from simple mental states, much as chemical compounds am built up from chemical elements, led by Wilhelm Wundt.

Structured interview: An interview *in* which the interviewer entirely controls the wording and sequence of the questions and the responses are confined to a pre-specified set of answers in a multiple choice format.

Stupor: The condition of extreme depression, in which a patient says and does nothing.

Stuttering: The involuntary repetition of a sound, syllable, or word.

Subconscious: That which is beyond the border of conscious attention, conceived by Freud as influencing, but not apprehended by personal consciousness.

Subconscious processes: Subconscious processes when distinguished from unconscious processes are those nearer to the margins of consciousness and distinguishable from the

Freudian unconscious. *See also conscious processes, nonconscious processes, unconscious processes.*

Sublimation: The redirection of the energy of a motive into other channels of action.

Subliminal perception: The consequences of stimulation below detection threshold; the effects have to be detected by their influences on other processes. *See also perception, registration.*

Subjective: The feelings, thoughts, and visions of an individual.

Subjects: The people or animals that participate in experiments.

Subvocalization: The habit of mouthing words silently while reading

Suggestion: The uncritical acceptance of ideas.

Superego: In Freud's tripartite division of the personality, this is the part corresponding most nearly to conscience, controlling through moral scruples rather than by way of social expediency. The superego is said to be an uncompromising and punishing conscience. See *also conscience, ego, id.*

Superordinate goals: The common goals shared by the parties to a conflict that are larger and more significant than their hostility and divergent goals. (This concept was proposed by Muzafer Sherif as an important factor in reducing intergroup conflict.)

Superordinate threats: The common threats shared by the parties to a conflict that are larger and more significant than their hostility and divergent goals.

Superstitious behaviour: Behaviour that develops as a consequence of accidental reinforcements.

Suppression: A process of self-control in which impulses, tendencies to action, wishes to perform disapproved acts, etc., are in awareness, but not overtly revealed. See *also repression.*

Survey research: A scientific research method of collecting information by interviewing a large sample of people largely with the aid of questionnaires; especially regarding their attitudes and opinions with respect to the burning problems of the day.

Syllogism: A basic form of logical reasoning; it comprises a major premise, a minor premise, and a conclusion.

Symbol: Anything that stands for or refers to something other than itself.

Symbolic Interaction: The process of interaction between human beings which is conducted at the symbolic level (for example through the use of language). The school of social psychology which is known as *symbolic interactionism* has stressed the implication of the symbolic interaction process for socialization. Man is seen as becoming fully human only through this interaction between the individual and his society.

Theories of Cooley and Mead. The foundations of social interactionist theory were laid by the American social psychologists. Charles Horton Cooley and. particularly, George Herbert Mead, who emphasized the role of society in shaping an individual's personality and sense of self.

Cooley formulated the concept of the *looking-glass self* to describe the process. Each individual, he argued, imagines himself as he appears in the minds of others, and his evaluation of this image leads to a continuing modification of his own behaviour. In this way we learn our identity from others and mold our identity in response to their subjective judgments.

Mead laid great emphasis on the role of language in the socialization process. Language he felt, makes available the tools – the shared symbols – through which a child achieves a fully human mind. The child, according to Mead, takes on the role of others, at first in play but later symbolically, that is, he learns to think and feel the way other people do. Initially, the child will experience only the viewpoint of particular others, such as his parents. Eventually, however, he will become aware of what Mead termed the generalized other, that is, he will gain a notion of the general expectation and attitudes of others in his society. In this way, the individual internalizes social attitudes and modifies his personality in accordance with them. Mead distinguished between the "I" – the spontaneous, natural, self-interested self, and the "me" – the socialized self imbued with the norms of the community and aware of the individual's social obligation. Symbolic-interaction theory has been particularly valuable for its emphasis on the manner in which language and cultural symbols Influence social relations.

Symbolic universe: The perception of a moral framework which exists as a reality independent of the individual.

Symmetrical distribution: A frequency distribution in which cases fall equally in the class intervals on either side of the middle; hence the mean, median, and mode fall together. *See also frequency distribution, skewed distribution.*

Sympathetic division: A division of the autonomic nervous system, characterized by a chain of ganglia on either side of the spinal cord, with nerve fibres originating in the thoracic and lumbar portions of the spinal cord. Active in emotional excitement and to some extent antagonistic to the parasympathetic division. *See also parasympathetic division.*

Sympathetic nerves: A division of the autonomic nervous system that runs the body on an emergency basis when triggered by extreme cold, pain, violence, or emotion.

Symptom substitution: The replacement of a symptom of mental illness by a patient after a prior symptom has been directly removed without treatment of the underlying illness. The extent to which symptom substitution occurs *is a* point of contention between behaviour therapists and other therapists who believe in the need for insight. See *also behaviour therapy, insight.*

Synanon: Group sessions aimed at changing the attitudes and behaviour of group members and characterized by extreme candor and honesty. Such sessions involve considerable attack and criticism, but also are conducted in a larger supportive context. Emphasis is placed on getting members to admit their faults and weaknesses: These sessions are usually held in Synanon houses, residences of an organization of former drug addicts who live together in a communal style.

Synapse: A gap at the junction point between two neurons where the axon of one cell meets the dendrites of the next cell. It is actually a gap between the two nerve cells, which provides a close functional connection between the axon of one neuron and the dendrites or cell body of another neuron.

Syntax: A study of the way morphemes are put together into coherent phrases or sentences.

Syringomyelia: A rare disease in which sensitivity to heat and cold is lost, but the sense of touch is kept.

Systematic desensitization: A behaviour therapy technique in which hierarchies of anxiety-producing situations are imagined (or sometimes confronted in reality) while the person is in a state of deep relaxation. Gradually the situations become dissociated from the anxiety response. See *also behaviour therapy, counter-conditioning.*

Systematically biased sampling: Sampling that misrepresents the characteristics of the population in some consistent way. For example, a sample drawn from lists of college alumni would not correctly represent the total population of adults in regard to educational level.

Systematic sampling: A form of probability sampling that involves choosing in a systematic but unbiased manner from a list that enumerates the whole population (for example, choosing every tenth name from an alphabetical list).

T

Taboo: Any social prohibition with generally, but not exclusively, irrational support and rather drastic penalties.

Tachistoscope: An optical projector used to present visual stimuli such as words, symbols, pictures, or other visually presented material to a subject for fractions of a second or minute; sometimes called a T-scope.

Tactics, interpersonal: Strategies deliberately adopted to influence another person.

Target act: The deed (e.g., a confession, a purchase, a favour, an opinion change) which is to be performed by the recipient of an influence attempt.

Target person: The person whom an influencing agent tries to influence.

Task-centred leader: A group leader who is primarily interested in seeing that his group accomplishes its given task.

Task divisibility: The extent to which a group task can be sub-divided in order to permit a division of labour.

Task leader: An individual who supplies ideas and guides the group towards a solution.

Task-oriented group: A group whose members are directed primarily towards the accomplishment of a given task. This is the opposite of a socioemotional group.

Task specialist: A particular group role, as observed by Bales, whose occupant assumes responsibility for generating ideas and for moving the group towards accomplishment of its task. This is the opposite of a socioemotional specialist.

Teaching machine: A device to provide self-instruction by means of a programme proceeding in steps at a rate determined by the learner; the machine is arranged to provide knowledge about the correctness of each of the responses made by the learner. See *also CAL.*

Telegraphic speech: A stage in the development of speech where the child preserves only the most meaningful and perceptually salient elements of adult speech. The child tends to omit prepositions, articles, prefixes, suffixes, and auxiliary words.

Telepathy: The claimed form of extrasensory perception in which what is perceived depends on thought transference from one person to another. See *also clairvoyance, extrasensory perception, precognition.*

Temperament: That aspect of personality revealed in the tendency to experience moods or mood changes in characteristic ways; general level of reactivity and energy.

Temporal lobe: A portion of the cerebral hemisphere, at the side below the lateral fissure and in front of the occipital lobe. *See also frontal lobe, occipital lobe, parietal lobe.*

Terminal button: A specialized knob at the end of the axon that releases a chemical into the synapse to continue transmission of the nerve impulse. See *also neurotransmitter.*

Territorial dominance: The phenomenon in which an individual dominates interactions with others when the interactions occur in the individual's own territory.

Territoriality: Our tendency to control the use of physical areas and maintain them as our own.

Territory: For many nonhuman species, a specific geographic region that an animal marks with scents or calls, uses as a nesting place, and defends against intrusion by other animals of the same species. For humans, it is an area whose occupant(s) perceive it as under their own control.

Test battery: A collection of tests whose composite scores, are used to appraise individual differences.

Test method: A method of psychological investigation. Its advantages are that it allows the psychologist to collect larger quantities of useful data from many people, with a minimum of disturbance of their routines of existence and with a minimum of laboratory equipment.

Test profile: A chart plotting scores from a number of tests given to the same individual (or group of individuals) in parallel rows on a common scale, with the scores connected by lines, so that high and low scores can be readily perceived. *See also trait profile.*

Test standardization: The establishment of norms for interpreting scores by giving a test to a representative population and by making appropriate studies of its reliability and validity. *See also norm, reliability, validity.*

Testosterone. The best known mate sex hormone produce ……….. are testes; it is important for the growth of the male sex organs and the development of the secondary male sex characteristics. It influences the sex drive. *See also androgens, secondary sex characteristics.*

Teratogenic effect: That which causes abnormalities in the development of an organism.

Tetrahydrocannabinol (THC): The active ingredient of marijuana.

Thalamus: Two groups of nerve cell nuclei located just above the brain stem and inside the cerebral hemispheres. Considered a part of the central core of the brain. One area acts as a sensory relay station, the other plays a role in sleep and waking; this portion is considered part of the limbic system. See *also hypothalamus.*

Thanatos: The death instinct – a tendency towards self-destruction – which Freud believed exists in everyone from birth. Turned outward, it can manifest itself as hostility, aggression, and war; turned inward, it leads to suicide.

Theelin: A female sex hormone, secreted through life until the menopause, that stimulates the reproductive organs and the breasts, determining the secondary sexual traits.

Thematic Apperception Test (TAT): A projective test of personality in which the subject is presented with a series of illustrations and asked to write a story based on each picture.

Theory: A systematic statement setting forth the apparent relationships and underlying principles of certain observed phenomena. A hypothesis is derived from a theory.

Theory X: An assumption held by some supervisors and employers that their subordinates do not want responsibility, dislike their jobs, and avoid working if they can. Thus, employers must arrange for their workers to be carefully monitored, controlled, and coerced. This term was used by Douglas McGregor. Compare with Theory Y.

Theory Y: An assumption held by some supervisors and employers that people seek out responsibility, enjoy their work, and will be committed to it if they have the proper opportunity. Thus, employers do not need to coerce their workers by means of surveillance, eternal control, or threat. This term was used by Douglas McGregor. Compare with Theory X.

Thinking: The ability to imagine or represent objects or events in memory and to operate on these representations. Ideational problem solving as distinguished from solution through overt manipulation.

Third party intervention: The intervention by a third party to try to help resolve a conflict between two other parties. The third party may utilize any means, including the various bases of social power. The third party can also serve as a conciliator, mediator, arbitrator, fact-finder, or message carrier (where communication between the parties has become difficult). Another method used by third parties is fractionation of conflict.

Threshold: The transitional point at which an increasing stimulus or an increasing difference not previously perceived becomes perceptible (or at which a decreasing stimulus or previously perceived difference becomes imperceptible). The value obtained depends in part on the methods used in determining it. See *also absolute threshold, difference threshold.*

Thyroid gland: An endocrine gland located in the neck, whose hormone thyroxin is important in determining metabolic rate. See *also endocrine gland.*

Tip-of-the-tongue phenomenon: The experience of failing to recall a word or name when we are quite certain we know it.

T-maze: An apparatus in which an animal is presented with two alternative paths, one of which leads to a goal box. It is usually used with rats and lower organisms. See also maze.

Tolerance: The need to take more and more of a drug to achieve the same effect. An important factor in physiological dependency on drugs.

Trace conditioning: A classical conditioning procedure in which the CS terminates before the onset of the US. *See also delayed conditioning, simultaneous conditioning.*

Trait: A persisting characteristic or dimension of personality according to which individuals can be rated or measured by a variety of personality tests. *See also trait profile.*

Trial-and-error thinking: The teeming process in which a subject solves a problem only after making many random responses.

Trait profile: A chart plotting the ratings of a number of traits of the same individual op a common scale in parallel rows, so that the pattern of traits can be visually perceived (syn. psychograph). *See also test profile, trait.*

Trait theory: The theory that human personality is most profitably characterized by the scores that an individual makes on a number of scales, each of which represents trait or dimension of his or her personality.

Trait theory of leadership: The view that a person emerges as a leader because of certain of has personality traits. The concept that "great men are born, not made" is the opposite of the more common social psychological position that a leader emerges because of a particular group situation and its effect upon individual members ("great men are made, not born)". Recent research indicates that leadership is actually best understood as a product of the interaction between personality and situational factors.

Tranquilizer: A drug such as chlorpromazine or reserpine used to reduce anxiety and relieve depression; hence useful in the therapy of mental disorders.

Tranquillizing drug: Any of a group of ataraxic drugs, which relax patients, giving them a feeling of peace and contentment, and freeing them from anxiety, or at least from its physical effects.

Transactional analysis: The model developed by Berne for interpreting interpersonal interactions as exchanges which can be categorized as belonging to the ego state of the child, the parent, or the adult.

Transcendental Meditation (TM): A form of meditation practised by some who follow Hindu yoga. The meditative state is induced by repeating a particular sound or phrase, called a mantra, over and over again. Each individual has his or her own mantra selected as most appropriate.

Transducer: A device such as an electrode or gauge that, in psychophysiology, converts physiological indicators into other forms of energy that can be recorded and measured.

Transfer: The application of material or methods appropriate to one situation to another situation.

Transference: In psychoanalysis, the patient's unconsciously making the therapist the object of emotional response, thus transferring to the therapist responses appropriate to other persons important in the life history of the patient.

Transfer of training: The effect of prior training or learning on new learning.

Transsexual: An individual who is physically one sex but psychologically the other. Transsexuals sometimes resort to surgery and hormonal treatment to change their physical gender. They do not, however, consider themselves to be homosexual. *See also homosexual.*

Transsexualism: A gender identity opposite to one's biological structure and hormonal balance. A person with male sex organs whose gender identity is female, or vice versa, is a transsexual.

Trauma: A severe, sudden shock that has permanent effects upon the personality.

Traumatic neurosis: The drastic disruption of personality caused by any sudden, severe shock that is interpreted as a real threat to continued existence. If caused by military experiences, is sometimes known as 'shell shock', 'battle fatigue', and 'war neurosis'.

Tribe (also called **Ethnic Group**): A comprehensive type of kin group, whose members live in several relatively contiguous towns, villages, and hamlets; they share a common ancestry, language, culture, religion, and name. There are several tribes in the whole world. Nigeria and Africa inclusive. Tribes were the major units of social organization in Africa prior to the 1884-5 Berlin Conference, which gave the main political and economic impetus to the scramble, partition, and colonization of Africa by the various powerful and imperialistic European countries, notably Britain, France, Germany, Italy, Spain, Belgium, Holland and Portugal. These imperialist European countries amalgamated several contiguous African tribes together to form most of the new nation-states of modern-day Africa, such as Nigeria, Ghana, Sierra Leone, Kenya, Uganda, Zimbabwe, the Republic of South Africa, etc. Largely because the patterns of social relationships and culture developed under the tribal organizations are older, much more firmly institutionalised, predictable, and psycho-socially satisfying than the much more recent, superficial, diffused and transient feelings of national patriotism and unity, tribal sentiments, affiliations, loyalties, and obligations tend to be generally stronger than the national ones. Such stronger tribal loyalties constitute a formidable obstacle to the development of national loyalties in most contemporary African nation-states, Nigeria inclusive. Among African countries, Nigeria contains the highest member of different tribes. According to the 1952/53 Nigerian census, there are more than 200 different tribes or ethnic groups in the country. They range widely from very small tribes of about 50,000 people, to very large or populous ones of up to 7 million people. The main tribes in Nigeria include the Ijo, Urhobo, Edo, Yoruba, Igbo, Tiv, Nupe, Hausa, Fulani, Kanuri, etc.

Trichromatism: Normal colour vision, based on the classification of colour vision according to three colour systems: black-white, blue-yellow, and red-green. The normal eye sees all three; the colourblind eye is defective in one or two of the three systems. *See also dischromatism, monochromatism*

Turner's syndrome: An abnormal condition of the sex chromosomes in which a female is born with one X chromosome instead of the usual XX. *See also X chromosome.*

Two-step flow of Information: Information is assumed to flow vertically from the national opinion leaders to the local opinion leaders through mass media and from the local opinion leaders to the people through personal influence.

Type: A class of individuals alleged to have a particular trait. According to psychologists, it is an invalid concept because individuals cannot be grouped into a few distinct classes.

Type-category unit: A unit of analysis in which one class of individuals in one class of situation is the focus of study.

Type theory: The theory that human subjects can profitably be classified into a small number of classes or types, each class or type having characteristics in common that set its members apart from other classes or types. *See also trait theory.*

U

Unconditional positive regard: Complete and total acceptance of anything that a client does or says in a client-centred therapy. This is a major approach of a therapist in a client-centred treatment.

Unconditioned response (UCR): In classical conditioning, this refers to the response given originally to the unconditioned stimulus used as the basis for establishing a conditioned response to a previously neutral stimulus. *See also conditioned response, conditioned stimulus, unconditioned stimulus.*

Unconditioned stimulus (UCS): In classical conditioning, this refers to a stimulus that automatically elicits a response, typically via a reflex, without prior conditioning. *See also conditioned response, conditioned stimulus, unconditioned response.*

Unconscious: A collective name for any mental activity which is thought to occur and to influence behaviour but which is not consciously experienced by the individual.

Unconscious motive: A motive of which the subject is unaware, or aware of in distorted form. Because there is no sharp dividing line between conscious and unconscious, many motives have both conscious and unconscious aspects.

Unconscious processes: (1) Processes, such as wishes or fears, that might be conscious but of which a subject is unaware. (2) Less commonly, physiological processes of the body (circulation, metabolism, etc.) that go on outside of awareness, preferably called nonconscious.   See *also* *conscious processes, nonconscious processes, subconscious processes.*

Undifferentiating item: In the description of persons, the lowest level of descriptiveness; refers to an individual's material possessions or social setting.

Uni-forming relationship: According to balance theory, two objects have a unit-forming (or U) relationship if they appear to be one unit. (Examples: Since I wrote this book, I have a Li-relationship with the book. Sometimes U-relationships depend upon the context: A Bendel delegate to a national convention probably has a non-U-relationship with a Kwara delegate; at an international convention, however, they would probably have a positive U-relationship (as Nigerians).

Universalistic orientation: A tendency to behave towards other persons in terms of widely shared societal norms. See *also* *particularistic orientation.*

Unobtrusive measure: A measure obtained without the awareness of the individual being assessed, thereby minimizing the possibility of measurement reactivity. (Example: One social researcher suggested that the popularity of a television special could be gauged by comparing the city water consumption immediately after the show with the consumption at the same one week earlier).

Unstructed interview: This term refers to the type of interview in which the interviewer and the interviewee are given very wide freedom in their questions and responses, but the interviewer is constrained to focus on the topic or area that is defined by the purpose of the interview.

V

Validity: In scientific research methodology, validity is said to exist when a test can be shown to measure that which it is claimed that it measures. Thus validity is the predictive significance of a test for its intended purposes. Validity can be measured by a coefficient of correlation between scores on the test and the scores that the test seeks to predict; i.e., scores on some criterion. *See also criterion, reliability.*

Value: A basic standard or criterion that states what is desirable (good) and what is undesirable (bad) in any culture. It serves as a guide to action and to the development and maintenance of attitudes towards people, events/and objects. Values are usually general criteria, and rarely refer to specific phenomena. Typical examples of values include freedom, equality, wisdom.

Variable: Any concept that can be measured or quantified, such as sex (male and female), colour (black, red, yellow, *etc*), and the like. Each of the different conditions that is measured or controlled in any research is a variable. *See also dependent and independent variables.*

Variable-interval schedule: A schedule of intermittent reinforcement in which reinforcements are presented in an irregular or variable interval of time regardless of an organism's response rate after the first correct response is made.

Variable-ratio schedules: A schedule of intermittent reinforcement in which the number of correct responses required before a reinforcement is received varies.

Variance: The square of a standard deviation.

Ventromedial hypothalamus (VMH): Area of the hypothalamus important to the regulation of food intake. Electrical stimulation of this will make an experimental animal stop eating; destruction of brain tissue here produces voracious eating, eventually leading to obesity. *See also hypothalamus, lateral hypothalamus.*

Verbal I.Q: Intelligence test scores based on subscales that require language usage, reasoning, comprehension, and information content, etc.

Verbal report: A statement made by a person about what was or is experienced, felt, perceived, believed, etc.

Verbal tests: Intelligence tests in which a great deal of the performance tested is in the form of words.

Verification: The process of collecting facts to support or refute theoretical predictions.

Vertigo: A feeling of dizziness.

Vestibular sacs: Two sacs in the labyrinth of the inner ear, called the saccule and utricle, which contain the otoliths ("ear stones"). Pressure of the otoliths on the hair cells in the gelatinous material of the utricle and saccule gives us the sense of upright position or departure from it. *See also equilibratory sense.*

Vicarious learning: Learning by observing the behaviour of others and noting the consequences of that behaviour (syn. observational learning).

Viscera: The soft inside parts of the body.

Visual area: A projection area lying in the occipital lobe. In humans, partial damage to this area produces blindness in portions of the visual field corresponding to the amount and location of the damage (syn, striate area*).*

Visual cliff: An experimental apparatus with glass over a patterned surface, one-half of which is just below the glass and the other half, several feet below. Used to test the depth perception of animals and human infants.

Visual field: The total visual array acting on the eye when it is directed towards a fixation point.

Visual purple: A chemical compound, normally found in a layer of the retina, which decomposes in the presence of light and recombines in darkness, and so is necessary for proper night vision. It depends upon vitamin A for nutrition.

Voice stress analyzer: A machine that represents graphical changes in a person's voice that occurs with emotion. Used in lie detection. See also *polygraph.*

Volley principle: A necessary part of the frequency theory of learning; the principle suggests that frequencies above the maximum rate at which a neuron is firing in sequence, to give a net rate higher than any single group. *See also frequency theory, place theory.*

Volumetric receptors: Hypothesized receptors that regulate water intake by responding to the volume of blood and body fluids. Benin, a substance secreted by the kidneys into the bloodstream, may be one volumetric receptor; it constricts the blood vessels and stimulates the release of the hormone, angiolensin, which acts on cells in the hypothalamus to produce thirst. *See also osmoreceptors.*

Voluntary attention: An attention which an individual gives voluntarily and freely in any action situation, without any motivation or conditioning.

Voluntary group: A group freely organized by citizens for the pursuit of some interests in contrast to a state established agency or a non-voluntary group based on birth, caste, creed, language, etc.

Voluntary process: Activities selected by choice and controlled or monitored according to intention or plan. *See also control processes.*

W

WAIS (Wechsler Adult Intelligence Scale): A widely used intelligence test for adults. A similar Wechsler Intelligence. Scale for Children (WISC) is also widely used.

Wants: The initiating and sustaining forces of behaviour. Wants may be positive (desires) or negative (fear or anxiety). It is the wants (drives or motives) which impel a person towards the achievement of a goal.

Weber-Fechner law: A psychophysical function stating that the perceived magnitude of a stimulus increases in proportion to the logarithm of its physical intensity.

Figure 20: **W communication network.**

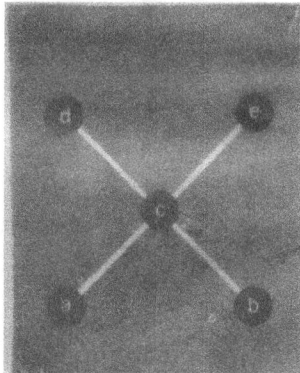

Source: Raven and Rubin (1976), page 271

Weber's law: A law stating that the difference threshold is proportional to the stimulus magnitude at which it is measured. The law is not accurate over the full stimulus range. See *also difference threshold.*

Wheel communication network: A centralized communication network in which one person is at the centre of all communication channels, and the other members of the group can communicate only with him, his position is comparable to the hub of a wheel.

Withdrawal of love: A form of parental discipline in which a parent explicitly or implicitly implies dislike for a child because of some specific unbecoming action performed by the child.

Working through: In psychoanalytic therapy, the process of re-education by having patients face the same conflicts over and over again in the consultation room, until they can independently face and master the conflicts in ordinary life.

X

X chromosome: A chromosome that if paired with another X chromosome, determines that the individual will be a female. If it is combined with a Y chromosome, the individual will be a male. The X chromosome transmits sex-linked traits. *See also chromosome, sex-finked trait Y chromosome.*

XYY syndrome: An abnormal condition in which a male has an extra Y sex chromosome; reputedly associated with unusual aggressiveness, although the evidence is not conclusive. *See also Y chromosome.*

Y chromosome: The chromosome that combined with an X chromosome, determines maleness. *See also chromosome, sex-linked trait, X chromosome.*

Y communication network: A communication network arranged in such a way that it forms "Y". In a five-person Y network, three persons can communicate only directly with one central person, and the fifth person can communicate only with one of the three peripheral persons (as at the bottom of the Y). The Y is a centralized communication network, but less so than the wheel communication network.

Figure 21: **Y Communication network**

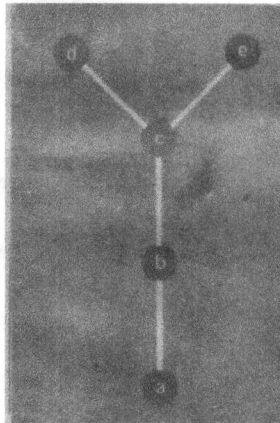

Source: Raven and Rubin (1976), page 271

Yerkes-Dodson Law: The name usually given to the inverted U relationship between stress and performance.

Young Helmholtz theory: A theory of colour perception that postulates three basic colour receptors, a "red" receptor, a "green" receptor, and a "blue" receptor. *See also opponent-process theory.*

Z

Zero sum game: Any game (or interaction) in which the gains and losses of the players sum to zero.

Zoophobia: A fear of animals and zoos.

Zygote: A fertilized, ovum or egg. *See also dizygotic twins, monozygotic twins.*